Hobbs, Brockunier & Co., Glass

IDENTIFICATION AND VALUE GUIDE

Neila and Tom Bredehoft

COLLECTOR BOOKS

A Division of Schroeder Publishing Co., Inc.

The current values in this book should be used only as a guide. They are not intended to set prices, which vary from one section of the country to another. Auction prices as well as dealer prices vary greatly and are affected by condition as well as demand. Neither the Authors nor the Publisher assumes responsibility for any losses that might be incurred as a result of consulting this guide.

Searching For A Publisher?

We are always looking for knowledgeable people considered to be experts within their fields. If you feel that there is a real need for a book on your collectible subject and have a large comprehensive collection, contact Collector Books.

On the Cover: Group of Peach Blow and Coral pieces. Courtesy of the Huntington Museum of Art, Huntington, WV.

Book design by Mary Ann Dorris
Cover design by Beth Summers

≈Contents≈

‎Acknowledgments‎

When we embarked on our project for documenting the history and products of the Hobbs, Brocknier & Company, we knew we would depend on many knowledgeable people to help us. We have also had cooperation from many museums and libraries who have been helpful in locating glass for photography, catalog illustrations, and trade journals.

We wish to give our heartfelt thanks to the following individuals and institutions for their help in our quest. Two people deserve special mention because of their help: Frank Fenton for allowing us to reprint his Hobbs, Brockunier & Co. catalog pages and G. Eason Eige who let us study and photograph Hobbs' glassware at the Huntington Museum of Art in Huntington, WV. We also thank those who helped but wished to remain anonymous.

Scott Brown
Howard Cusic
G. Eason Eige of the Huntington Museum of Art, Huntington, WV
Margaret and James Forkner
Tom Felt
Frank M. Fenton of the Fenton Art Glass Co., Williamstown, WV
Mart Groesser
Dorothy Lee Jones of The Jones Gallery of Glass and Ceramics, Douglas Hill, ME
Mary Ann and Dick Krauss
Marilyn and Charles Lockwood
R. J. McAuliffe
Holly McClusky of the Oglebay Institute, Wheeling WV
Sister Catherine Marie Paumier
Duane Reeves
Linda Sandell
Jo and Bob Sanford
C. R. Sargent, Jr.
Ray and Eileen Secrist
Dean Six
Hazel Tellier
Rick and Ricki Thompsom
Ross Trump
Libby and Abe Yalom
The Carnegie Library, Pittsburgh, PA
The Henry Ford Museum, Dearborn, MI
The staff of the Rakow Library, Corning Museum of Glass, Corning, NY
The Winterthur Museum, Winterthur, DE

ᗌ Foreword ᗍ

In 1864 in South Wheeling, West Virginia, a revolutionary new process for pressing glass was developed that would change the American glass industry forever. In December of that year, William Leighton, Sr., a partner and chemist with J. H. Hobbs, Brockunier and Company, developed a formula that set up well in moulds and produced a clear, almost flint-like quality of glass that could be mass produced at one third the cost of lead crystal. This formula is known as lime glass.

While this unique achievement alone brought national recognition, Hobbs, Brockunier is remembered for much more. The versatile firm produced elaborate cut and engraved pieces, fancy chandeliers, standard apothecary ware, pressed tableware, lamps, and colorful Victorian art glass.

It also was a major production company. In 1879, the Crockery and Glass Journal reported that J. H. Hobbs, Brockunier and Company was the largest glass firm in the United States, which boasted 330 employees and produced 60 tons of glass per week. According to the article, Hobbs also had the largest cutting shop in the country and had recently purchased the country's largest gas furnace.

Although the firm closed in 1893, shortly after merging with the U. S. Glass Company, many of Hobbs, Brockunier's products — Wheeling Peachblow in particular — are highly sought after by American glass collectors today.

Hobbs, Brockunier and Company clearly deserves recognition comparable to that of Sandwich, Mt. Washington, and New England as one of the most significant glass firms in America for its innovative products and the effect that the lime glass formula had on mass production of tableware.

In the words of Charles W. Brockunier, dated August 31, 1886, *"The South Wheeling Glass Works has made the name of Wheeling a familiar word much beyond the limits of the United States by the excellence of her product: in Cuba, in South America, the distant continent of Australia, in England; and only last week an application from Paris, the seat of the finest artistic products in the world, was made for the sale of these goods manufactured in Wheeling."*

Much of the company's glassware was not documented or even attributed to the firm until this publication. This book will surprise readers who aren't fully aware of Hobbs' tremendous range and versatility. The authors, Neila and Tom Bredehoft, deserve our gratitude for producing this well-researched volume.

A book on this company has been long overdue, and is a welcome addition to our growing knowledge of the American glass industry.

April, 1996
Holly Hoover McCluskey
Curator of Glass
Oglebay Institute
Wheeling, West Virginia

⌐Introduction⌐

The pressed table glass industry in the United States attained its majority after the Civil War with the development of an inexpensive lime glass which rivaled in clarity, if not tone, the standard flint, or lead glass, of the time. William Leighton, Sr.'s formula substituting bicarbonate of soda for litharge in the manufacture of glass reduced the cost of materials to approximately 25% of what it had been. Glassware now could be had by everyone, and to fill the need, glasshouses sprouted everywhere and those glass houses which were already established, flourished. J. H. Hobbs, Brockunier & Co., of which Leighton was a partner, went from making standard wares to making art glass which is eagerly sought today. Hobbs, Brockunier & Co. became one of the most prestigious houses in the Midwest, if not in the entire country. Before the company joined the U. S. Glass Co. in 1892, they had made wares which not only rivaled the best imported wares from England and Bohemia, but were sold in this country as having been imported from Europe!

To be fully appreciated, Victorian glassware, including that made by Hobbs, must be studied not only as a whole, but as it developed, a year or two at a time. For instance, at the Centennial exposition in 1876, acid etching became popular as a decoration. Before the year was over, most American glasshouses were etching portions of their wares. But it was 1880, four years later, before the idea of etching patterns on plain glass was developed. Before 1878 "fancy colors" meant primarily Ruby. By 1884 most glasshouses were making amber, blue, and canary, and some were making amethyst, sea green, and other colors. Hobbs, Brockunier & Co. boasted of 25 colors and treatments at this time, many more than most glasshouses. Glass colors, effects, and patterns must be understood in relation to those same colors, effects, and patterns which were made before and after.

For most of the South Wheeling Glass Works' life its name was J. H. Hobbs, Brockunier & Co. or Hobbs, Brockunier & Co. In this book, we have tried to use the correct name (according to time period) wherever possible. It is easy to say "Hobbs" when we mean "Hobbs, Brockunier & Co.," however, and it slips in from time to time. Brockunier, by the way, is pronounced "Brock COON yer" by members of the family.

After 1887 the company's name was changed to Hobbs Glass Co. This was a major turning point in the history of the company. Two of the three partners left and because the remaining partner was unable to organize a new company immediately, many of the employees, including some of the management, found work elsewhere. Many of the wares which were made after this time owed their ancestry to the earlier company, notably in their shapes. But there were few wares continued after this time which had been made before, except the for old standards, molasses cans, tumblers, etc.

Among shards found at the Hobbs/Northwood site, in South Wheeling, were a large number of opal (white glass cased with crystal) lamp shade shards. We have been unable to determine whether these were made by Hobbs, Brockunier & Co. or Northwood.

About The Book

We have included patterns which we can positively attribute to Hobbs, Brockunier & Co. or patterns for which we have good reason to credit to Hobbs, Brockunier & Co. Major and minor patterns are listed chronologically in the Patterns chapter. In all cases we have attempted to provide basic information about each pattern: the date it was introduced, the colors in which it was made, any known decorations, patent information, pertinent comments, and reproductions.

We have tried to maintain the original company and industry terminology not only for pattern names but the names of the pieces. For instance, Hobbs used the term comport rather than compote. Also, what is now called a barber bottle was then a bitter — indicating an entirely different use for this form. In the case of jugs or pitchers, the company itself used both terms and we have used whichever term they used in catalogs with each pattern.

The Lighting chapter forms the next largest section of this book. We have included lighting devices which we can document. We know there were other lamps and globes made by Hobbs, Brockunier & Co., but in the interests of accuracy, we have only shown those of which we are certain.

We have included a Miscellaneous chapter to cover the odd pieces and short lines that do not fit well into the major sections of the book. Again, we are certain that many other items were made at Hobbs, Brockunier which would fall into this category, but at this time we have not been able to document them. This company was in business for many, many years and certainly made many standard designs and items which are unrecognized today. This is partly due to incomplete catalog documentation and partly because similar wares were made by many companies.

A short chapter is included at the end of the book which lists and illustrates several patterns and/or pieces of glass which have been attributed to Hobbs, Brockunier & Co. or which are confusing in their similarity to Hobbs' pieces. There are also a few outright copies of Hobbs' pieces and patterns shown.

Several points need to be made about the prices given in this book. First, remember that prices of glass vary from area to area in the country. Prices listed are for pieces in perfect or near-perfect condition. In order to furnish realistic prices, we have asked several knowledgeable collectors and dealers to give prices for most patterns. We are indebted to these people for their help.

The History of Hobbs, Brockunier & Co.

The South Wheeling Glass Works

Hobbs, Brockunier & Co.'s display embraces everything in the glass line from a common crystal set to the finest combination of colors in glassware ever produced in this country. Their wares are displayed in all the principal cities of the United States and Canada, and large quantities are exported to Great Britain, South Africa, and Australia. The steadily increasing trade of the company is evidence sufficient that their goods are all they are represented to be. Mr. C. W. Brockunier, the active business head of the firm, is regarded as one of the shrewdest men in the business, while Mr. Wm. Leighton, the metal maker and designer, is believed to have no equal in the art of producing rich and clear colored or crystal glass. Mr. John H. Hobbs, the senior member of the firm, is the oldest glass man still engaged in the business in the west, and Mr. Hobbs knows the business thoroughly from the cellar to the garret, so to speak.

Crockery & Glass Journal, December 1, 1887

Hobbs, Brockunier & Co., its predecessors and its successors, had a long and varied history. Much of the early history is now recorded only in legal records and a few contemporary accounts of the company, its products, and the men who were involved in the firm. The company began with little fanfare in a time when glasshouses were failing with remarkable regularity. Quietly, the company began producing standard, plain wares which were needed by both housewives and businesses, and it prospered.

The name of the company changed several times over the succeeding years as partners either left the company or were added to it. However, during its many years in business, a complete reorganization only took place twice — the first being at the end of 1888 when the original company charter expired and the second when the company was absorbed into the U. S. Glass Co. combine.

Hobbs, Brockunier & Co. was one of the most important of the American glass companies in the Victorian period. While most companies specialized in one aspect of glass manufacture, Hobbs, Brockunier & Co. made almost everything in glass except bottles and window glass. Their production ranged from the mundane to the exotic, from common tumblers to art glass such as Wheeling Peach Blow and to massive chandeliers sold in every corner of the world.

Eventually, the fate of the Hobbs Glass Co. was due in part to the very thing that made it unique and important. The fancy glass items it made required extensive hand work, and therefore were expensive to produce. By 1891, however, the U. S. Glass Co. was interested in producing glass using only the most modern equipment — requiring relatively unskilled workmen. Hobbs, Brockunier and Co., known for wonderful patterns and types of glass created by William Leighton, Jr. and Nicholas Kopp, became outdated and was consequently phased out of existence. An era of American glass making came to an end.

PROLOGUE — 1840 to 1845

Wheeling, Virginia (later West Virginia), first grew and gained importance because of its location on the Ohio River. People were settling the Northwest Territory and moving into the South. Travel overland was slow, expensive, and difficult, but it was made easier by following navigable rivers. Riverboats moved both people and merchandise, and Wheeling became an important river-front town. Wheeling's importance increased even further after the National Road was built with Wheeling as its western terminus.

Wheeling became attractive to investors and manufacturers with not only glasshouses, but iron, nail making, and other industries being established. At this time there were no railroads west of the Allegheny Mountains, so alternative transportation for manufactured goods was a necessity.

One of the most important features contributing to the success of the South Wheeling plant was its location very near the Ohio River. Riverboats and barges offered cheap transportation to markets in the West and South. These newly settled areas created a demand for glassware of all kinds. Operating a factory near the river substantially lowered the cost of shipping glass compared with the high costs of shipping from the eastern factories.

As late as 1883, a quote stated: "The recent rains in this section and in the Southwest have made all the streams navigable, and many goods now go West and South on the steamboats plying between Pittsburgh, Wheeling, Cincinnati, St. Louis and New Orleans. Shippers as a rule prefer shipping by boat as a measure of safety and economy. Goods are handled more carefully, and carried more safely, and the rates are much less than those given by rail."

The history of Hobbs, Brockunier & Co. goes back almost to the beginning of glassmaking in Wheeling. The property which would later become the Hobbs, Brockunier & Co. factory site was first developed when Francis Plunkett & Horatio Miller began construction of a new glass factory in January of 1839 in Ritchietown near the corner of what became 36th and Wetzel Streets. This factory was the first glasshouse built south of the town of Wheeling. The timing, though, was unfortunate as a severe depression gripped the country in 1839, and there were many bank and industry failures nationwide. Plunkett and Miller were forced to mortgage their new factory and its equipment in mid-1840, and they had defaulted on these loans by 1841. The factory and property were sold in October of 1841. Plunkett had no further involvement with glassmaking in Wheeling, but Miller soon bought the property with borrowed capital. He briefly tried to make glass at the factory, but also defaulted on loans within a year.

For unknown reasons, James B. Barnes and John L. Hobbs visited the Wheeling area in the early 1840s and decided to invest their money in the growing town. Both had been employed at the New England Glass Co. in East Cambridge, Massachusetts, prior to the 1840s. Barnes was superintendent of the pot room and worked closely with Deming Jarves in designing and building the plant. John L. Hobbs found work at the factory as a cutter when he was a boy. By his twenty-first birthday he was made superintendent of the cutting shop and a salesman for the company. Surely he must have had great talent for glass decorating or this important job would not have been entrusted to so young a man. When they came to Wheeling, the two men, along with James F. Barnes (son of James B.), formed the partnership of Barnes, Hobbs & Co.

BARNES, HOBBS & CO. — 1845 to 1849

The bankers, having acquired the property after Miller's default on his loans, eventually leased the Plunkett & Miller factory to Barnes, Hobbs & Co. in April 1845. Barnes and Hobbs named the factory the South Wheeling Glass Works. The factory at this time had only one furnace with a capacity of seven pots. Articles made at the time were solar chimneys, jars, vials, tumblers, pungents, tinctures, lamps for lard oil, salts, and cologne bottles. Early accounts also indicate the factory made purple, green, and olive glass, in addition to crystal flint (lead) glass.

The South Wheeling Glass Works was situated below a hill from which the company mined its own coal to fuel its furnaces. The area around the factory was developed and provided enough lots for homes and boarding houses so the workers could live nearby. Plunkett & Miller early on had built brick row houses near the factory for workmen.

The cost of coal for the factory in 1845 was 35 cents per ton, while the cost of wood for the lehrs was $1.50 a cord. Very early payrolls of the factory stated that skilled workers received from 75 cents to $1 per move while unskilled laborers received much less. A few workers' names were listed along with their wages: "On the first pay rolls are the following: Chas. Butler, 75 cents per move; Henry Leasure and Wm. Elson, 15½ cents per move; Andrew Baggs, 25 cents per move; Peter Cassell, 18¾ cents per move; William Kryter, mould maker, $30 per month." A move at that time was for six hours work, not the four hours of the later years when unions negotiated wages and moves.

According to old accounts, the business had its share of problems, but it survived. One of the setbacks was the defeat of Henry Clay for president of the United States in 1844. Clay had espoused a protectionist attitude on imports — a view dear to the hearts of glass manufacturers. Following his defeat several prospective investors did not invest money with Barnes & Hobbs. Eventually Barnes and Hobbs purchased the factory site and coal mining rights in January of 1848 for $11,000.

HOBBS, BARNES & CO. — 1849 to 1856

James B. Barnes died in early 1849, and the firm was reorganized with the name becoming Hobbs, Barnes & Co. The partners were John L. Hobbs, James F. Barnes, and John H. Hobbs. At this time the company was increasingly successful in supplying the demand for glass to the southern and western markets, and enlarged the capacity of their works. Cut, plain, and fire polished flint and fancy colored glassware were being made. In 1853 the Baltimore & Ohio Railroad finally came to Wheeling, providing much needed rail transportation.

BARNES, HOBBS & CO.; HOBBS & BARNES — 1856 to 1863

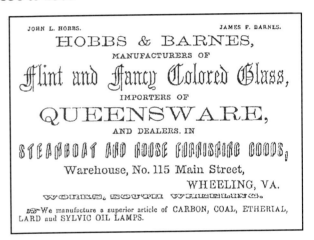

1859 ad for Hobbs & Barnes.

J. K. Dunham joined the company in 1856, and the name was returned to Barnes, Hobbs & Co. In addition to Dunham, the other partners were still John L. Hobbs, James E. Barnes, and John H. Hobbs. This name only survived for about a year, and as in 1857 the name again became Hobbs & Barnes. Lamp chimneys became a staple of the firm during this period as the discovery of oil and its useful by-products resulted in a large market for lighting devices and glass chimneys. By this time the factory occupied about an acre of land. Already it had three furnaces totaling 24 pots, a mold shop, and a cutting shop. There were several buildings for various factory functions, including an engine house, a building for refining batch ingredients, and a packing and warehouse. Access to the coal mine owned by the company was through one of the buildings. By mining its own coal on site, Hobbs & Barnes paid only about $7.50 per day while eastern factories were charged $45.00 per day for the same amount of fuel. According to old accounts Hobbs & Barnes manufactured glass valued at $100,000 in 1857. By 1860, the annual production value had increased to $120,000 and 115 persons were employed.

One of the most interesting of the non-production pieces known to have been made during the period of Hobbs & Barnes is a small clear glass bell engraved "1860 Bell & Everett". This bell was made for the presidential campaign of 1860 when the lesser-known John Bell of Tennessee opposed Abraham Lincoln.

1860 financial note, Hobbs & Barnes.

Many Wheeling residents, including many glasshouse workers, became soldiers in the Civil War. The glass factories were left with few workers, the most able-bodied and youngest having left the area for military service. The factory was forced to close for six months in 1861 because of lack of manpower and the general upheaval in the country. The work force was greatly cut back and the factory was forced to rely on elderly men and incompletely trained young men and boys to make glass. During this period, Barnes apparently became convinced that the glass factory was a poor investment and withdrew. He eventually established a retail store in Wheeling dealing in glassware and crockery.

The state of West Virginia was formed in 1863 from a portion of Virginia, and Wheeling increased in importance, having become the new state capital.

J. H. HOBBS, BROCKUNIER & CO. — 1863 to 1881

James F. Barnes sold his interest in the South Wheeling Glass Works to the Hobbses in 1863 for $15,000. During this period, John L. Hobbs established a separate firm, J. L. Hobbs, Son and Company. This company became one of the local outlets for the glass company. Invoices state "J. L. Hobbs, Son & Co. Flint Glass Manufacturers, and Importers of Queensware. Wareroom, No. 115 Main Street." The elder Hobbs turned much of his attention to this new venture and left the running of the glass factory to his son, although he retained his financial interest in the glass company.

In 1863, Charles W. Brockunier joined the firm as a partner. He and John H. Hobbs, along with other investors, had previously formed a company which found oil, giving both the financial capital to join as partners in the reorganized firm. The company name was again changed, this time to J. H. Hobbs, Brockunier & Co., reflecting the elevation of J. H. Hobbs to head of the firm. At this time, several men left to start their own company, Oesterling, Henderson & Co. This firm eventually became Central Glass Co. in Wheeling. The men leaving included John Oesterling, John Henderson, William Elson, Roy Combs, and Henry J. Leasure.

This year was perhaps the most momentous in the history of the company since in the fall William Leighton, Sr. and his son, William Leighton, Jr., were induced to come to Wheeling from the New England Glass Co. The association of Brockunier, with his astute business and financial acumen, combined with the talents of the Leightons in designing glass, formulating colors, and developing glass effects, brought Hobbs, Brockunier to its greatness in the coming years.

William Leighton, Sr. was the chemist for the firm and was remarkably successful in developing new glass formulae. He developed a successful formula for making glass using lime instead of lead in 1864. Clear, beautiful pressed glass was made from this formula, and the low cost of this recipe revolutionized the glassmaking industry. For the first time, excellent quality pressed glass was able to be made at a fraction of the cost of lead glass. This innovation made glass for table use within the economic reach of most people. No longer was glass found only on the tables of the rich, but also in the homes of the middle and lower income classes. Most of what we know about the development of the formula and its effects on the industry comes from an article written in 1880 by William Leighton, Jr. describing the history of glassmaking.

"In the winter of 1864, Mr. Wm. Leighton, Sr., of the firm of J. H. Hobbs, Brockunier & Co. made a course of experiments in the composition of flint-glass, the result of which was so successful that the manufacture of lime-glass was commenced by his firm, and ware was produced equaling in beauty the finest lime-glass [sic... lead glass was meant]. The most important feature in the composition of this new lime batch was the use of bicarbonate of soda in place of soda-ash, until that time universally used in lime-glass; this and better proportion of all the materials constituted the improvement, and led to the most important results. As the improved lime-glass was much cheaper than flint-glass, being less than half its cost, other factories commenced using the same material and learned the new composition. The ware thus manufactured could only be distinguished from flint-glass by its less specific gravity, and by the peculiar tone of its sound when struck; the flint-glass having a full metallic tone or ring, while the lime-glass emits a dull, dead sound, destitute of vibratory tone. From the time of this improvement in lime-glass the flint-glass factories began to languish. The larger number of them, perceiving that the era of flint-glass was passed, gave up the old composition, and commenced the manufacture of bicarbonate glass, as it was then called. But a few factories still clung to the old lead-glass composition, fondly hoping, and perhaps believing, that lime-glass would run a brief course and that there would be a return to the time-honored flint-glass. It soon became evident however, that lime-glass had gained the ascendant by merits that would stand the test of time, and those who still persevered in the manufacture of lead-glass found their ware could no longer be profitably made, and gained the experience that, in an age of progress, whoever clings to the methods of the past

will soon be neglected and forgotten. Besides advantage of cheaper material, lime-glass has the property of chilling and becoming rigid more rapidly than flint-glass, thus enabling and even compelling, the workmen to finish the ware more rapidly, and hence making a greater production. As the specific gravity of lime-glass is less than that of flint-glass, articles made of the former have the

Exterior of J. H. Hobbs, Brockunier & Co., from the Hayes Atlas of 1877.

advantage of this lightness of weight. The result of all these advantages, together with improvements in furnaces, tools, and methods of manufacture, has been to reduce the cost of glass-ware to about one-fourth part of what it was when the invention and introduction of bicarbonate glass took place in 1864. With this reduced cost, and consequent reduced price, the use of glass-ware has been extended correspondingly. New factories have been built, old factories have increased their capacity, and a sufficient supply of glassware has been produced to meet the demand which the reduced prices created. No kind of ware, even if composed of the most common materials, can now compete in cheapness with lime-glass for drinking vessels and table ware; while for beauty of material, finish, shape, and ornamentation, glassware is more than equal to, and for cleanliness far beyond, any other."

Little is known of the patterns made prior to 1870. Certainly many of the individual pieces illustrated in the Miscellaneous Patterns and Pieces chapter were first made during this period. In 1870 Hobbs and Leighton patented two patterns, Grapes with Overlapping Foliage and the famous Blackberry, both made in clear and porcelain (opal). Lamps were already an important part of the factory's production, and John H. Hobbs was granted Patent No. 103,460 on May 24, 1870, for a lamp connector. This device allowed the base and font of a lamp to be joined by an interlocking mechanism requiring no plaster of Paris. Many of Hobbs' early opal footed lamps are found with this connector which was used for many years.

In early 1871, Paneled Wheat was patented by J. H. Hobbs. Mr. Hobbs also secured a mechanical patent during this year for the manufacture of lithophane lamp shades.

In 1872 John H. Hobbs patented new pharmacy graduates. Previously these had been made at Hobbs, but the measuring lines had been engraved on the exterior of the graduates. In Hobbs' new process, the lines were pressed on the interior of the graduate, eliminating the necessity of engraving the lines and also resulting in more accurate measures.

A pressed glass flower and fruit stand was also patented early in 1872 with John H. Hobbs and C. W. Brockunier listed as inventors (Patent No. 162,234).

The financial panic of 1874 caused several of Wheel-

ing's glasshouses to fail, but J. H. Hobbs, Brockunier & Co. continued in business.

In 1875 J. H. Hobbs, Brockunier & Co. exhibited a case of table glass ware at the Massachusetts Charitable Mechanic Association fair and was awarded a silver medal (the highest award) for their exhibit of pressed "Table Glass Ware, manufactured from Soda Glass…. These examples are the best ever exhibited here by a class of goods entering more largely into consumption than any other, and are worthy of special notice." These wares may have included examples of some pieces shown in one of the earliest Hobbs ads: patented shell-handled pitchers, lemonades, and sauce dishes. These shell handles are now called reeded handles. The Massachusetts display may have also included some of Hobbs' opal footed lamps with the patented brass lamp connector.

By 1875 the company had enlarged dramatically from its humble beginnings in 1845, and now owned about 60 acres around their factory site of four acres. About 300 persons were now employed and produced glassware valued at $325,000 annually. The factory had three furnaces, each of 10 pots. Benzene was used as fuel in the glory holes since it contained no sulfur which would discolor the glass. In addition to making glass, the factory produced all its own pots and molds, mined its own coal, and sawed lumber from which it made its packing boxes. All of these secondary activities made J. H. Hobbs, Brockunier & Co. almost self sufficient, greatly reducing overhead. Their sample rooms at the factory were described as:

"…a magnificent display of glassware of every variety, ranging from the 'Cordial' to the large 'Preserve' and of patterns plain and beautiful design, which will equal the production of foreign countries. Here we find all kinds of fancy table-ware,

Interior of J. H. Hobbs, Brockunier & Co., from the Hayes Atlas of 1877.

glasses, shades, all styles of lamps, frosted ware, tumblers, druggist's graduates, and a thousand and more articles which space forbids us to enumerate."

In 1875 J. H. Hobbs, Brockunier & Co. advertised their porcelain glass. Porcelain is what we now call milk glass, or opal. Hobbs' opal wares are made of a very dense, opaque white glass. It is sad to realize that Hobbs was producing large quantities of cut and engraved glassware during this period, and that today we have no way of identifying these patterns. Only a few specimens survive that are known to be of Hobbs' manufacture, mostly in museums. They are identifiable because of their history, having been passed down in Wheeling families for many years. Several examples may be seen in the Oglebay Institute in Wheeling which has an extensive collection of Wheeling-made glassware.

"The operation of these works has in all these years been strictly confined to the production of wares of the finest quality and most elaborate workmanship. Only the most skillful workmen have been employed, and many of them brought directly from the best establishments in Europe." This report from mid-1875 also noted that the foreign workers in turn trained local men in the glassmaking and glass-decorating arts. The result of this was a work force of highly skilled and competent glass workers in the Wheeling area. Many men trained at Hobbs, Brockunier & Co. went on to establish or work in other glasshouses nearby.

At this time reports also noted that J. H. Hobbs, Brockunier & Co. was the first company in the United States making delicate, blown tumblers to rival those imported from Germany and France. This is just one more indication that this company was a leader in glassmaking of the time. It produced superb wares which competed very successfully with the best imported wares and the excellent products from the glasshouses of the East. At this time they maintained sample rooms in Boston, New York, Philadelphia, San Francisco, Baltimore, and Havana, Cuba. Since the products of this company were well known and the excellence of its wares unequaled, the company itself did not do much advertising in trade journals, and often the reports are less than enlightening as to what patterns and items were being made.

Hobbs exhibited their wares at the Centennial Exposition in Philadelphia. Early in 1876 the extremely popular No. 76 Viking pattern was produced and almost certainly was on display at the Exposition. Also advertised in 1876 was "a full line of 'iced' and opal wares." This reference to "iced" may refer to acid finish on clear glass or Tree of Life, or possibly an unknown design. A record of some wares exhibited included cut ware described as "strawberry diamond," "silver diamond,"

Early cut glass water pitcher, possibly of the type shown at the Centennial. Courtesy of Oglebay Institute.

and "prism." Also exhibited were No. 58 Mitchell tableware, No. 86 – specifically a "10 inch bowl with 16 OG scallops," No. 49 decanters, and No. 5 stemware.

One of the major improvements in glassware by Hobbs occurred in September of 1876 when they began to produce glass "trimmings or mountings, constructed for attachment to brackets and bracket-arms" for chandeliers and gas lighting fixtures. These quickly became a "specialty" of the company and were widely marketed. The fixtures were made in innumerable styles with many lights, "from two to twenty four," and eventually up to 32! Naturally, Hobbs patented such a lucrative and novel idea. Three patents were issued for the processes of making glass to enclose the metal tubes on gas fixtures and chandeliers. Another patent was issued for a decorative circle of joined prisms to be used as a pendant to decorate the base of the gas fixture, enhancing the brilliance of the light.

In early 1877 J. H. Hobbs, Brockunier & Co. built a warehouse 100 feet by 50 feet at their factory. By February of 1878 reports stated that the company was running three furnaces and employing 650 persons.

The new pattern for January of 1878 was a variation of Viking, called No. 79 Goat's Head. Also in 1878 William Russell patented his one-piece flower pot with attached saucer. Reports also mentioned the manufacture of "salvers, wines, goblets, mugs, epergnes, etc." in canary (vaseline). Iridescent glassware was also mentioned, but this glass is unknown today.

In 1879 several men at J. H. Hobbs, Brockunier & Co. left the firm to establish the new Riverside Glass Co. at Wellsburg. These included William Brady, Charles Brady, John Brady, James Ratcliff, John Dorn, James Flannigan, and Austin McGrill.

By September of 1879, J. H. Hobbs, Brockunier & Co. installed a new furnace "with original features, the largest in this country, if not in the world." This was a new Gill furnace using producer gas, of which only four had previously been built. At this time, reports also stated that the Hobbs plant was "possibly the largest, as it is among the best known, of the table-glass manufactories of the country." The furnace was of 13 pot capacity, and it was claimed that "it could turn out as much glass as any two of the old style furnaces." The installation of this furnace required the building of a new room to house it, 100 x 100 feet. In the basement underneath the furnace were stored the pots and other articles needed for the furnace. Including the two smaller Gill furnaces at Hobbs, the factory now had a capacity of 39 pots working about 60 tons of glass weekly. The *American Pottery & Glassware Reporter* published a letter from the company in early November 1879:

"In your issue of the 30th of October there is the following item:

"'It is rumored here that the new thirteen-pot gas furnace of Hobbs, Brockunier & Co.'s factory in Wheeling is not working satisfactorily. Some Pittsburgh experts say it is not constructed on the right principle, and doubts are expressed whether it will ever do any good. This is unfortunate, as the firm have a large number of orders on hand and more coming in.'

"Allow us to say that our furnace has worked to our entire satisfaction ever since fire was put in. Time only will prove whether the opinion of 'Pittsburgh experts' amounts to anything. When we first made crystal glass, used oil in glory holes, wind on our molds, &tc., &tc., there were not a few wise men who predicted failure. Only so far as the publication of your item may prevent our customers from sending in orders do we care for it. We can promise them that their orders will be filled with our usual promptitude."

"Yours, Respectfully

"Hobbs, Brockunier & Co."

Hobbs apparently felt they had to dispel rumors coming out of Pittsburgh from their competitors. Not only did they refute the allegation that their furnace was poorly designed, but they took the opportunity to remind all readers about the many innovations that J. H. Hobbs, Brockunier & Co. had initiated in the glass industry. Competition, rumors, and dirty politics were all alive and well back in the 1870s!

In the fall of 1879, J. H. Hobbs, Brockunier & Co. launched a new pattern which became very successful — Tree of Life with Hand. This pattern has been ascribed to various factories over the years; but it is uniquely Hobbs, including the Little Samuel comports and lamps.

Some time during the year of 1879, J. H. Hobbs, Brockunier & Co. exhibited their products at the International World's Fair in Sydney, Australia, for which they received a bronze medal. This may have been financially worth the effort as later reports were that large shipments of chandeliers were sent to Australia.

"Some of our oldest and most reliable glasshouses run on a single design for months at a time. One firm finds all it can do in a single design while Hobbs, Brockunier & Co. bring out a design weekly, and yet do not provoke their customers." Throughout the years, reports of J. H. Hobbs, Brockunier & Co. were laced with references to the tremendous variety of glass made by the firm — from the mundane to the exotic. This endless variety is certainly what gave the company the ability to withstand the ups and downs of business. If tableware was not selling, maybe lamps and chandeliers were, and vice versa.

In 1880 the factory survived a fire which at first report stated the factory would certainly be lost, but in actuality only a pile of rubbish below the pot room caught fire and was quickly put out, thus saving the buildings from the most-feared disaster of glass manufacturers. The estimated loss was $1,500. In August of that year another accident occurred in

which the roof collapsed during the night shift, slightly injuring two boys.

In March of 1880 J. H. Hobbs, Brockunier & Co. shipped a large consignment of wares to Edinburgh, Scotland. Previously in 1879 a report indicated that a shipment had been made to Persia "strange to say, not a single article was broken, after its long and rough voyage."

While J. H. Hobbs, Brockunier & Co. had used hydrofluoric acid to finish portions of a pattern's design as early as 1876 with Viking, by the spring of 1880 they began making a pattern with an intricate etched design on plain, non-figured pieces. Collectors now call this pattern Flamingo Habitat, although the company called the bird a stork and referred to the pattern as "in Japanese style."

In the middle of 1880, J. H. Hobbs, Brockunier & Co. added a sandblast department at a cost of $5,000. The Dolphin pattern, new in the fall of 1880, was decorated by this process. Magnification of the frosted areas of this pattern reveals a rather coarse, pitted surface, not visible to the naked eye nor to the touch. The finish is very different from the smooth, even surface of Viking which was done by hydrofluoric acid.

The old coal-fired furnace was renovated into a Gill gas furnace in 1880 because of the success of the larger furnace J. H. Hobbs, Brockunier & Co. had added the previous year. Later in the year it was announced that another new factory building, 100 x 100 feet, was being built to house another 15 pot Gill furnace. Apparently the new furnace improvements were working well and business was good, enabling J. H. Hobbs, Brockunier & Co. to expand and renovate in a short period of time. The management was wisely reinvesting its profits into the business rather than taking them for personal use. By keeping the factory up to date with modern machinery, they were able to produce an unusually high quality product with few flaws. "There are now three improved Gill gas furnaces in this factory, which is also furnished with all the most recent appliances and patents for the speedy and ingenious manufacture of bar and table ware" (April, 1881).

Strikes and other worker unrest at J. H. Hobbs, Brockunier & Co. were not often reported. However, there seems to have been a major problem in April of 1881. With no explanation as to the circumstances, a short announcement was made that all the employees of the cutting department were fired and that cutting would now be done on contract with an entirely new group of cutters.

In June of 1881, "At the request of Mrs. L. W. Washington, Vice regent for this state, a water set of fine cut glassware was made by our leading glass firm, J. H. Hobbs, Brockunier & Co., and sent to Mount Vernon, where it will be placed in a conspicuous position as a specimen of the beauty and brilliancy of West Virginia glassware. The goblets were of the 'Lavellier' pattern, cut in fine diamonds, hollow flute and fan, with slop bowl to match. The pitcher was the celebrated 'Fifth Avenue' design made by this firm, cut richly and very artistically engraved by Mr. Otto Jaeger, who is as skillful with the wheel as with the rifle. The inscription by request of Mrs.

Washington, was, 'Presented to the Vice Regent of West Virginia for the Ladies' Mount Vernon Association, by J. H. Hobbs, Brockunier & Co.'" This set of glassware has disappeared over the years, as Mount Vernon no longer seems to have this in its possession. It is unfortunate that this cannot be traced so that identification of some of the cuttings done by Hobbs could be documented. Throughout most of its existence the company produced much cut and engraved ware but little is known about the designs today.

One short reference was found in May of 1881 about knife handles made by J. H. Hobbs, Brockunier & Co. "A knife-handle, beautifully embossed and figured, is being manufactured at the factory of Hobbs, Brockunier & Co. for a cutlery factory in Connecticut."

In the fall of 1881, J. H. Hobbs, Brockunier & Co. introduced a new decorative effect in glass which they called Craquelle. This beautiful, delicate glassware was made in the many colors of the time, old gold (amber), crystal, sapphire blue, marine green, and ruby (cranberry). Reports indicated that prior to this time no ruby craquelle pitchers were made in this country. The remarkable Hobbs' chandeliers remained popular. The company also filled "a very large" order for chandeliers for a "large public building of Nashville, Tenn." which resulted in other orders from that area.

In November of 1881 John H. Hobbs died at the age of 77. "The business will be continued by the surviving partners, and as soon as possible the new firm will be announced." "The firm style of J. H. Hobbs, Brockunier & Co., Wheeling, W. Va., has been changed to Hobbs, Brockunier & Co." (November 24, 1881, *Crockery & Glass Journal*).

HOBBS, BROCKUNIER & Co. — 1881 to 1888

These years in the company's history are the most important. The most dramatic and artistic designs and types of glasses were made during this time. Leighton continued to experiment with exotic colored glasses and finishes and also designed molds and equipment to make some of the distinctive Hobbs pieces. During this period, the company was the largest maker of art glass in America, especially in the ruby (cranberry) glass so sought today.

The company continued to make improvements at the factory. "Hobbs, Brockunier & Co. are putting up and repairing steam pipes, putting in new boilers, and in every way providing for the heating of their buildings, thus securing the health and comfort of their employees. About five hundred hands, of whom one hundred are women, are employed at the glass works of Hobbs, Brockunier & Co." At Christmastime Hobbs provided their employees with a "Christmas table...for the benefit of their employees contains many beautiful sets of glassware." Apparently the employees were able to choose a Christmas gift from the company.

On March 2, 1882, the company suffered a substantial fire. "The mould room, engine house and factory were now completely wrapped in flames.... The factory was a ruin." Actually, portions of the factory remained intact. Many of the molds were only partially damaged, the cutting and engraving building survived, and one warehouse was saved. Unbelievably, the glass in the pots was intact and the men kept the furnaces fired to keep the glass molten. Even more incredible were the actions of more than 50 employees trying to save the factory. When a fast mail train approached the factory and threatened to cut the water hose lying across the tracks, the men bravely stood on the tracks, forcing the train to stop. All in all, C. W. Brockunier's estimate of the loss at the time of the fire was $40,000.

Crockery and Glass Journal, March 2, 1882:

"It is with much regret we mention the partial burning of one of Wheeling's most thriving and first-class establishments, the Glass works of Hobbs, Brockunier & Co., which occurred on Friday evening, about five o'clock. Just before the alarm was sent in, a small tongue of flame was discovered on the roof, near the south end of the factory, just where the pipe from the glory hole furnace pierces the roof. It was but a small blaze and might easily have been extinguished. The factory was well supplied with hose and water cocks, besides Babcock extinguishers, but when a hose was made ready not a drop of water responded to the turning of the cock. Someone seized a Babcock and mounted to the roof, but he slipped and fell, bringing the extinguisher with him. By this time the reel arrived and made its connection, but there was no water, and it was powerless. Prayers, curses, and entreaties were showered upon our Water Works, but without bringing the much needed fluid, and in the meantime the flames had slowly crept over the entire roof and were pursuing their devouring way. A garden hose would have quenched the flames when discovered without the loss of fifty dollars, and the large crowd which had assembled grew exasperated at the sight of the destruction of thousands of dollars worth of property, without an apparent chance of salvation. Creeping to the east or rear, the flames attacked the chemical room, where saltpetre was stored, and on taking hold there roared and hissed in unappeasable fury. The mold room, engine house and factory were now completely wrapped in flames, and the sight was one of unparalleled splendor and horror. To understand the situation I will give you an idea or plan of the works. The factory, warehouse, and mold shops together formed a right-angled triangle, with a hypotenuse toward the river; on the south was the mold room; then came the factory; then the packing room; then on the northern side are the warehouse and office, separated by an alley; and running parallel with the factory is the large two-story building devoted to cutting and grinding, mixing, engraving, sandblasting, etc. The south end of this building is of wood and though it took fire several times it escaped by a miracle. But the flames had completely burned out the south angle of the triangle, mentioned, and up into the right angle of the triangle leaving intact only the warehouse nearest the railroad and the adjoining office. Across Thirty-Sixth Street from the office is the large new etching building, which with the cutting room, escaped. It was connected by a bridge with the warehouse,* *but this structure was cut away to destroy communication. After the fire had been stopped at the warehouse by a fire-proof wall it was in condition to be successfully fought and then after two hours of fierce burning was subdued, and nothing remained of its former fury but the smoulderings on projecting woodwork. The factory was a ruin. Fortunately the floor was heavily arched with brick, and was therefore inde-structible, and the furnaces with their solid build, were their own safety. The glass in the pots is uninjured, and men are engaged firing the furnaces to maintain the glass in fusion. The presses and most of the molds and patterns were removed and a heavy loss averted. Stored in the solid arches mentioned were $50,000 worth of wood patterns, and after the fire they were discovered to be safe and sound. The molds were in tolerable condition, with portions lost, but not men-tionably damaged. At this time it is impossible to say what the loss will be. Mr. C. W. Brockunier informed your corre-spondent that he thought $40,000 would cover actual losses. The walls, with the exception possibly, of the south one, were in good condition, and the furnaces all right. This glasshouse is one of the largest in the country, and is now the pioneer establishment of the West. It gives employment to 450 or 500 men, boys and girls. But very few of these will be out of work for any considerable time, as the work of rebuilding will begin today. Mr. Brockunier says the company can loose no time in getting to work, and with a temporary roof the com-pany can go on as soon as the debris is cleared away. The multitude of hands employed in the cutting, grinding, engraving, etching, packing and shipping departments will lose no time. The losses are covered by insurance. The ware-house, cutting house, and etching room are fully insured, but as they are unharmed it is unnecessary to elaborate on that. The cutting shops and the burned portions together are insured for $33,000, of which $20,000 is on the latter.”*

By March 9, 1882, the south furnace was once more under roof and glass being made from it — seven days after the fire! Repairs had been made to four lears, and foundations were begun for four more. Expectations were that the other furnaces would be ready for making glass within the week. The mold shop was working and the cutting shop had enough ware on hand to continue work at full time.

Repairs continued through March of 1882 with the work-ers busy making glass in the midst of the construction, work-ing glass from two furnaces. The company not only made repairs to their factory following the fire but took advantage of the situation to make improvements. “The west end of Hobbs, Brockunier & Co.’s warehouse is being built up very rapidly, as are also the mold rooms on the south end of the factory.” “The new mold shop will be one story higher than the one that was destroyed by the fire, and the east end of the warehouse, which was also destroyed, will be the same size as it was making no change in the appearance of the structure. They expect to have it finished in two weeks.”

Construction and rebuilding continued in May: “The new iron roof over the engines at Hobbs, Brockunier & Co.’s. Glass

Works was finished yesterday, and the sides of the room will be boarded up as rapidly as possible. The brick masons started to work on the second story of the mold room yesterday. This portion of the factory is being pushed very rapidly, as they are badly in need of it. The new building that was completed about a week ago is 55 x 10 feet and is used for storing ‘snap-dragons.’ It is fireproof throughout.”

By August, Hobbs, Brockunier & Co. was running the fac-tory to full capacity and had a large number of orders on hand.

Today examples of engravings done at Hobbs, Brockunier are few. But in 1882 two reports were given which indicate to us today the extent and the variety of the decorated glassware made by Hobbs. The first is from June, 1882: “The South Wheeling Glass Works have just turned out some beautiful specimens of engraved glass ware particularly interesting at this time, during our races. Your correspondent was shown one piece yesterday. It was a fine cut glass decanter with a beautiful horse engraved upon it. The workmanship is perfec-tion, and we could well judge of the beauty of the whole set of glassware so exquisitely ornamented. But this is only in keep-ing with all the work done by this firm.” A September 1882, report is quite detailed in its reports of products and decora-tions. In addition, it gives some indication of the work of Otto Jaeger and the early works of Harry Northwood. Jaeger was considered to be the best glass engraver at Hobbs at this time. Northwood had recently come from England and was employed as an etcher.

“Mr. Harry Northwood, of the etching department of Hobbs, Brockunier & Co., had on exhibition some fine designs of workmanship which arrested the attention of all of artistic taste, and struck even the casual observer forcibly. The glass is not engraved as many supposed, nor is it etched by the ordinary process now in vogue in this country. It sur-passes in artistic design, fine workmanship and beauty of effect any work done by any other process. Mr. Northwood came from England less than a year ago, and brought the new idea with him. Among the ware shown is a pair of pitch-ers, one having a representation of ‘Lampetia complaining to Apollo,’ from the Odyssey, and the other ‘Neptune rising from the Sea,’ from the Iliad, which show they are produced by an artist. Another ‘Rebecca’ pitcher is surrounded with a wreath of roses, and for delicacy of work and beauty of design rivals anything we have ever seen. There is also a pitcher having an aquarium with fishes etched on the side, the effect being peculiarly beautiful when it is filled with water, and another with stags under trees show [sic] three distinct processes of etching. A novel and attractive set of ware called the ‘Vermi-celli’ set also attracted comment. He had also on display some genuine Wedgwood Rockingham ware, and etched by himself with an ornamental design on the edge. The differ-ence between this work and the etching produced by the ordi-nary process consists not simply in the superior artistic work, but in the peculiar bright outlines which surround all the figures. In the stag scene and in some of the other pieces

three effects, one, a sort of mottled, one gray and one bright rounded line, appear. Some of the wine glasses and other small pieces are perfect gems. This gentleman has carved a cameo by hand with chisels on dark blue glass that is wonderful, having taken six weeks' continuous labor. Mr. Otto Jaeger, of the same establishment, had another display in the way of engraved ware. Mr. Jaeger is known throughout the whole country as the most noted engraver of the day. This display was larger than the centennial display of the same kind — in fact the largest display ever made in this country…. In looking over the display the following choice bits are noted down; a pitcher has two birds hovering over a nest perched on the limbs of a tree on which are two of their young; the plumage and poise of the birds is such that one is almost deceived into believing them natural. Several water sets were displayed, consisting of a pitcher, tray, two goblets, and bowl. The bird is standing in a very natural position. The design is especially tasty and neat, being made so by the bluebells and Scotch thistles which are engraved in. A pitcher with two bald eagles fighting surrounded by a wreath of holly is a very bold and attractive design. An elaborate water set showing the most careful and accurate work has a deer and panther engraved surrounded by foliage. This is a very choice and expensive piece. A pitcher that is made plain is made very handsome by the engraving thereon of a halting stallion; the manner in which the action of the muscles is brought out is wonderful and a matter of curiosity as to how it is done. A fancy cut decanter with a horse engraved in a small medallion is very fine. A miscellaneous collection of egg-shell goblets on which is some very rare work in the shape of ostriches, cranes, bouquets, palm trees, and lilies of the valley. These goblets give to the display a very fine and rich appearance; also half a dozen goblets on which full rigged ships are engraved. The skillful workmanship, steady hand, and true eye that it took to engrave the article are wonderful to contemplate. A water tumbler with dolphin and crown was very plain but rich. It was highly polished, and the minute points in the crown gleamed like the diamonds they were intended to represent. A Whiskey decanter with tray and twelve glasses, with fuchsias engraved on them, is very beautiful. A goblet with merely a pheasant is magnificent. Every feather of the bird is shown, and every fibre of the ferns is seen, the same as if it was a piece of nature's handiwork. A goblet with the steamer Bristol is certainly worthy of notice."

Hobbs, Brockunier & Co. seems to have suffered fewer strikes by workmen than many other factories. This may be partly explained by the way in which they treated their workers as evidenced by this 1882 quote: "The largest furnace at Hobbs, Brockunier & Co.'s glass works is being repaired. It will be ready for service again by the middle of January. This firm still keeps the men employed that have worked at this furnace, so that no man employed by them ever loses his time." In actuality, the men from this furnace shared their time with the men who worked at the other furnaces so that while none had full time, all had some employment. This also helped keep the men available to Hobbs rather than having them look for employment elsewhere.

By October of 1882 Hobbs, Brockunier & Co. was making items in Optic, Venetian, Craquelle, and, according to an ad, were making the colors of sapphire, rose, marine green, and old gold.

The factory had been rebuilt and was completely ready for

Ad announcing Hobbs, Brockunier & Co.'s holiday colors and patterns for 1882. *Crockery and Glass Journal, October, 1882.*

business by January of 1883. However, trade was slow in the spring. Uncertainty about tariff legislation pending in the U. S. Congress helped delay glass production. The large 16 pot furnace was not lit and repairs were made to it. Early in the year Hobbs depended on sales of their staple items: lamps, chandeliers, and the relatively new Craquelle. Hobbs also depended heavily on their foreign business. "Hobbs, Brockunier & Co. have been engaged for years in the shipment of goods to the various English colonies, extending their shipment in many instances to Australia and the islands of New South Wales. Almost weekly they send goods to South America."

In February of 1883 William F. Russell applied for a design patent for producing decorated glassware. The patent was assigned to Hobbs, Brockunier & Co. The process described a method to form ribs or "corrugations" on the exterior surface of the blown glass. Spiral exterior ribs are sometimes found on bowls similar to the No. 205 bowls and some lamp globes.

Hobbs, Brockunier & Co. usually seemed to have business even when business was bad enough to force other factories to close. In May of 1883, reports stated: "Hobbs, Brockunier & Co. are doing probably as good a trade as any glasshouse in the West. They have been in the business so long that they have customers who have been buying from them for nearly if not quite a half century." "Hobbs, Brockunier & Co. have their entire producing capacity at work, and there is no complaint of dullness or prices at this factory. They run and have run right along for years, never complain, never boast, produce plenty of ware and sell it. In short, they are ideal glass manufacturers."

Two new lines of lamps were introduced in mid 1883, but these are not identifiable today. Also mentioned were new styles of fancy shades, and particularly, new designs on etched globes. For several weeks new goods were alluded to without details. By the end of August more specific details began to emerge. Spangled glass was the first described.

William Leighton, Jr., was granted a design patent for spangled blown glassware. He had applied for both design and mechanical patents for this glassware on the same day, September 28, 1883. His design patent was granted for 14 years, so American glass companies were unable to make any spangled blown glassware until after late 1897, unless they ignored the patent. His process, according to the patent, resulted in "A new article of manufacture, a piece of glassware having spangles or flakes of infusible crystalline material embedded between upper and lower layers or strata of its mass." Leighton specifically mentioned mica as the "infusible crystalline material" but did not limit the patent to the use of mica only. His patent was specifically for blown ware, not pressed ware.

Sales improved in the latter part of 1883: "They have been very, very busy." All furnaces were in production and orders for lamps were particularly large, with business being described as the best in two years.

In October 1883, reports were given about the art-type glassware being made by Hobbs. "The item of expense does not seem to go for much with purchasers of these goods. All they appear to care for is the quality, and the more expensive the work, the more unique the design, the better they like it. 'The infinity of changes that molten glass is susceptible to is something phenomenal,' said a gentleman at the factory. 'All that a designer has to do is to furnish an idea, and that idea is made tangible in a moment.... No person is obliged to have a set of ware of the same design as that of his neighbors.... The educated designer is the man who is always in demand about a factory, for by the result of his lucubrations are the factories maintained.'" The variety of types of glass made by the company always seemed to impress reporters. In late 1884, reports stated: "The advantage this firm has over most of its Western (and Eastern, too, for that matter) competitors is that it can make ordinary glass and at the same time glass of the finest manufacture. No greater variety is made in any other factory in the world."

In late October and early November, Craquelle and Spangled were being suggested as excellent Christmas gifts. Craquelle was so popular that several shops at Hobbs, Brockunier & Co. were making it exclusively. This is an interesting detail since Craquelle is quite hard to find today. Another puzzle for today's collectors is that Opal was in great demand for the Christmas season of 1883. Exactly what items or patterns were made in Opal at this time are not known today.

Hobbs, Brockunier & Co. were also exhibiting "Roman, Grecian and Trojan vases" in their sample room. At least three patterns which are unknown today were introduced in 1883 — Nos. 126, 127, and 128. No. 126 was described as "diamond and waterfall" design. These patterns may not have been pressed ware but cut designs.

Hobbs, Brockunier & Co. narrowly escaped disaster in October of 1884 when "The oil tank sprung a leak and the oil ran down a hill and into the gutter by the B. & O. R. R. track, where it caught fire in some manner, and at once the flames ran alongside the gutter until for a space of nearly a square a blaze about five feet high marked its course. Two empty freight cars took fire and were entirely destroyed, and the good work by the home company early saved the factory." Hobbs, Brockunier & Co. was again spared in early 1884 when the Ohio River rose to within 30 yards of the factory. The factory stood on relatively high ground, but two of the salesmen, W. S. Brady and B. M. Hildreth, lost many of their household possessions to the flood which inundated most of the city. Certainly many workers and their families who lived in the lower areas were also devastated by their losses during this flood.

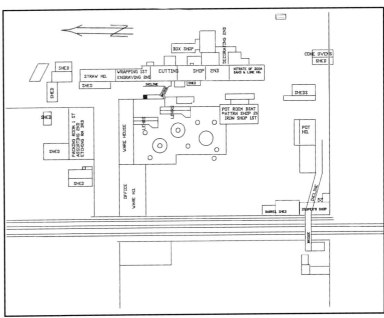

Layout of various buildings of Hobbs, Brockunier & Co. redrawn from an 1884 Sanborn Fire Insurance map.

The new patterns and effects brought out in the year of 1884 continued to be innovative and striking. In April, Polka Dot was introduced in its various colors, including crystal, old gold, sapphire, marine green, canary, ruby, rubina verde, and aurora. Polka Dot is often called Inverted Thumbprint today. Hobbs, Brockunier & Co. used the Polka Dot optic to enhance many existing and new blown ware molds, including lamp shades and globes. "Aurora colors" were mentioned in reference to Polka Dot — what was meant by Aurora is unknown today.

By the end of September announcements were made about amberina followed closely by mentions of the entire No. 101 Daisy and Button pattern, which Hobbs called Hobnail Diamond. Hobbs, Brockunier & Co. had been granted permission from the Libbey Co. to make amberina in pressed ware only. The Libbey Co. had developed and patented amberina and made the color almost exclusively in blown ware. Hobbs, Brockunier & Co. made a number of blown items, especially in Polka Dot, which look like true amberina which is a heat-sensitive glass. However, close examination of the Hobbs, Brockunier & Co. pieces reveals that these are actually Ruby Amber — an amber glass body plated with a gather of ruby lining part of the body. This technique gives a very close visual approximation of true amberina glass but lacks the delicate shading between the colors. Mention was made that the rubina verde color was new at this time and was especially used for lamp globes.

Bringing out No. 101 Daisy & Button and Polka Dot patterns, along with all the new colors, gave Hobbs, Brockunier & Co. excellent sales during the last months of 1884. "The holiday articles…this season surpass in originality of design and beauty of finish, any goods yet got out for the trade by this firm."

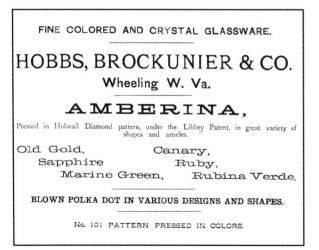

Ad for Hobbs, Brockunier & Co.'s amberina, referring to the Libbey patent. *Crockery & Glass Journal*, October 1885.

Fuel at a reasonable cost was always a concern for glass factories. While Hobbs, Brockunier & Co. had ample supplies of coal, recent improvements in gas furnaces made this the fuel of choice. Since 1880 when the first Gill furnace was installed in the factory, Hobbs had been using producer gas to fire its furnaces, made by heating coal in a closed vessel and then burning the fumes given off. The use of natural gas would improve the clarity of the glass produced because it did not contain sulfur and burned cleanly. Hobbs, Brockunier & Co. apparently owned some land in the Wellsburg area and in the fall of 1884, a gas well was struck there. While the gas was an important find, it was not deemed possible to move the massive factory to Wellsburg because of expenses. Instead, plans were made to pipe the gas to Wheeling. By February, 1886 the gas still had not been brought to the factory. "It is a pity that, with the enterprise exhibited by the several Wheeling glass firms, and the many fine, skilled workmen resident here, that no successful effort has been made to bring natural gas here…. The finest table ware, including color combinations, is made here, and workmen are often compelled to lay idle while those making fine ruby ware 'warm in' and reheat in the open mouths of pots filled with molten glass, so as to avoid sulphuring the ware. Besides, some trouble is often experienced with the gasoline 'glory holes.' Natural gas would be an immense thing for the Wheeling glass firms." It was not until November of 1886 that Hobbs ran an ad announcing that they were running their three furnaces and "our entire plant with NATURAL GAS, and yet find it difficult to fill orders as promptly as we could wish."

Charles Brockunier was always interested in the sales of the company and the politics of the country. In 1885 it was reported: "Mr. Brockunier thinks that the great need of the glass business today is a good foreign trade, with cheap rates of transportation, revised navigation laws and rapid mail facilities. The manufacturers of the United States would supply South America and Australia with most of their manufactured articles. He hopes Cleveland, reform and a new Congress will see to it that we get these." Brockunier was also the president of the Manufacturers' Gas Co. of Wheeling which supplied natural gas to the factory. In 1883 he served as president of the National Glass Manufacturers' Association; in 1887 he was vice president.

Already in January of 1885 reports indicated that the successful lines brought out by Hobbs, Brockunier & Co. in 1884 were being copied, but "the results have been so futile as to excite only a feeling of derision on the part of the manufacturers." This reference is probably to both Polka Dot and Daisy and Button which were widely copied by many companies of the time and later. At the same time indications were given of plans to come for 1885: " [Hobbs, Brockunier & Co.] distanced for years all ordinary competition…. It will be diversified, both in color and articles made…. While the common grades of ware will still be made, they will not be turned out so largely as heretofore." During these few years from 1883 to 1888, Hobbs, Brockunier & Co. was at its most innovative.

The focus was turning from staple wares to exotic glasses and unusual patterns. During this period William Leighton, Jr. was able to make many of his most unusual glass colors and decorative effects commercially successful. "This firm may be expected to show to the trade this year the finest goods made on this continent."

Announcements were made of opalescent glass being introduced in "new goods" while color was reported selling well with special mention of sapphire being in demand for use as decorative "parlor ornaments."

Following the trade shows early in the year, March reports told of the expanding line of colors now available — up to "twelve or fifteen." Hall lights, cylindrical globes, and an umbrella shade in Daisy and Button were among the new products listed.

Despite the glowing reports of new wares and new colors, sales appear to have been slow during early 1885. By June ruby amber, the copy of true amberina, was introduced. "Decorated wares" were also listed as being in the line although the type of decoration was unspecified. Trade remained moderate through September, but by early November the factory was in full blast with all three furnaces running.

In September of 1886, the *Wheeling Daily Intelligencer* published a major review of the glasshouses of Wheeling, tracing the history of glassmaking in the area from its beginnings until the present time. One of the most interesting items in this history was the description of the Hobbs factory at that time. "From the little concern of 1836 these works have grown in the manufacture of table ware and fine goods until their capacity excels that of any other single glasshouse in the country. The buildings cover an area of several acres. The works are now composed of three furnaces with a melting capacity of 150 tons per week, clay room and pot manufactory, mold shops, cutting shops, etching rooms, decorating rooms with necessary kilns to burn decorated ware, etc. Six hundred and fifty hands are employed. About four hundred car loads of goods are shipped annually to every part of the United States, Cuba, South America, Australia, and Europe. Sample rooms are kept by this firm in Boston, New York, Philadelphia and Baltimore, with traveling salesman in the West and North."

The same article described some of the ware that was being made by the company. "Several thousand dollars worth of gold bullion is used annually in coloring the fancy ware, producing a pure ruby. This firm makes a larger amount of ruby glass annually, than all other houses in this country combined."

"Some six or eight years ago the importers began to bring more largely of fancy colored articles made in France, England, Bohemia, Belgium and Germany, and American taste for these goods becoming aroused, this factory was the first in this country to reproduce the imported ware. Latterly it began to improve on foreign designs, reversing the order of things, leaving foreign manufacturers to imitate Wheeling. The trade built up in this country for colored ware has excelled even the expectations of the firm, and a growing demand is the reward

of their enterprise. The larger part of the production of the works is of this style of goods."

In late November a mention was made of "their latest novelties in coral ware, which for elegance of shape and beauty of coloring cannot be excelled anywhere. They have a line of pitchers in this ware of exquisite finish, the colors rivaling the bloom on the peach." Another short mention stated that this new ware would be ready for sale January 1, 1886. Trade journals referred to this exotic and sought-after glass relatively infrequently. Originally Coral was a copy of glass imported from England made by Thomas Webb & Sons. But the sale of the Oriental porcelain Morgan Peach Blow vase for the then extravagant amount of $18,000 and Hobbs' glass copy, however, spurred sales and interest in the new glass.

In February of 1886, W. L. Libbey & Son sent announcements to the glass trade concerning a lawsuit against the Mt. Washington Glass Co. and Frederick Shirley. The court upheld Libbey's patent for blown amberina or rose amber (Libbey's term). Libbey advised that they had licensed only Hobbs, Brockunier & Co. to make pressed amberina and that they would prosecute anyone who tried to make or sell blown amberina in this country. Interestingly, Gillinder did make at least a moderate amount of pressed amberina in Daisy and Button, apparently in direct conflict with the warning from Libbey or causing the warning.

In contrast to the rather cursory mentions of coral (Peach Blow), starting in March extensive reports were given to the new Dew Drop and Pineapple lines. Dew Drop (today called Hobnail) was patented by William Leighton, Jr. and William F. Russell on June 1, 1886, and given patent number 343,133. Prior to this patent, opalescent effects were produced using spot molds and then blowing the article to the finished shape. The new method used molds with the "nodules" already in the mold and the glass was pressed, not blown. There has been great confusion over the years with many referring to Hobbs' Dew Drop as blown, but it is not — all of it is pressed but often hand tooled into final form.

Dew Drop, No. 323, is one of few patterns that lived up to its advance publicity. It truly was an innovation in glass and customers loved it. Much of it is available today — along with

AMBERINA.
Pat. July 24, 1883

INJUNCTION GRANTED.

To the Trade: Boston, February 24th, 1886.
   We hereby call your attention to the decision of Judge Colt, of the U. S. Circuit Court, given February 19, 1886, granting a preliminary injunction in our suit against the Mt. Washington Glass Co. and F. S. Shirley for the infringement of our patent on "Amberina Glass." The decision declares our patent to be valid, and in accordance with it the Mount Washington Glass Co. and Mr. Shirley are now enjoined from manufacturing or selling "Amberina" or "Rose Amber" Glassware. We take this opportunity to caution all Manufacturers and Dealers against infringing our patent by manufacturing "Amberina" Ware or selling any such ware unless the same is obtained from us or some manufacturer duly licensed by us. We have granted no license to manufacture "Blown Amberina Ware," of which we are the sole manufacturers, but have licensed Messrs. Hobbs, Brockunier & Co., of Wheeling, W. Va., to make pressed "Amberina," they being the only authorized manufacturers of these goods. Any Amberina Ware made, sold, or offered for sale by other parties is a direct infringement of our patent, and we shall enforce our rights against all such. We shall be pleased to receive your orders and give them our prompt attention.
   Yours, etc., W. L. LIBBEY & SON.

Injunction notice from Libbey regarding Amberina. *Crockery & Glass Journal*, 1886.

19

its myriad imitations. It is fascinating to collect Dew Drop. It was made in more colors and effects than any other of Hobbs' patterns. At least 18 color variations are known, and most are also available with allover satin finish. Crystal was enhanced with Frances decoration, and also plain crystal with amber rims was made.

The mid-year pattern introduced was No. 102 which we have christened Maltese and Ribbon — using descriptive terms used by Hobbs, Brockunier & Co. in the patents. This pattern was overshadowed by Dew Drop, as little of it is found today, especially in colors.

In September references were made to: "323 'Richelieu' is a superb line, and the 323 'Rubina' is a very pretty combination." The reference to Richelieu is vague, but seems to refer to a color or an effect of glass, not the pattern, as it is used to describe pieces in No. 323 Dew Drop. Richelieu also is used to describe the No. 205 bowls. Since the bowls are often found in ruby with white rims and Dew Drop also comes in ruby with opalescent decoration, Richelieu may refer to the ruby/white color combination reminiscent of a cardinal's robes. It later appears to also refer to other colored bodies with different color rims. The original meaning of the word remains obscure.

During the fall of 1886 Hobbs, Brockunier & Co. operated all three furnaces, "a fact that has not occurred for years." Their offerings included "Richelieu, coral, and novelties in rare representations of fruit in glass." Pears, apples, etc., in Coral glass are extremely rare today. "The past two years have been eventful ones in the history of this firm. They have been making finer goods and realizing more for their pains and ingenuity than for several years previous. The new designs in all the colors known to the trade require much time, labor and money to properly present, and the trade never loses anything by the introduction of new and fine goods."

In 1887 the company was exceedingly prolific, bringing out several new lines of both pressed and blown ware. Also announcements were made — "They have also gone largely into the decorating business, which adds richness to the appearance of the glassware." At this time, the decorations referred to were enameled decorations both on pressed ware patterns and blown ware. A new "handsome line of spiral glassware in delicate colors" was announced in February 1887. This was pattern No. 207 Murano which was first promoted in a Hobbs, Brockunier & Co. advertisement in March.

An intriguing, unknown line was advertised in April of 1887 as the new Choncha line. Hobbs, Brockunier & Co. also introduced their new Acorn lamps at this time, replacing their former Fairy lamps.

By mid year the new pressed pattern, No. 115 (now called Wheeling) was introduced along with several decorations, including enamels and engravings. The blown ware pattern introduced at the same time was No. 230 Neapolitan described as "decidedly the richest colored line we have seen." Charles W. Brockunier was appointed by the Wheeling Chamber of Commerce to head a committee to extend an invitation to President Cleveland to visit Wheeling. Brockunier had a shad-

ed ruby satin Neapolitan vase decorated with a written inscription in black old English letters. After being displayed in Wheeling, the vase was sent to President Cleveland, but he did not visit the city. The vase survives today in the collection of the Oglebay Institute in Wheeling.

Suddenly in September of 1887 the boys working at Hobbs, Brockunier & Co. went on strike. As can be expected, the trade journals took a dim view of this strike, as they did of all strikes. "Without any note of warning the boys, ranging from twelve to sixteen years of age, at one of the largest establishments here deliberately walked out of the factory, leaving the skilled workmen idle and closing the establishment. It was afterward learned that they wanted an advance of wages, and notwithstanding terms were satisfactory to the workmen, the small boys who hold the molds, carry wares to the ovens, and do what is called 'snapping' quit in a body, and as there are two or three hundred of them, and a change in the wages they are paid here means a change elsewhere, it assumed a matter of much importance. A full week's wages was lost to all the skilled workmen about the factory, as well as the product being lessened that much." Indeed, the next week's issue reported that the strike had ended. "The loss to the employees was fully $8,000, and the boys who caused the trouble and annoyance gained nothing."

John H. Hobbs celebrated his sixtieth birthday in October of 1887, "Mr. Hobbs was the recipient of elegant and numerous presents, among which was a water pitcher on which is painted an excellent likeness of himself as he appeared last summer on a tour round St. Clair Springs, Mich."

The first months of 1887 were very good for Hobbs, Brockunier & Co. with good sales and full employment. However, the last months of the year were plagued with unrest in the glassworkers' union. An industry-wide strike was threatened and labor unrest accelerated during the last quarter of the year. Finally, at midnight on December 31, the union declared its strike and completely shut down the tableware industry.

The charter for Hobbs, Brockunier & Co. expired at the end of December 1887. With the strike beginning at almost the same time, it was difficult to attract investors and money in order to organize a new company. Charles Brockunier and William Leighton chose not to remain as active partners in the new corporation, but continued to have money invested in the company. Dalzell Bros. & Gilmore had relocated to Findlay, Ohio, following the lure of cheap land, cheap gas, and cheap labor. Leighton and his son, George, became associated with the new company, renamed Dalzell, Gilmore & Leighton. Brockunier retired from an active part in the glass business at this time. He had been in ill health for some time and had also suffered the death of two sons.

Several men left the company during this period to join Fostoria Glass Co. including two salesmen, Benjamin Hildreth, becoming sales manager of Fostoria, and Lucien B. Martin eventually becoming the president of Fostoria Glass Co. by 1891. James Russell had departed in 1885 to manage a factory in Melbourne, Australia, but returned and was associated with the Fostoria Glass Co. William Russell left to join Dalzell, Gilmore & Leighton in Findlay, Ohio, as factory manager in 1888.

HOBBS GLASS CO. — 1888 to 1891

The Hobbs Glass Co. applied for its new charter at the end of February 1888. At the time of application the stockholders were listed as J. H. Hobbs, C. W. Brockunier, and William Leighton, Jr., Howard Hazlett, and Walter H. Rinehart. Attempts were made to raise $75,000 in addition to the $75,000 allocated to the physical assets and good will, but the attempt failed. By August the investors were still trying to reorganize the company and had listed the capital stock as $100,000, evaluating the plant at $42,000. This time they were able to raise the needed capital by selling stock and the company was then chartered. By this time Leighton and Brockunier had given up active involvement in the company although reports indicated that they still had money invested in the venture. Announcements were that H. E. Waddell would become secretary, leaving a similar position at Central Glass Co. Nicholas Kopp became the "glass maker" or

Hobbs Glass Co. letterhead.

chemist, taking the place of William Leighton, Jr. Nicholas Kopp immediately began working on several new lines. Stockholders were now listed as J. H. Hobbs, William Leighton, Jr., Henry Schmulbach, A. J. Clark, and Howard Hazlett. Smith Butler became the factory manager at this time.

The factory was restarted in late August making standard lines in crystal and colors with only the large 15-pot furnace, but two furnaces were in use by October. A report of a line of new tumblers in opalescent was given in late October. In December advance reports of two new lines were presented. "They are engaged in some new patterns in crystal and colors that will astonish the trade.... One is blown, the other is a pressed set, while a variety of novelties are intermingled. The entire stock of this company is brand new. None of the stock of Hobbs, Brockunier & Co. was purchased, indeed, there was none left to purchase."

In January the company was advertising two new lines, No. 326 Swirl in "10 different effects," No. 327 Quartered Block with Stars and many other specialties including shades and water sets. Soon the company was running its two larger

furnaces to full capacity. In March of 1889 reports of machine-made glass were given: "A flat celery and olive dish made by a new machine of this company are taking well with the trade everywhere." These pieces were probably the forerunners of the new Crystalina line.

John H. Hobbs at this time was dividing "his time between the glass works and the new Windsor Hotel, of which he is principal owner." Hobbs apparently was taking a great interest in the hotel and its continued renovation. "Mr. John H. Hobbs, president of Hobbs Glass Co., and one of the proprietors of the new Hotel Windsor, is gratified at the increasing popularity of the new hotel. Traveling men who stop there once always go back again." A later comment noted, "Mr. Hobbs gives personal attention to the entertainment of guests."

The Windows lamps were brought out in May of 1889: "No. 326 the new line of fancy lamps.... These lamps are made in crystal opalescent, sapphire opalescent, ruby opalescent and plain crystal. There are five sizes, besides a night lamp." A few months later Hobbs Glass Co. announced three new lines: "No. 330, in imitation heavy cut, No. 331 in ruby, pink, ornate and crystal, blown, and No. 332 in crystal, plain and engraved, pressed." No. 330 is now called

Ad for the Hotel Windsor. *Crockery & Glass Journal,* 1890.

Hobbs' Block and No. 332 is known as Oglebay. The Oglebay pattern is made from reworked molds of the No. 115 Wheeling pattern. The herringbone ridges were removed, leaving broad, plain panels.

In December, Hobbs Glass Co. announced their No. 334 tableware, now called Crystalina, and No. 335 Hexagonal Block. Crystalina was patented April 1, 1890, by H. E. Waddell and given patent number 19,749.

By December of 1889, Kopp was referred to as the "factory boss and metal maker" and H. E. Waddell the "secretary and general manager."

In early 1890, Crystalina and Hexagonal Block were advertised, along with a new line of lamps, No. 338, made in crystal, blue, and ruby in coral (Seaweed).

In May of 1890 reports were that Hobbs Glass Co. was drilling a gas well on their property. "Mr. Waddell, the efficient secretary, said that they proposed finding gas, oil, or China before stopping. This will be the first gas well bored in the city of Wheeling."

In October of 1890 Hobbs again suffered a major fire. At this time a loss of $30,000 was estimated. "The fire started near the entrance to the long building located in the rear of the main factory, which is used for the engraving, etching, decorating and mixing departments. It is thought that the fire originated from natural gas, which, however, was turned low when the place was closed up. The loss to the buildings, machinery, stock, etc., will amount to from $25,000 to $30,000. The total insurance on the burned section is $12,000, and the bulk was held by foreign companies [companies not of the Wheeling area]. Glassmaking was resumed on Sunday night as usual at Hobbs Glass Works, and temporary arrangements are being made for engraving and cutting. The fire will not interfere with glassmaking...."

Three weeks later, reports were that glass was being made. H. E. Waddell apparently was given much credit for saving the factory and held in high esteem by the other employees at Hobbs Glass Co. for his efforts during the fire.

Pattern No. 339 Leaf and Flower was announced in December of 1890, with special mention of its four bottle caster set. New decorations on No. 334 Crystalina were also mentioned at this time.

The Ohio River flooded the city of Wheeling again in February of 1891, although Hobbs Glass Co. was not affected except for being isolated from all communication. The workers were prevented from reaching the factory, so glass could not be made for most of a week.

On February 12, 1891, a charter was issued in Harrisburg, PA, to a new company to be known as the United States Glass Co. Hobbs Glass Co. became a charter member in the company and was hereafter designated as Factory H of the U. S. Glass Co. John H. Hobbs was a director of the new firm. H. E. Waddell was retained as factory manager of Factory H.

Following the formation of U. S. Glass, several key men at the Hobbs Glass Co. left to take positions at other factories. Nicholas Kopp immediately left to join the Fostoria Shade and Lamp Co. in Fostoria, Ohio.

During April and May of 1891, announcements were made of a new "ice cream tray and saucers, made in crystal, plain or with gold finished edge." The No. 341 square font lamps were also introduced at this time in "blue opalescent, ruby opalescent and white opalescent" — now called Snowflake lamps. These were made with a metal screw socket joining the bases and fonts. This metal sleeve was covered with a glass collar. No. 341 Mario was introduced in July, one of the last major patterns introduced by Hobbs Glass Co.

Sales were slowing for Hobbs Glass Co. during the middle of 1891, although the lamps were still selling well. "Sixteen moves of lamps are made here every 24 hours, which means a large output." Sales seemed to improve for a few months during the fall season, but shortly reports indicated that trade was only fair. The beginning of the end was now upon Hobbs Glass Co. — now only Factory H of the immense U. S. Glass Co. Early in 1892 reports were optimistic about production and sales, but these were probably not entirely truthful. By March 1892, a small sentence spoke volumes: "Factory H is doing very well but not as busy as it might be." Terse optimistic reports continued through the first half of the year but hints were that business could have been better.

On August 8, 1891, Mr. James D. Wilson, the auditor for U. S. Glass Co. sent a request to each member glass factory requesting statements showing sales by month for the preceding year — July, 1890 through June, 1891. He also specifically requested sales for July, 1890 and July, 1891. Hobbs Glass Company complied with this request on August 12, 1891, with the following accounting:

Enclosed please find statement of sales from June 30'/90 to June 30'/91.

July 1890	*8,504.58*
Aug 1890	*11,707.58*
Sept 1890	*24,408.09*
Oct 1890	*21,607.51*
Nov 1890	*17,483.67*
Dec 1890	*7,762.77*
Jany 1891	*7,879.91*
Feby 1891	*19,463.21*
March 1891	*19,264.25*
April 1891	*13,826.85*
May 1891	*7,626.16*
June 1891	*24,717.49*
	$184,253.07

Yours respt.
Hobbs Glass Co.
Adams

From another account, the July 1890 sales were reported as $8,804.08 and the July 1891 sales were only $2,604.83. The auditor also compiled the annual expenses of each company. Hobbs Glass Company paid its manager, Mr. Waddell, $3,000; the bookkeeper received $1,200. The day factory manager received $2,000, and the night manager $1,600. The three salesmen received respectively: $1,500, $2,000, and $2,000. The superintendent of packing received $720. The invoice clerk received $480; the shipping clerk, $780; the night foreman, $1,100; and the superintendents of the mold shop, $1,250 each, for day and night shifts. Office expenses were calculated at $10,960 and factory expenses, $3,800 annually. Hobbs Glass Company had some of the highest expenses of the member factories. Only Central paid its manager more and the expenses for both the factory and office were quite high compared with most of the other factories.

Some time within the first year of the existence of U. S. Glass, the company sent out one or more representatives to visit each factory to give an unbiased evaluation of each. This was done to help the executives decide whether the member factories were productive or were losing money. When Hobbs Glass Co. joined U. S. Glass it was given a total value of $175,498.66. The breakdown of the evaluation was as follows:

Value of buildings	$66,244.24
Machinery	65,735.89
Land	30,218.80
Good Will	13,299.73
Total Value	$175,498.66
Value of Materials	$15,342.01
Value of Glassware	35,650.24
Total Rec'd from Hobbs Glass Co.	$226,490.91

Other calculations included the annual taxes from July 1, 1891, to June 30, 1892, as $323.10, but from July 1, 1892, to June 30, 1893, the taxes had risen to $1,104.17. Fire insurance was listed as $17,000. Expenses are enumerated below:

Total annual cash carrying while idle:

Salaries & Wages	$5,511.40
Taxes	1,104.17
Insurance	238.00
Repairs	1,026.74
Total	$7,880.31

The opinion rendered by the representative seems to have sealed the fate of the Hobbs Glass Co. "This is an expensive plant. The goods are colored and fancy that are not made elsewhere — as a rule. Its product is high priced but each sale is a small one. Its record as a money maker shows up fairly well with the others in the combination. The plant is old and a new factory with its capacity could be built for one half of the investment. My own opinion is that if the product of this plant could be taxed with the exact cost of selling its goods, that its net showing would be poor in the way of profits."

Hobbs Glass Company actually was in the middle range of income with six factories selling more annually. Certainly their high expenses combined with the lower income was a factor in deciding to close it permanently. The evaluator apparently felt that much money would have to be spent on improvements to make the factory competitive, especially since U. S. Glass was building new, more automated factories and updating existing ones to limit the number of workers. Hobbs, because of its fancy art-type products, necessarily was not adaptable to machine-made glassware but its wares required much hand working and finishing.

The U. S. Glass Co. was formed in the spring of 1891. For the January 1892 glass show in Pittsburgh, most of the member companies brought out a new pattern. These first 12 patterns became the basis for the new company's wares, the patterns having been developed by each member factory.

These patterns were given numbers in the 15,000 series. Factory O contributed their new Silver Age pattern — now called U. S. Coin — and was designated as pattern No. 15,005. Factory H (Hobbs) did not have a pattern in the 15,000 series.

On May 26, 1892, the *Wheeling Daily Intelligencer* reported the seizure of the coin glass molds. *"A set of glass molds belonging to the U. S. Glass Company and used at the Central works and another set used at the Hobbs factory were seized yesterday by a special officer of the United States government, and will be destroyed today under his supervision.*

"Several months ago the Central Glass Company brought out a novel series of sets of glassware, the distinguishing feature being the ornamentation of all the pieces with representations of silver coins, from dollars down to dimes, according to the sizes of pieces of ware. The dies were very faithful representations of the coins, and the imitations were etched white. The effect was very novel and pretty, and the ware became popular at once, and has had a large sale.

"The moulds cost several thousand dollars. The moulds for lamps with similar ornamentation were taken to the Hobbs factory, and the other ware continued to be manufactured at the Central.

"On Tuesday a special agent of the treasury who was at Pittsburgh, received a telegram telling him to look into the question whether this ware did not come within the prohibition of the law which forbids the making of any design or representation in imitation of United States coin. The officer called at the company's office in Pittsburgh, and from there came down here and examined the ware and the moulds. He said the ware could do no harm, and was not in itself illegal, but the existence of the moulds could not be allowed under the law. He therefore took possession and to-day the moulds will be destroyed under his superintendence. Possibly other designs will be substituted for the coin ornaments.

"Manager Scott, of the Central factory, said last night that the company had about cleared enough to pay for the moulds. The only thing serious about the seizure was that it stopped the manufacture of a line of glass which was proving very profitable." While the molds were destroyed, the glass which had been made was not seized, nor destroyed, and the company continued to sell its remaining stock.

This report clarifies what coin glass was made at the Hobbs (Factory H) works. Central made all pieces in the pattern including some of the lamps, but Hobbs made only lamps. Other accounts specify that the molds themselves were not destroyed, but that the coin design was chiseled off all the molds. The molds were reused to make the pattern now known as Columbian Coin.

Adding to Hobbs' difficulties was the fire in early April 1893, which damaged the decorating department. "The decorating department of Factory H of the United States Glass Co. recently damaged by fire is again in running order. Temporary sheds have been erected over the kilns which were found still to be in good condition to allow burning of ware which had been colored in another portion of the factory. As soon as the work of adjusting the insurance is completed, the erection of a fine corrugated iron building will be started." In August comment was made: "Operations will be resumed at Factory H of the United States Glass Co. [after the summer shut down] about the 15th, by which time the works will be in better shape than ever. The new building measures 200 by 30 feet, two stories high, and will be used for cutting and engraving."

Actually, work did not resume at Hobbs at that time. In fact, none of U. S. Glass Company's factories were started immediately after the summer break. In mid-September, notice was taken that "They [U. S. Glass] have neither started that [Hobbs] nor any other of their factories, nor will they do

Catalog illustration, Silver Age, No. 15,005 (U.S. Coin) table set.

so until the matters in dispute between the Associated Glass Manufacturers and the workers are satisfactorily adjusted." By October reports were: "Fires were drawn in Factory H of the U. S. Glass Co. last week…. It begins to look like a number of the glass factories in this neighborhood would start non-union when they do resume."

Matters were not satisfactorily adjusted between U. S. Glass and the glassworkers. U. S. Glass was quickly erecting large automated factories at Gas City, Indiana, and Glassport, Pennsylvania. Both these large plants were to be equipped with the latest automatic equipment and thus would require fewer skilled glassworkers. Naturally the union was opposed to such actions. While it was never openly spoken of in the trade journals — who were anti-union — U. S. Glass had certainly been formed to oppose the union and to introduce the automated equipment. It also had been formed to help hold prices down for glassware since the country was in a depression. The union was so powerful that individual companies could not oppose it. The union had a large strike fund and could successfully keep striking members from one or two companies from returning to work for lack of money. The union provided it. However, it could not withstand the consolidation of so many factories under one management and act-

ing as one unit in negotiating contracts and wages. The union called a strike on October 12, 1893. It was a long and bitter strike, the union not admitting to defeat until January 1897. However, U. S. Glass had continued to make glass with its automated machinery and untrained workers and was in a stable financial position.

H. E. Waddell continued as manager of Factory H until mid-1893, when he left to join Elson Glass Co. as manager along with Percy Beaumont who had succeeded Kopp as chemist at Factory H. Both went to Elson Glass Co. along with Smith Butler who became factory manager and Edward Miller the foreman of the mold shop. At this point, glass was no longer being made at Factory H. Remaining stock was sold as late as May 1894 by Augustus G. Frohme who succeeded Waddell as manager.

If it was made of glass, Hobbs, Brockunier & Co. made it. If it was a decoration that could be done on glass, likewise Hobbs, Brockunier & Co. did it. Their approach to their products seems to be much as their approach to the physical holdings of the company — everything. They controlled their own destiny by making their own pots and machinery, owning their own fuel, and also making any type of glassware needed short of bottles and window glass. Much of what they produced will never be able to be attributed properly. There was simply too much of standard wares made, both in volume and variety. The lack of advertising and catalogs existing today also hampers attribution of glass to Hobbs, Brockunier & Co.

EPILOGUE

Hope continued for several more years that the old Hobbs, Brockunier & Co. factory would reopen. Many reports sporadically appeared in the trade journals describing schemes about raising money to purchase the old factory from U. S. Glass. Money always seemed to be a sticking point — the investors wanting to purchase the site for much less than U. S. Glass thought it was worth. Interestingly, U. S. Glass was continuing to maintain and even update the property as late as early 1895. Eventually the factory site was sold to Harry Northwood who had severed his connections with the National Glass Co. in late 1901. Northwood and Thomas Dugan purchased the factory in April 1902 for $40,000, only $10,000 of which was paid by them. U. S. Glass agreed to hold a $20,000 mortgage, and $10,000 was furnished by the Wheeling Board of Trade.

After several successful years, the H. Northwood Co. came on hard times following the death of Harry Northwood. The last glass of the company was made in December 1925. Thus ended the making of glass at the old Hobbs, Brockunier & Co. site.

November, 1893: "A largely attended meeting of the citizens of Wheeling was held in the offices of the Chamber of Commerce on November 20 to see what could be done toward purchasing Factories O and H, in this city of the United States Glass Co. A letter from the company stated that O cost them $274,000, including $40,000 for good will, leaving $232,000 and H cost

$178,300, including $13,000 for good will, leaving $165,300. Molds and etchings at the former cost $45,584 and molds at the latter $28,177, this to be deducted. The company offers to sell at 25 per cent off, leaving $244,154 for the two plants. Twenty eight business men subscribed stock. It was decided to apply for a charter at once and buy or build new factories."

May 23, 1894: "The last unsold glass at the old Hobbs plant owned by the United States Glass Co., was shipped a few days ago. A. G. Frohme has been in charge."

April, 1895: "The United States Glass Co. continues active work on the repairs at Factory H, in this city. The roof covering the entire plant has been put on and work commenced on repairs inside the factory. An entire set of new pipes to carry wind for cooling molds and ware from the fans has been contracted for, and A. H. Aube began work on them on the 28th. All other machinery and appliances are to be completely overhauled and the factory gotten ready for operation. Just when the factory will be started is problematical, of course, but it is now too late for spring trade and work on ware for fall trade seems unlikely to begin before July. However, the repairs are progressing so that work may begin on ten days' notice."

October, 1897: "Another effort is being made by the citizens of Wheeling, W. Va., to purchase the old Hobbs glass factory in that city from the United States Glass Company and put it in operation. About $50,000 has already been subscribed to a fund to start the works of which the A.F.G.W.U. [American Flint Glass Workers' Union] has subscribed $15,000 and Henry Schmulbach has taken $10,000 worth of stock. The amount required is $80,000. It is said that the plant can be purchased from the United States Glass Company as it stands for $38,000."

November, 1897: "The deal to purchase the old Hobbs glass factory and operate it has finally been declared off. The local union of glass workers at Wheeling headed the list with $15,000, but notwithstanding that sufficient encouragement could not be had to warrant further effort and the matter has finally been dropped."

September, 1898: "United States Senator N. B. Scott, unable to wean himself entirely away from the glass trade, and impelled by a patriotic motive to assist the business enterprises of his home city, last week took up the matter of securing control of the old Hobbs glass plant with D. C. Ripley, of the United States Co. The lowest cash price was asked for, and if this is reasonable Senator Scott, backed by local capitalists, will revive that industry. If the owners do not place a fair value upon this plant the spirit is such now that it is quite probable a new one will be built. There is no doubt that the necessary capital to organize a strong company is now at command. They prefer to revive that long idle plant, but they are determined men, interested in the material welfare of Wheeling, and they will not permit an unreasonable demand on the part of the present owners to baffle their efforts."

October, 1899: "The United States Glass Co. fixed $65,000 as the price of the bare plant formerly known as Hobbs-Brockunier & Co.'s, reserving three very valuable lots on the north side and all the equipment about the dismantled factory. This was regarded as too stiff and was promptly rejected. Since that time Senator N. B. Scott, who is spokesman for those who will start it, has been seriously ill, and is still unable to attend to affairs. If Mr. Ripley can give better terms they have not been communicated."

November, 1899: "It is definitely settled now that the Hobbs-Brockunier plant will not be acquired under the present conditions, and it is not absolutely certain that the new move will be carried to a successful issue. There is not the slightest doubt of money enough being in sight to put a new factory in operation, but the division of sentiment as to acquiring the three Hobbs furnaces or putting up an entirely new plant is the rock that may split the project wide open. What the final outcome will be is a matter of conjecture at this time."

The People

Few if any of the men involved achieved anything like national prominence. They were important only to the Wheeling area, and many of them mattered only to their families. Any examination of a piece of antique glass made in Wheeling, however, will confirm that the men and boys who worked in the glasshouses made their own memorials.

-Robert DiBartolomeo

Most of the men, women, and children who worked for Hobbs, Brockunier & Co. and its forerunners and successors are today nameless. Over the period of its life, the company employed many hundreds of people, most in hard, unfulfilling, hot jobs. The hours were long and the conditions poor — even dangerous.

The importance of Hobbs, Brockunier & Co. and the education in glassmaking that working at the factory gave the men is recognizable when one realizes that men from Hobbs went on to either own, manage, or hold responsible positions in more than 18 glassmaking factories including Central Glass Co., Elson Glass Co., Northwood Glass Co., Beaumont Glass Co., Fostoria Glass Co., Consolidated Glass Co., Dalzell Gilmore & Leighton Glass Co., Iowa City Glass Co., Belmont Glass Co., Riverside Glass Co., Hazel-Atlas Glass Co., La Belle Glass Co., Nickel Plate Glass Co., Model Flint Glass Co., Jefferson Glass Co., Buckeye Glass Co., Crystal Glass Co., Ohio Flint Glass Co., and Bonita Glass Co.

Today we are indebted to the anonymous workers who willingly endured hardships we can only imagine to produce the glass we so admire and covet. In an effort to give at least some of these people recognition, we have included biographical information on the following people who were either important at Hobbs, Brockunier & Co. or achieved fame in the glass world after their employment at the Wheeling factory.

The Barnes Family:

JAMES B. BARNES, 17 – to 1849. James B. Barnes had worked at New England Glass Co. from 1818 as superintendent of the pot or crucible room. He was credited by Deming Jarves with having engineered the factory's furnaces. In conjunction with J. L. Hobbs, J. F. Barnes (his son), and J.H. Hobbs, he purchased the former Plunkett and Miller glass factory at the corner of Wetzel Street and 36th Street in South Wheeling (Richietown) — the eventual site of Hobbs, Brockunier & Co. — and formed Barnes, Hobbs & Co. in 1845. The plant was named the South Wheeling Works after 1845. He died in 1849.

JAMES F. BARNES. James F. Barnes was the son of James B. Barnes. He succeeded his father in Barnes, Hobbs & Co. which was reorganized on his father's death as Hobbs, Barnes & Co. He sold his interest in this company for $15,000 in 1861. After selling his interest, he opened a retail store in Wheeling which sold glassware, among other things.

The Hobbs Family:

JOHN L. HOBBS, 1804 to 1881. John L. Hobbs was born in South Carolina and grew up in East Cambridge, Massachusetts. At an early age he was employed by the New England Glass Co. where he became superintendent of the cutting department and salesman on his twenty-first birthday. He visited the Wheeling area about 1844 along with James B. Barnes. He was an original partner of James B. Barnes in Barnes, Hobbs & Co. in 1845. He became the senior partner in Hobbs, Barnes & Co. in 1849. John L. Hobbs retired from active participation in the glass company in 1867, leaving the running of the business to his son, J. H. Hobbs. He opened a retail store selling crockery and glass, along with other items and supplies. Mr. Hobbs continued to be associated with J. H. Hobbs, Brockunier & Co. until his death in 1881, at age 77, in Philadelphia.

"DEATH OF A PROMINENT GLASS MANUFACTURER WHEELING, November 7, 1881

"John L. Hobbs, one of the most prominent glass manufacturers in the world, died at Philadelphia last Tuesday, in the seventy-seventh year of his age. Mr. Hobbs has been so long so prominently connected with the manufacture of glass in this country that we deem it but right to give our readers an epitome of his history.

"He was a gentleman widely known outside of this vicinity on account of his connection with the glass interests of the country — being one of the pioneers in the manufacture, and the inventor of several improvements. His parents were in South Carolina, his father doing some engineering work, in 1804. They were stationed at Fort Moultrie, and it was here that John L. Hobbs was born. They soon after moved back to New England, their home, where his brothers now reside.... His boyhood was passed in East Cambridge, Mass. When quite young he entered the employment of the New England Glass Co. So favorably impressed was this famous company with his capacity that they made him superintendent of their extensive cutting department and salesman the day he attained his majority.... In 1844 he turned his attention to the rapidly growing West, and after careful thought concluded to commence the manufacture of glass in Wheeling. He united with him Mr. James B. Barnes, and in April, 1845, they leased the then idle glassworks in South Wheeling, formerly owned by Plunkett and Miller. Here commenced a prosperous and brilliant business career.

"The works at that time consisted of two furnaces, containing fourteen of the small pots then in use. The glass manufactured was known as 'flint,' 'lead' or 'Full crystal,' and articles manufactured were solar chimneys, jars, and vials.

"In 1849 Mr. J. B. Barnes died, and the firm became composed of John L. Hobbs, James F. Barnes, and John H. Hobbs, and continued to do business under the firm name of Hobbs, Barnes & Co. until 1856. During that time the works were enlarged and new and improved furnaces built. In 1856 the firm became Barnes, Hobbs & Co., with the same gentlemen at the head, with the addition of J. K. Dunham. Later the name changed to Hobbs & Barnes. In February, 1863, the present firm of J. H. Hobbs, Brockunier & Co. was formed; and it was this firm that became famous for almost completely revolutionizing the character and the methods and appliances of finishing it. It was at this time that Mr. Hobbs became convinced that the glass of the future would be a glass in the manufacture of which lime would be one of the principal ingredients used, and that lead would be discontinued. He purchased material, and in spite of several very unsuccessful experiments, he was not discouraged in eventually attaining success. The efforts of Mr. Hobbs attracted much attention and were warmly seconded by other members of the firm. In the fall of 1863, William Leighton, Sr., was admitted into the firm, and taking charge of the manufacturing department, entering readily into the prospect of finding a glass pure in color and durable, without lead being a component part of the mixture. Numerous experiments were made, and at last sand, Spanish whiting, and bicarbonate of soda, with the other usual ingredients, were found to make a brilliant and durable article.

"As before stated, Mr. Hobbs, with his early partners, had many difficulties to meet and overcome; but by his well-known steady and conscientious work he moved continually forward. In 1867 he retired from active service at the glassworks, and thenceforth devoted himself to travel and to his investment....

"His funeral took place on Thursday, from his late residence. It was one of the largest and most notable that has taken place in the city for a long time. The deceased was known to everyone, and all were his friends.... The body was in a plain casket of walnut, and laid out in the front room. The floral decorations were magnificent, especially a crown, cross, and pillow. Appropriate music was rendered very sweetly. At the conclusions of the ceremonies the halls were cleared, and the male employees of the South Wheeling Glass Works, an institution of which John L. Hobbs might be said to be the founder, filed slowly in, and passing on either side of the casket, took the last look at their old employer. Two hundred and sixty two men and boys filed by. It was really an imposing scene. Each department was by itself. In line were old gray-headed men of seventy, and from that age down to boys of ten. Each one was decorated with a mourning rosette. They filed out of the rear of the building and marched to Chapline street, where they waited until the cortege came

along. The men then marched to the foot of Wheeling Hill, where they lifted hats, and with bowed heads waited for the remains to pass. Messrs. Wm. Leighton, Jr., and C. W. Brockunier, proprietors, marched at the head. The pall bearers were all grandchildren of the deceased, being Messrs. Howard, Samuel, Edward, and Robert Hazlett, Walter and Frank Rinehard, Charles Hobbs, and T. W. Phinney."

JOHN H. (HENRY) HOBBS, 1827 to 1910. The son of John L. Hobbs, he succeeded his father and became senior partner in J. H. Hobbs, Brockunier & Co. in 1863. Under the direction of Hobbs and his partners, C. W. Brockunier and William Leighton, Jr., the glasshouse flourished, becoming one of the largest manufacturing companies in the Wheeling area and achieving national prominence in the American glassmaking industry. He was active in the company until it became part of U. S. Glass in 1891. On the opening of the United States Glass Co., Mr. Hobbs became a director of that firm. In 1890 he became part owner of the Windsor Hotel in Wheeling. By 1903 he had retired and was living with his daughter in Massachusetts.

J. HARRY HOBBS. He was the son of John H. Hobbs. Little is known of J. Harry Hobbs although we do know that in 1875 he was "studying the glass trade" in the Baltimore office under J. A. Dobson & Co., the agents. In 1882, he "accepted a position in Hobbs, Brockunier & Co.'s glass works."

CHARLES HOBBS. He was another son of J. H. Hobbs. He was married in June of 1886 and he and his wife were presented to Wheeling society at a large fete in his father's home. By May, 1899 he had moved to Cicero, Indiana, to take charge of the mold shop of Bonita Glass Co. being run by Otto Jaeger. His father was also involved in Bonita, but probably only in a financial way.

JAMES HOBBS. He was superintendent of J. H. Hobbs, Brockunier & Co. in 1875. He may have been a brother of J. H. Hobbs.

The Leighton Family:

WILLIAM LEIGHTON, SR., 18 – to 1891. He and his father, Thomas H. Leighton, Sr., developed the first ruby glass formula in 1848 while still with the New England Glass Co. He joined J. H. Hobbs, Brockunier & Co. in the fall of 1863 as factory superintendent and partner in the company. He developed the lime glass formula in 1864 which revolutionized table glass manufacture. William Leighton, Sr., left the Wheeling area in 1888 and returned to New England. In 1880, it was said that he was "probably the oldest practical glass manufacturer in the United States." An announcement of his death in 1891, stated simply, "Wm. Leighton, Sr., formerly connected in the glass business at Wheeling with John L. Hobbs, died at Concord, Mass., on February 23. He was the father of William Leighton, Jr., of Dalzell, Gilmore & Leighton Co., Findlay, O."

WILLIAM LEIGHTON, JR. He was the son of William Leighton, Sr., and had worked at New England Glass Co., Cambridge, Mass., with his father. Along with his father, he joined J. H. Hobbs, Brockunier & Co. as a chemist in 1863.

In 1868 he became a partner in the firm. Eventually he succeeded his father as plant manager. He held design patents for Blackberry, Spangled ware, and many mechanical patents. While at Hobbs, he was responsible for most of the colors and glass formulae used in the plant. He was also a well-educated man who wrote poetry and translated German works into English. In March of 1888 he was listed as an incorporator of the successor to Hobbs, Brockunier & Co.; but by July 1888 he had left the firm and became associated with Dalzell, Gilmore & Leighton of Findlay, Ohio.

PETER LEIGHTON, 1822 to 1891. He came to Wheeling in 1854, probably the first of the Leightons to settle in Wheeling. He also had worked at the New England Glass Co. in Massachusetts. He is said to have started with Hobbs, Barnes & Co. in 1858 as a glassblower. In February, 1886, the following was said in *American Glass Worker:* "Peter Leighton, one of the oldest glass workers in the trade, and one who toiled when the art of modern glassmaking was in its infancy, and who can go back in memory and reminiscences long before the days when the first tumbler was pressed, is working at Hobbs, Brockunier & Co.'s, and wears the silver crown of reverent age with a knightly grace." He died December 15, 1891, at age 69. He was probably a brother of William Leighton, Sr.

GEORGE W. LEIGHTON. George was the son of William L. Leighton, Jr. By 1886 he was working as a chemist at Hobbs, Brockunier & Co. By July, 1888, he had left Hobbs to join Dalzell, Gilmore & Leighton in Findlay, Ohio. He patented the famous Onyx art glass for Dalzell, Gilmore & Leighton. He resigned from Dalzell, Gilmore & Leighton in 1889.

J. HARVEY LEIGHTON, 1849 to – He worked at Hobbs, Brockunier & Co. prior to 1877. He moved to Iowa, and in 1880 helped found the Iowa City Flint Glass Co. and served as its superintendent. He also organized a bottle factory in Ottawa, Illinois. He founded the first trade journal devoted entirely to glass, the *American Glass Worker*, in 1882. He returned to the Wheeling area and became manager of Belmont Glass Co. in Bellaire, Ohio, in 1884. He eventually established several glass marble factories between 1890 and 1911 in Akron, Navarre, and Steubenville, Ohio. In about 1906 he organized the Leighton Glass Co. in Shadyside, Ohio, at the site of the old Pultney plant.

The Brockunier Family:

CHARLES W. BROCKUNIER. Said to have been a bookkeeper at Hobbs, Barnes & Co. He became a partner in 1863 in J. H. Hobbs, Brockunier & Co. Brockunier was active in various glass organizations, being vice president of the National Flint and Lime Glass Association in 1882, and president of the National Glass Manufacturers' Association in 1883. During this period he lost two sons and suffered ill health, sometimes being confined to his home for extended periods. He remained as partner until 1888 when the charter for the company expired. Originally he was listed as an incorporator of the new firm, Hobbs Glass Co., but by July of 1888 he had retired as an active partner and invested in real estate in the interior of

West Virginia. In November 1892, he was elected to the West Virginia senate.

WILBER C. BROCKUNIER. He succeeded William Brady as bookkeeper of Hobbs, Brockunier & Co. in late 1886. In December of 1886 it was reported: "Mr. Wilber C. Brockunier, who has been connected for many years with the Top Mill, one of the largest iron industries of this section, becomes the cashier at the South Wheeling Glass Works today (16th inst.) Mr. Brockunier was connected with the pay department of the army during the war, and is a very capable man. He is a brother of Mr. Chas. W. Brockunier of Hobbs, Brockunier & Co."

The Brady Family:

CHARLES N. BRADY, 1849 to 1938. As early as 1870, his name appears as witness on several J. H. Hobbs, Brockunier & Co. patents. In 1875, he was the Western salesman for the firm. He resigned his position in 1880 to become president of the newly formed Riverside Glass Co. in Wellsburg, West Virginia. During his career he was active in starting several glass companies, namely: Hazel Glass in Wellsburg, West Virginia, in 1885; Atlas Glass Co. in 1896. He withdrew his position in Riverside in 1887, and moved to Washington, Pennsylvania. In 1897 he was a director of Beatty-Brady Glass Co., of Dunkirk, Indiana. In 1902 he was president of Hazel-Atlas Glass Co. and was chairman of the board in 1911.

WILLIAM S. BRADY. In 1880 he joined J. H. Hobbs, Brockunier & Co. as a bookkeeper. He left in late 1886 to become general manager of Riverside Glass in Wellsburg, West Virginia. He was succeeded by Wilbur C. Brockunier as bookkeeper. By May 1888 he was the secretary and a director of Fostoria Glass Co. In 1890, he was vice president of Fostoria Shade and Lamp Co. In 1891, he was secretary of Fostoria Glass Co. at Moundsville, West Virginia. In 1900, he helped incorporate Republic Glass Co., in Clarksburg, West Virginia, along with his brother James C. Brady. In 1901, he succeeded Lucien B. Martin for a short time as president of Fostoria Glass Co. In 1906, he was vice president of Hazel-Atlas.

Others:

ANDREW BAGGS, 1833 to 1883. He originally worked as a glassblower and eventually a glass cutter at Barnes & Hobbs as early as 1845 and continued until 1863 when he left to help form the precursor of Central Glass Co., of Wheeling, Oesterling, Henderson & Co. He left Central in 1872, and helped found La Belle Glass Co. in Bridgeport, Ohio. In 1879 he designed the well-known Queen Anne pattern for La Belle Glass.

PERCY J. BEAUMONT. He succeeded Nicholas Kopp. He worked at Hobbs Glass Co. as metal maker and decorator, but left in July of 1893 to go to Elson Glass Co. as a chemist and glass decorator, being succeeded by Henry Findt at Hobbs, formerly with Northwood Glass. Beaumont was a brother-in-law of Harry Northwood. He founded Beaumont Glass Company in 1895, selling his interest in 1906, and becoming factory manager of Union Stopper Co. until its closing in 1916.

SMITH BUTLER. He became factory manager at Hobbs Glass Co. in 1888. He may have come with Hansen E. Waddell from the Central Glass Co. as he left Hobbs Glass at the same time as Waddell in mid-1893. He became factory manager at Elson Glass Co. in Martin's Ferry, Ohio.

CHARLES BIRCH. In late 1882 he had taken charge of the mold shops of Hobbs, Brockunier & Co.

PETER CASSELL, 1830 to 1912. He began work at Barnes, Hobbs & Co. as a boy of 15. In the 1850s he worked as a presser at Hobbs, Barnes & Co., eventually becoming a glassblower. He left the company about 1861. In 1886 he was one of the directors of Central Glass Co. in Wheeling. He helped found Nickel Plate Glass Co., of Fostoria, Ohio, in 1888, and helped incorporate the new Central Glass Works in 1896.

ROY COMBS. He was a glassblower at Barnes, Hobbs & Co. He left in 1863 to help form Oesterling, Henderson & Co., the forerunner of Central Glass Co. in Wheeling.

JAMES CUMMINS. For a few months in 1880, he was Western salesman for J. H. Hobbs, Brockunier & Co. He resigned the same year. He was a noted glass and china dealer in Wheeling.

ANDREW DEGENHART. He was a mold maker for Hobbs, Brockunier & Co. He left and found work in Findlay, Ohio, and subsequently in Indiana. Father of John Degenhart who founded Crystal Art Glass Co. in Cambridge, Ohio, after John left the Cambridge Glass Co., Cambridge, Ohio.

JOHN DORN, JAMES FLANNIGAN, AUSTIN McGRILL, JOHN BRADY. It was reported in October 1879 that these men were leaving Hobbs to manage a new firm at Wellsburg, West Virginia (Riverside). They had been employed at J. H. Hobbs, Brockunier & Co. John Brady was probably related to Charles and William Brady.

J. K. DUNHAM. Partner in Barnes, Hobbs & Co. in 1856. His interest in the glass firm was probably entirely financial. He opened a retail store after severing his connection with Barnes, Hobbs & Co.

SEYMOUR C. DUNLEVY. Traveling salesman for Hobbs Glass Co. in 1888. He had formerly worked for La Belle Glass Co. in 1878, and was secretary in 1880. He became president and general manager in 1886 for a short period, then traveling salesman. He held this post with the Northwood Glass Co., of Martin's Ferry, Ohio, before he went to Hobbs Glass Co. He was described as "an old timer on the road." He resigned from U. S. Glass in August 1892.

WILLIAM K. ELSON. As a boy of 12 he was employed at Hobbs, Barnes & Co. in 1845, when they were organized, and earned 15½ cents per turn. He left the company in 1863 and helped found Oesterling, Henderson & Co., the forerunner of Central Glass Co. in Wheeling, West Virginia. He joined Belmont Glass Co. and became manager in 1879. He left Belmont in 1882 to found Elson Glass Co., serving as president and general manager. In 1893 he left Elson Glass Co.

HENRY FINDT. Succeeded Percy J. Beaumont as chemist at Factory H of U. S. Glass Co. (Hobbs) in 1893. After leaving Hobbs, he worked for Central Glass Works, and eventually was in charge of the factory department of Jefferson Glass Co. of Steubenville, Ohio, in 1904.

AUGUSTUS G. FROHME. Before 1886 he was a traveling Western salesman for Hobbs, Brockunier & Co. He continued in this capacity for Hobbs Glass Co. In December of 1891 for a short time he went to Pittsburgh to take a place in the Commercial Department (sales) of U. S. Glass Co. under A. H. Heisey. In July of 1892 he ran Factory H (Hobbs) while H. E. Waddell was ill. By August, he was back on the road as traveling salesman. In August of 1893 he was promoted to general superintendent after the departure of H. E. Waddell. The factory was not making glass at this time. In November of 1893 it was reported that he was selling out the stock on hand. In 1895 he was secretary of Beaumont Glass Co., which he left in 1900 to become traveling salesman for U. S. Glass Co. In 1905 he became president of Jefferson Glass Co. in Steubenville, Ohio, and he retired from the glass business in 1907.

HOWARD HAZLETT. He was a grandson of John L. Hobbs. He was involved in Hobbs, Brockunier & Co. and became one of the incorporators of Hobbs Glass Co. in 1888. His father, R. W. Hazlett, was a son-in-law of John L. Hobbs and one of the executors of his estate.

JOHN HENDERSON. He was probably an engineer at Hobbs & Barnes in 1860. He was the father-in-law of Peter Cassell. He was a partner with John Oesterling and formed Oesterling, Henderson & Co. in 1863, the forerunner of Central Glass Co. of Wheeling. Others who had previously worked at Hobbs, Barnes & Co. and were involved in Oesterling, Henderson & Co. and eventually Central included Theodore Schultz and Westcomb Attwell.

BENJAMIN M. HILDRETH. He was a brother-in-law of William S. Brady. He was working in the office of Hobbs, Brockunier & Co. in 1883 and in April of 1885, he became a traveling salesman the firm. He became sales manager for Fostoria Glass Co. in 1888. He returned to the Wheeling area in 1894. In 1897 he became traveling salesman for the Ohio Flint Glass Co. In 1900 he was salesman for the Beaumont Glass Co., and later he became secretary of that company. He resigned in 1901.

STEPHEN HIPKINS, JR. In 1876 he closed his own mold shop in Bellaire, Ohio, and worked for Hobbs, Brockunier & Co. designing and making molds. He probably worked on the molds for Viking and Goat's Head, among others. By 1882 he had left Hobbs, Brockunier and was working at Buckeye Glass Co., Martins Ferry, Ohio. With his three sons, he opened his own mold shop in 1884, making molds for many renowned patterns.

OTTO JAEGER, 1853 to —. He came to Wheeling in 1877, and was employed at Hobbs, Brockunier & Co. For 11 years he was in charge of the etching, engraving, and cutting departments. In 1882 it was said: "Mr. Jaeger is known throughout the whole country as the most noted engraver of the day." In 1888 he was traveling salesman and president of Seneca Glass Co. in Fostoria, Ohio. He left Seneca by September of 1896 and organized Bonita Art Glass Co. in Indiana, and later in Wheeling in 1901, serving as secretary-treasurer and decorating manager. This factory eventually moved to Huntington, WV, in 1930. He was listed in the Tiffin (Ohio) City Directory in 1911 – 12 as a glassworker employed by Tiffin Cut Glass Co. In 1919 he was involved in organizing the Mountain Glass Co. of Kingwood, WV. In his day he was a renowned marksman.

NICHOLAS KOPP, 1865 to 1937. In August of 1888 he was a chemist for Hobbs Glass Co., taking William Leighton, Jr.'s place. He was succeeded by Percy Beaumont at Hobbs. By July 1891 he had left Hobbs after it joined U. S. Glass and became factory manager of Fostoria Shade & Lamp Co. in Fostoria, Ohio, and continued as factory manager after Fostoria Shade and Lamp was purchased by Consolidated Lamp and Glass Co. in 1894. In 1897 he developed a selenium red glass. While associated with Consolidated he developed many new colors, especially for lamps. In 1900 he founded Kopp Lamp and Glass Co. which became part of Pittsburgh Lamp, Brass and Glass Co. Kopp continued as a director. After the closing of this firm, Kopp organized the Kopp Glass, Inc., which is still in business, making, among other things, lenses for traffic lights.

HENRY JAMES LEASURE. He was employed at Hobbs, Barnes & Co. as early as 1850. He left, along with others, in 1863 to found Oesterling, Henderson & Co., the forerunner of Central Glass Co.

LUCIEN B. MARTIN, 1853 to 1923. The city of Martin's Ferry, Ohio, had been named for his father. In 1870 he started working for J. H. Hobbs, Brockunier & Co. He was a salesman for the company. He was president of Fostoria Glass Co. in May of 1888. In 1901 he left Fostoria and became manager of the Commercial Division of National Glass. He also served as a director of the Crystal Glass Co. of Bridgeport, Ohio. After the dissolution of the National Glass Co. in 1904, he became president of Ohio Flint Glass Co., of Lancaster, Ohio. He left the next year to found and serve as sales manager of the Hocking Glass Co. also in Lancaster. In 1908 he and several others founded the Lancaster Glass Co. in Lancaster, Ohio. Mr. Martin became president of the company.

EDWARD MILLER. He was mold shop foreman at Hobbs Glass Co. He left to join Elson Glass Co. in July 1893.

HARRY NORTHWOOD, 1860 to 1919. He worked at Hobbs, Brockunier & Co. in the etching department in 1882. He worked as a designer at La Belle Glass Co., Bridgeport, Ohio, in early 1884; and he became manager by 1886. In the interim he may have worked at Phoenix Glass Co. in Phillipsburg, Pennsylvania. After La Belle burned in 1887, Northwood founded the Northwood Glass Company in Martin's Ferry, Ohio. It continued in business until mid-1892. Northwood and his other partners opened a new factory in Ellwood City, Pennsylvania, in late 1892. He left this concern in 1896 and went to Indiana, Pennsylvania, establishing the Northwood Co., which became a member of the National Glass Co. combine in late 1899. He left National in 1902 and bought the old Hobbs plant from U. S. Glass. The firm name became H. Northwood & Co., with Harry Northwood as its vice president. He continued with this company until his death in 1919. This, the last Northwood glass factory, closed in 1926, bringing to an end glassmaking on the old Hobbs factory site.

JOHN OESTERLING. He worked at Hobbs, Barnes & Co. in the mold room at a salary of $7 per week. He left in 1863 and founded Oesterling, Henderson & Co., the forerunner of Central Glass. He served as Central's president. According to old accounts, he made the first molds for his new factory at his home on his kitchen table.

THEODORE "DOREY" OREM, – to 1883. He was head of the mold shops at Hobbs, Brockunier & Co. prior to 1882. He left in November of 1882 to join Belmont Glass Works at Bellaire, Ohio, in a similar position. He died June 20, 1883. "Mr. Orum [sic] was one of the oldest and most skillful and best known glassmakers in the country."

MICHAEL J. OWENS, 1859 – 1923. Michael J. Owens began work at J. H. Hobbs, Brockunier & Co. at the age of 10. At age 29 he joined E.D. Libbey in Toledo, Ohio, and almost immediately was put in charge of a factory to make electric light bulbs in Findlay, Ohio. While Owens was not an educated man, he was a mechanical genius. He invented and built an automatic bottle blowing machine which revolutionized the glass bottle industry. At the time, it was reportedly the most complex machine ever made. Indirectly, this invention resulted in the reduction of the use of child labor in the glass industry. Owens-Illinois Glass Co., organized by Owens and Libbey, became the worlds largest manufacturer of bottles.

JAMES E. RATCLIFF. In 1878 he was thought to be associated with Hobbs, Brockunier & Co. He helped found Riverside Glass Co., in Wellsburg, West Virginia, in 1879; and served as secretary until his resignation in 1899.

WALTER H. RINEHART. He was the grandson of John L. Hobbs. Involved in Hobbs, Brockunier & Co. and one of the incorporators of Hobbs Glass Co. in 1888.

JAMES B. RUSSELL. Russell was night manager of J. H. Hobbs, Brockunier & Co. in 1880. He left to become manager of Fostoria Glass Co., Fostoria, Ohio, in 1887. He then left Fostoria in 1894 to manage Dithridge-Smith Co. in Kent, Ohio.

WILLIAM F. RUSSELL. He held patents at Hobbs, Brockunier & Co. He became manager of Dalzell, Gilmore and Leighton in Findlay, Ohio, in 1888. He held the same position in Model Flint Glass Co. in Findlay in 1891, and continued at this company after its relocation to Albany, Indiana, until 1901 when it joined National Glass Co.

HANSEN E. WADDELL. From 1878 to 1888 he was associated with Central Glass Co., Wheeling, West Virginia — most of this period as manager and secretary. In August of 1888 he left to become secretary and general superintendent of Hobbs Glass Co. After the merger with U. S. Glass Co., he continued as manager of Factory H (Hobbs). In July of 1893 he left to go to Elson Glass Co. to be "in full charge." By 1896 he was a traveling salesman for McKee & Brothers, and became a salesman for A. H. Heisey & Co. of Newark, Ohio, in 1900.

HARRY WADDELL, 1872 or 73 to 1893. He was the son of H. E. Waddell. He worked as a bookkeeper for Hobbs Glass Co. from the age of 15. He left Hobbs in 1893 with his father to become salesman for Elson Glass Co. He died "on the road" at age 21 in October, 1893.

…In 1880 Mr. Charles Brockunier while in the East was attracted by a unique set of colored glassware and purchased it for his own use. In the fall of 1881 the first colored glassware made in the valley was turned out at the factory of Hobbs, Brockunier & Co. It was the cynosure for all dealers that came this way and attracted so much attention, that other manufacturers rapidly fell into line in its manufacture until now the delicate tints can be found in every sample room. This line of goods has commanded an excellent trade, and has really bridged the chasm of disaster into which several firms, at least, would have plunged but for its introduction…. The ruby, gold, and sapphire admit the introduction of prices that are the means of salvation for many regretful experimenters. But for this fact there would hardly be an oasis in the desert description of the struggling glass trade of the Ohio valley….

-Crockery & Glass Journal, July 1885

Still ahead. Hobbs, Brockunier & Co. The first to make the modern colors in Table and Fancy Glassware, we have continued adding to our variety. In addition to old gold, sapphire, canary, opalescent, ruby, amberina, we announce our newest and in many respects most beautiful coral ware, which will be ready for sale January 1, 1886. Pressed & Blown ware decorated in various designs.

-American Pottery and Glassware Reporter, December 3, 1885

The first pattern referred to above is Craquelle — the first of Hobbs' tableware patterns to be made in several colors. Color production remained very important to Hobbs, Brockunier & Co. until the factory closed. The second quotation lists many colors and introduces Coral.

Hobbs, Brockunier & Co. made some of the most beautiful glass and beautiful colors of any glass company in the United States. They not only made a tremendous variety of colors but developed many of them in their factory. William Leighton, Sr., William Leighton, Jr., and Nicholas Kopp developed wonderful colors and color combinations that were not made elsewhere. In March of 1886 the company was making about 25 different colors and combinations of colors. What a remarkable variety! At this time, this listing did not include their many variations of spangled and spattered glass — an almost endless variety of color combinations in just these two types of glass.

COLOR LIST AND DESCRIPTIONS

Most terminology used in the following descriptions of Hobbs' colors is taken from either trade journal quotations or from the Leighton formulas.

A few terms need defining in order to properly interpret the descriptions given:

Acid Etched Often called satin glass. This effect is produced by exposing clear glass to hydrofluoric acid or its fumes, resulting in a translucent, satiny finish.

Alabaster We have used this term to describe an effect used by Hobbs which is a variation of opalescence. Often, especially in Dew Drop, the article of glass is plated (lined on the interior with a translucent opalescent layer) but the raised portions on the exterior remain clear which differs from usual opalescent treatment.

No. 323 Dew Drop sapphire finger bowl, glossy; covered sugar, acid etched.

No. 207 Murano celery ruby alabaster, No. 314 spoon ruby glossy.

Engraved This decoration on glass differs from standard cut cutting. The engraving itself is done with multiple small metal wheels, usually copper, resulting in intricately detailed decorations. Engravings are usually kept gray. Engravings are often more detailed than cuttings, but lack the brilliance of highly polished cuttings.

Engraved tumbler, ruby amber.

Opalescent Colored or crystal glass is formed with raised portions which are quickly chilled after blowing or pressing. The piece is then reheated to develop the milky-white effect, especially on areas most cooled in the previous step. Blown pieces are then reheated and blown into a final finish shape mold. Examples: Blown: Polka Dot, Pressed: Dew Drop.

No. 323 Dew Drop sapphire, small nappy glossy; spoon opalescent.

Plating/Plated A cased glass which has had a second, or third, layer added to the first gather, resulting in an interior and exterior of different colors. Example: Peach Blow. Plating can also be applied on the inside of a nearly finished piece.

Spangled A plated glass which has mica between the layers resulting in a silver or gold flecking, depending on the color of the exterior

Coral tumbler with opal plating.

gather. This was patented by William Leighton, Jr. for Hobbs, Brockunier & Co.

Spatter A plated glass which can have several layers. The initial gather is rolled into one or several colors of glass which is in small pieces. After this, the entire gather is again plated with another layer of glass. The result is a glass which has several small spots of color or colors spread over the entire piece. Spatter and Spangled glass can be combined for stunning effect.

Striking/Struck Glass which is reheated, usually only on rims or partial surfaces, to develop a new color from the original

Modified No. 11 vase, opal and ruby spatter with amber plating, also spangled.

color of the glass gather. A heat-sensitive ingredient in the original formula makes this possible. The result is a glass of at least two distinct colors with a gentle blending of colors where they meet. Example: amberina.

Most Hobbs colors can be found both with a glossy surface or with an acid etched (satin finish) surface. Many were also made in both a clear color and an opalescent color. In addition to all the colors possible by combining these two effects, Hobbs also sometimes plated two different colors (either clear or opalescent) to provide an entirely new color effect.

Hobbs made color combinations that are called struck or heat-sensitive glass. Struck glass needs to be reheated in the glory hole after the piece is finished in order to develop the color. If not reheated, the glass retains its uniform original color. Usually the color is not developed over the entire piece, but it is developed on the edges. The result of this technique is a gentle shading of color from one to the other with a subtle gradation where the two colors meet. Hobbs, Brockunier & Co. made only Coral (Wheeling Peach Blow) and Amberina in heat sensitive glass.

Other Hobbs, Brockunier & Co. color combinations such as rubina, rubina verde, ruby amber, and ruby sapphire were made by plating (usually the interior of an article) with ruby (cranberry). These combinations are not heat sensitive glass. This plating technique results in the colors having a sharper boundary between the two and not the gentle blending of colors resulting from a true heat-sensitive glass which has been struck.

Amberina Amber shading into fuchsia ruby edges. This is the original name for this color. Amberina was made by Hobbs under license from New England Glass Co. who developed and patented this color and the process for making it in 1883. It is a true heat-sensitive glass, made only in pressed ware by Hobbs, Brockunier & Co.

No. 101 Daisy and Button toy tumbler, amberina.

However, one formula given by Leighton refers to "Amberina for blown Garnet Shades, etc." It is interesting to note that Leighton used at least three amberina formulas — two of which used coral plated cullet (Peach Blow). It is remarkable that economic use was made of this expensive cullet, as most heat-sensitive or plated cullet could not be reused to make colored glass. Note that the formula "most frequently used" containing the coral cullet uses a significantly smaller amount of gold in the batch. Economically, the company saved money both by using less gold and utilizing the cullet which would have otherwise been thrown away.

Canary Called vaseline by collectors. Canary is the original term used for this glass color. It is a bright yellow with green highlights. It was made by using uranium salts in the batch as the coloring agent. Canary was made in acid etched finish, opalescent (glossy or acid finish), and plated alabaster lining (see Lemon Yellow, below). It is also sometimes found plated with turquoise and pink and possibly other colors.

Coral A heat-sensitive glass which is amberina plated with opal

Small coral vase.

(milk glass). Coral is the original name used by Hobbs, Brockunier & Co. Coloration of coral pieces shade from a pale amber to a deep fuchsia mahogany. This color is comparable to plated amberina (made by the New England Glass Co.) but without ribs. The longer a piece was reheated, the deeper the final color of the item. Some cruets (oils) appear to have been intentionally made entirely mahogany since these have dark amber handles and stoppers. Leighton gives the formula for the white lining or plating, also. Coral has a glossy finish. See also Peach Blow. Most people today do not differentiate between coral and Peach Blow.

Green Opaque Seen in plated, spangled glass. This is a pale opaque green.

Indian A red amber plated over spangled blue. This is the original name of this color taken from William Leighton's formula.

Lazuline A medium blue plated over spangled blue. This is the original name of this color taken from William Leighton's formula.

Lemon Yellow Canary plated inside with an alabaster layer, resulting in a translucent glass. It may be found with glossy or acid finish. This color seems to have been primarily used for the No. 205 or 206 bowls which are often seen with a ruby edge.

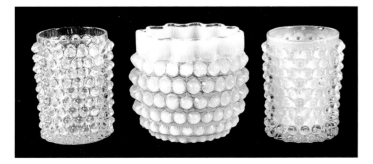

No. 323 Dew Drop tumbler, canary; No. 323 Dew Drop spoon, opalescent canary; No. 323 Dew Drop tumbler, canary alabaster.

No. 205 plate, lemon yellow with ruby rim.

Marine Green Called apple green by collectors-a pale blue-green. This is Hobbs' original name for this color. Marine green has almost the same formula as sapphire except for the addition of uranium. May be found with acid finish, opalescent (glossy or acid finish), and plated with alabaster. The color was developed by William Leighton.

Marine green, No. 101 toy tumbler, glossy; No. 236 Polka Dot tumbler, opalescent; No. 323 Dew Drop finger bowl, alabaster.

Old Gold Called Amber by collectors. This is the original Hobbs' name for this color. It was made in acid etched finish, opalescent (both glossy or acid finish), and plated alabaster lining.

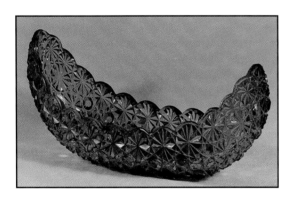

Old Gold No. 101 Canoe, glossy.

Opal (Porcelain) A dense, milk white glass. Examples glow pink under ultraviolet light. Hobbs used the term porcelain for this color in the 1870s, but later used the more general term, opal. Hobbs used this color for Paneled Wheat, Sawtooth, Blackberry, and Grapes with Overlapping Foliage. In addition to these patterns, many early oil lamps using the patented brass connector had opal standards (bases).

Opal footed lamp.

Peach Blow Coral glass with an acid etched finish. We believe Hobbs made this distinction since they did not use the term Peach Blow until after they started producing a copy of the Morgan vase in acid etched finish. See Coral for the description of the color.

Peach Blow salt and pepper shakers, silver plate holder. Courtesy of Mary Ann and Dick Krauss.

Rose An opaque pink color, found spangled and plated outside with crystal. Leighton's notes say this was difficult and expensive to make. We have also used the term pink to indicate the plated ruby glass which was used extensively in the Neapolitan pattern to differentiate it from Rose.

No. 319 jug, rose spangled.

Rubina A combination of crystal and ruby. This is the original name for this color. It is a plated color, not a heat-sensitive one. It may be found with acid etched finish, and in opalescent (both glossy or acid finish). It also may be found plated with alabaster.

No. 323 Dew Drop jug, rubina. Courtesy of Jo and Bob Sanford.

Rubina Verde A combination of canary and ruby. This is the original name for this color. It is not a heat-sensitive color, but rather, the ruby is plated on a portion of the interior of the canary item. May be found with acid etched finish, opalescent (glossy or acid finish). This color is most often found in the Dew Drop pattern.

No. 323 Dew Drop celery, Rubina Verde.

Ruby Called cranberry by collectors. Ruby is the original name used by Hobbs and by other companies making this color at the time. This color was developed by William Leighton, Sr. sometime in the 1850s at New England Glass Co. It was made by using gold in the formula, and so was more expensive than most other glasses. It is a plated glass, the outer layer being crystal. At one time, trade journals stated that more ruby glass was made at Hobbs, Brockunier & Co. than by all the other glass companies in the United States.

Upper left clockwise: No. 323 bitter bottle, ruby; No. 323 jug, ruby satin; No. 314 Polka Dot hotel celery, ruby; No. 331 salt, ruby; No. 323 Dew Drop tumbler, ruby.

Ruby Amber A combination of amber and ruby. This is the original Hobbs' name for this color. This is a plated color combination, not a heat-sensitive glass. Today it is often mistaken for amberina. Hobbs' method of producing the same color effect in blown wares did not infringe on the patent for amberina held by Libbey. It produced a color similar enough to amberina that, even today, it takes study to determine if a piece is true amberina or ruby amber. Hobbs, Brockunier & Co. used this color in the Dew Drop pressed pattern, among others.

No. 323 Dew Drop 4" square nappy, No. 314 Polka Dot celery, No. 323 Dew Drop tumbler in ruby amber.

Ruby Sapphire A combination of sapphire and ruby. Collectors sometimes call this bluina or bluerina. The descriptive name ruby sapphire is more in keeping with other Hobbs' color names such as ruby amber. Ruby sapphire is sapphire plated with ruby. Opalescent examples are unknown, although this effect is a possibility. This color may be found acid etched. This color is extremely hard to find today and is very costly.

No. 216 Polka Dot salt shaker in ruby sapphire. Courtesy of Hazel Tellier.

Sapphire Clear, copper-sulfate blue, using "verdigris" as the coloring agent. This is Hobbs' original name for this color. Hobbs' sapphire is very striking and deeper in tone than many other blue colors of the period. It may be found with acid finish, opalescent (glossy or acid finish), and plated with alabaster lining. This is another color developed by William Leighton, Jr. Sapphire is often found in Daisy & Button and Dew Drop patterns.

No. 323 Dew Drop tumblers in sapphire: glossy, opalescent, alabaster.

Turquoise Sapphire plated with opal to make it opaque. This is the original Hobbs' term for this color. It was often used on bowls which have rims of white or opaque yellow. Turquoise can also be found plated with canary. Other color combinations are to be expected.

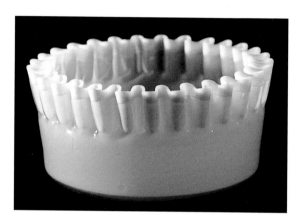

No. 205 7" bowl, turquoise Richelieu. Courtesy of the Huntington Museum of Art.

Yellow (Opaque) While this color has not been found in either trade quotes or catalog references, a few examples are known in Hobbs' shapes. The color is an opaque, bright yellow. This color might have been developed by Nicholas Kopp.

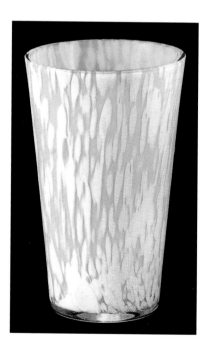

No. 247 champagne tumbler, yellow and opal spatter.

THE EVOLUTION OF COLOR AND DECORATIONS

The following list of colors and decorations is taken from several trade journals of the period. We have found it helpful to list colors and patterns in chronological order to clarify our understanding of the company's growth and its products.

This list contains the earliest reference we have found for any color. In the case of decorations, particularly cuttings and engravings, we have listed the named patterns we have encountered. Unfortunately, illustrations and examples of these decorations are not known today.

March, 1875: Porcelain (Opal).

Decorations: Frosted ware, cutting; engraving including fruit, flowers, monograms.

"This firm also manufactures ware called porcelain, rivaling in beauty either crystal or flint ware. It is of a transparent and white color, and equal in strength to china" Actually porcelain is not transparent, it is a quite opaque opal (milk) glass. "This porcelain is made from that wonderful product of the far North, the ice stone of the Esquimaux, or the kryolite of modern geology. To the visitor, the most interesting portion of this vast establishment is its extensive cutting shops, where one becomes almost bewildered in contemplating the never ending variety of shapes and patterns into which the glass is cut; and where the engraving wheel works out the most delicate patterns fruit, flowers, fanciful tracery, beautiful letters and monograms, which have made these goods rival the best work of eastern factories and scarcely excelled by the finest imported ware." — *Crockery & Glass Journal*, May 13, 1875

March, 1875: An ad for the South Wheeling Glass works stated: "Flint and Fancy Colored Glassware, Cut and Engraved Goods."

The ad, however, was not specific as to what colors were made at this time.

1876: Strawberry diamond, Silver diamond, Prism cuttings.

Accounts of the time listed these cuttings done by Hobbs which were displayed at the Centennial Exposition in Philadelphia.

February, 1877: Diamond pattern cutting.

"Among the cut goods I noticed full lines of duplicates of the sets, exhibited by this company at the late Centennial Exhibition. These are mostly in the favorite diamond pattern, and would grace any table. Finely engraved crystal ware of all kinds is made here, from table sets down to exquisite paper weights and ink stands in which the most critical eye will fail to detect a flaw." — *Crockery & Glass Journal*

January, 1878: Iridescent glassware

"They show some very elegant iridescent glassware, which sparkles in the light with all the colors of the rainbow." *Crockery & Glass Journal*

Again, Hobbs' iridescent glassware is unknown at this time.

July, 1878: Canary; sand blast decoration

"One of their novelties is a new shaped globe. These globes are etched and ornamented by the sandblast process, and present a rich and beautiful appearance.... They have just brought out a great variety of ware in canary color, such as salvers, wines, goblets, mugs, epergnes, etc" — *Crockery & Glass Journal* While most pieces are unknown in canary, it is likely that the rarely found Little Samuel epergnes in that color were made at this time.

June, 1881: Cuttings

"The Goblets were of the 'Lavellier' pattern, cut in fine diamonds, hollow flute and fan." — *Crockery & Glass Journal* From a set presented to Mt. Vernon from the Ladies' Mount Vernon Association of West Virginia.

October, 1881: Old Gold (amber)

"We have a sample before us in old gold color that is as fine as anything yet shown." — *Crockery & Glass Journal*

December, 1881: Ruby

"Hobbs, Brockunier & Co. have for some time been experimenting in the manufacture of ruby crackled pitchers. These pitchers are of a beautiful ruby color and have a crackled appearance." — *Crockery & Glass Journal*

June, 1882: Engraving

"The South Wheeling Glass Works have just turned out some beautiful specimens of engraved glass..., a fine cut decanter with a beautiful horse engraved upon it." — *Crockery & Glass Journal*

September, 1882: Engravings

Many engravings done by Otto Jaeger and Harry Northwood for the State Fair Exposition.

October, 1882: Ad listing: "Optic, Venetian, Craquelle, Sapphire, Rose, Marine Green and Old Gold Ware." — *Crockery & Glass Journal*

August, 1883: Spangled

"The latest addition to the list of novelties is what they call spangled glass. A very unique effect is produced by flecking gold or silver foil on a ground of dark blue or green and covering the spangles with a thin coating of crystal glass. Malachite effects are produced by taking a ground of malachite blue and flecking spangling it with silver foil and coating in crystal." — *Crockery & Glass Journal*

January, 1884: Opal

Opal pieces in this time period are not known except for some items made in spangled ware. Whether other patterns were made in Opal in the 1880s is not known today.

June, 1884: Aurora

"...we notice a fancy vase in the Aurora colors, polka dot pattern." — *Crockery & Glass Journal* Aurora has been one of the most tantalizing mentions of color we have encountered. At this time, Aurora remains a mystery.

September, 1884: Amberina

"The Amberina goods are in special demand this season." — *Crockery & Glass Journal*

October, 1884: Rubina Verde

"A new ware called the 'Rubina-Verde' has just been introduced." — *Crockery & Glass Journal*

December, 1884: Decorated ware-unspecified

"Decorated ware of great merit has also been added to its infinity of products." — *Crockery & Glass Journal*

January, 1885: Opalescent ware

"The opalescent ware will be one of the leading features of the new goods." — *Crockery & Glass Journal*

March, 1885: Alabaster (opalescent white); canary opalescent.; rubina, rubina and sapphire; decoration: gold band.

"They have been extending their line of colors till they now have twelve or fifteen different shades of color. Among the varieties of new ware which your correspondent noticed this week is a pitcher in polka-dot of alabaster white glass.... The ware is given a soft, mellow tint of canary in some instances.... A very handsome toilet bottle rimmed with a gold band is expected to take an immediate hold upon the popular fancy.... Among the other colors are old gold, sapphire, marine green, canary, ruby, aurora, Rubina, Rubina Verde, and a new color almost nameless being a combination of Rubina and sapphire, the latter predominating." — *Crockery & Glass Journal*

May, 1885: Gold

This is not described well, but it seems to refer to the gold rims which are often seen on imported European goods. "Among the new patterns...amberina and rubina fruit dishes tinted with gold-the richest goods we have ever seen in the tableware line." — *Crockery & Glass Journal*

June, 1885: Ruby amber

"The ruby-amber recently put on the market is receiving the highest praise from the trade."— *Crockery & Glass Journal*

December, 1885: Coral

"In addition to their usual lines of unrivaled colored and crystal wares they have a line of coral ware, the beauty and elegance of which is really superb." — *Crockery & Glass Journal*

February 1886: Burmese

"Their sample rooms this season glitter with rich colors and tasty patterns of every known piece of glassware, and the intermixture of colors, comprising ruby, amber, sapphire, marine green, and Burmese, make a combination of rare beauty." — *Crockery & Glass Journal*

While this quote names Burmese, we feel that the reference is actually to coral, as there is no other documentation that Hobbs made what we call Burmese colored glass.

March, 1886: White tinted with ruby, blue, etc.— unknown

"They have just added some new lines, among them a beautiful white tinted with ruby, blue, etc." — *Crockery & Glass Journal.*

March, 1886: About 25 different colors and combinations of colors, including opalescents; decorations No. 6, No. 7, and No. 2 painted.

"They have about 25 different colors and combinations of colors.... Their No. 101, No. 6 and No. 7 decorated sets...No. 290 tumblers, beautifully engraved...another table line known as decorated No. 2, painted and kiln burned.... The 'Dewdrop,' 'Pineapple' opalescents of all kinds and the Coral goods" — *Crockery & Glass Journal*

June, 1886: Peach Blow Ad: "Hobbs, Brockunier & Co.'s Peach Blow Vase, Coral and Lusterless. Fac-similie of Celebrated Morgan Vase." — *Crockery & Glass Journal*

September, 1886: Richelieu

"The 323 'Richelieu' is a superb line." — *Crockery & Glass Journal*

At this point, we do not know for certain what Richelieu is. Bill Heacock speculated that it was a satin white opalescent, but other ads and catalog pages than the one he cites do not agree with this interpretation.

February, 1887: Decorations (unspecified)

"They have also gone largely into the decorating business, which adds richness to the appearance of the coral, blue and white glassware. The decorated water and toilet bottles are rich ornaments and lose none of their usefulness by this additional artistic touch, while it adds materially to their popular favor."— *Crockery & Glass Journal*

March, 1887: Ruby ware and combinations of rubies in rich effects.

Described in an ad along with "Murano (No. 207) in very delicate tints." — *Crockery & Glass Journal*

January, 1890: Decorations: Gold etched

"An entirely new feature has been added called the 335 gold etched novelties." — *Crockery & Glass Journal*
This is the amber stain with etched design found on 335 and others.

September, 1891: Ruby stain

"The ruby stained table line is a good seller." — *Crockery & Glass Journal*

EXTRACTS FROM WILLIAM LEIGHTON'S COLOR NOTES

The following are color formulas from William Leighton recorded and given to his sons. At the time, glass formulas were closely guarded secrets, so William was giving his heirs a priceless gift. There were many more formulas written down in the original along with a treatise on tests to run on glass chemicals to determine purity. The other formulas were not listed as being made at Wheeling, but at the New England Glass Company.

The following formulas were designated as being used at Wheeling. The original lists were typed, but a few notations were handwritten. These handwritten additions are shown in italics. The spelling used is taken exactly from the original. Numbers are assumed to be pounds per batch.

It might be interesting to note that the ruby batch used gold valued at $5332.50 in 1996 ($395.00 per ounce). In other words, the addition of gold to the batch added 12 cents per pound in 1887. In 1996 that would equal $2.38 per pound. Ruby glass was to be plated inside crystal, making perhaps 10% of the total glass in a piece.

A few words need clarification. **Tartar** is potassium bitartrate; **Verdigris** is copper sulfate; **Litharge** is lead oxide; **Alumina** is aluminum oxide; **Saltpetre** is potassium nitrate. **Arsenic** was used as a flux, to facilitate the fusing of ingredients. **PD Blue** is powder blue or cobalt blue, used as a whiting agent. **Manganese** is used as a decoloring agent. Note the three different recipes for amberina glass.

1887
Old Gold
Dry Sand	.2000
Soda Ash	.925
Lime	.100
Arsenic	.4½
Red Tarter	.35

When color was required dark, 16 lbs. extra tartar was put in each pot.

Saphire [sic]
Dry Sand	.2000
Nitrate	.133
Soda Ash	.880
Lime	*.100*
Arsenic	*.4½*
Verdigris	*.11*

Marine Green
Dry Sand	.2000
Nitrate	.100
Soda Ash	.890
Lime	.100
Arsenic	.4½
Uranium	.4
Verdigris	.4½

Opalescent Crystal
Dry Sand	.2000

Soda Ash	.772
Fluorspar	.260
Alumina	.200
Manganese	.8
PD Blue	.6 OZ

Canary
Dry Sand	.2000
Nitrate Soda	.20
Soda Ash	.912
Lime	.100
Arsenic	.4
Uranium	.10

Opalescent Canary
Dry Sand	.2000
Nitrate Soda	.293
Soda Ash	.532
Fluorspar	.215
Alumina	200
Arsenic	.5
Uranium	.12

Opalescent Sahire [sic]
Dry Sand	.2000
Nitrate Soda	.293
Soda Ash	.532
Arsenic	.5
Fluorspar	.240
Alumina	200
Verdigris	.16

All preceeding batches may be plated outside of ruby batch given below.

To dissolve gold use ½ oz Aqua Regia per dollar.

AQ. REG =
    1 HNO
    3 HCL
    3 H20

CA $5. gold piece [indecipherable] weighs 130 grains

Ruby
Dry Sand	.1058
Litharge	.486
Soda Ash	.150
Nitrate Soda	.318
Dissolved Gold	
Valued in Dollars	.270
Metal Antimony	.112½
Manganese	.112½
Arsenic	.1½

For mand. use gold 34 and mand the same
When plain work hot into lumps.
Put lumps through lears 12 times. which will develope [sic] color.

Rose
Rose Cullet	.225
Dry Sand	.450
Litharge	.360
Soda Ash	.67

Nitrate 243
Metal Antimony 9
Manganese 3
Dissolved Gold
In Value $5.6

When plain press into lumps in mold.

Work hot. Lear until red. Lumps are used by reheating and pressing into shape.

Slow & Expensive to work.

Amberina

Dry Sand 1820
Litharge 1820
Nitrate 560
Dissolved Gold
In Dollars 150
Ox. Antimony 64
Manganese 21
Arsenic 5
Crocus Matis 45
Alumina 156

Amberina must be worked hot; if cooled too much it don't color.

[In this batch, the gold added three cents cost to pound of glass in 1887. In today's gold that would be $.66 per pound of glass.]

Another amberina more frequently used.

Dry Sand 426
Litharge 426
Nitrate 130½
Dissolved Gold
In Dollars 60
Ox. Antimony 15
Manganese 5½
Crocus Martis 10½
Alumina 35½
Coral Plated
Cullet 1750

[In this batch, the gold added five cents cost to each pound of glass in 1887. In today's gold that would be $.97 per pound.]

Coral — White

Dry Sand 1200
Litharge 1066
Nitrate 390
Arsenic 84
Bone Ash 48
Crocus Matis 17
Manganese 10

Plated inside amberina makes coral-ware; melt in monkey. Eats pot badly.

Amberina for blown garnet shades etc.

Dry Sand 182
Litharge 182
Nitrate Soda 56

Gold–Dollars 15
Ox. Antimony 5
Manganese 1⁶/₁₆
Crocus 2¹⁰/₁₆
Alumina 15½
Coral Plated Cullet 100

1884
Plating white for spangled ware

Dry Sand 200
Litharge 130
Saltpetre 60
Borax 30
Bone Ash 12½
Arsenic 10

Flint to plate out side white for satin Spangled ware

Dry Sand 1800
Litharge 1200
Nitrate Soda 220
Pearl Ash 150
Soda Ash 150
Arsenic 1¼
Manganese 2¹/₁₆
PD Blue . . . . .1 OZ.

Plating Blue for Spangled ware

Dry Sand 420
Nitrate Soda 9½
Lime 18¾
Arsenic 1½
Cobalt 18¾
Soda Ash 170

Silver to plate ouside above blue

Dry Sand 1500
Nitrate Soda 15
Lime 75
Soda Ash 625
Arsenic 3
Manganese 1½
PD Blue . . . . .1 OZ.

Indian to plate ouside preceeding blue

Dry Sand 1800
Nitrate Soda 0
Lime 90
Soda Ash 762
Arsenic 3¹⁰/₁₆
Red Tarter 72

Lazuline to plate outside above blue

Dry Sand 1800
Nitrate Soda 120
Lime 90
Soda Ash 690
Arsenic 6
Verdigris 21

≈The Patterns≈

> *Of the variety and extent of the product of the South Wheeling Works I can only speak generally. A catalog of it would exhaust my limits. I have called it a tableware factory because the larger part of its manufacture is intended for table use, but its patents reach from glass chandeliers to glass coffins and monuments, and are sufficient to light the way into the world as well as to provide a decent exit from it.*
>
> -*Crockery and Glass Journal,* September, 1879

Hobbs, Brockunier & Co. began as a small, unremarkable glass company producing wares and patterns similar to other companies of the time. Through hard work and careful management the company grew into one of the most prestigious American glass companies, competing equally with companies abroad and in America making what we now call art glass.

By the 1870s Hobbs, Brockunier & Co. began to produce patterns which are distinctive and highly collectible today, including Blackberry, Paneled Wheat, Viking, and Goat's Head. With the shift of production to colored glass, the company reached new heights in sales and popularity of its products. Hobbs, Brockunier & Co., unlike most other companies of the 1880s, did not have a short color period followed by a return to crystal production. Hobbs, Brockunier & Co. continued to produce colored glass, developing new colors and opalescent effects until it eventually ceased business. The importance of Hobbs, Brockunier & Co. is still recognized today by the popularity of its patterns such as Wheeling Peach Blow, Daisy and Button Amberina, Windows opalescent, and others.

As you study the patterns made by Hobbs, Brockunier & Co., watch for the distinctive ogee scallop on the edges of many pieces. This seems to have been a favorite Hobbs' motif and occurs in several patterns such as Viking, Tree of Life, and others.

Many of Hobbs, Brockunier & Co.'s blown ware shapes are found in several patterns. Study the shapes shown in Polka Dot, Coral/Peach Blow, and others to become familiar with Hobbs' shapes. The blown ware patterns are not listed numerically but are found under the various patterns or effects in which they occur. Whenever possible, we have included the shape numbers after the item entries in the pattern lists. Hobbs, Brockunier & Co. used their standard shapes over and over to produce many different types of wares. Note the shapes of the oils, vases, pitchers, and syrups. Learning the shapes will help you identify Hobbs' pieces when you see them in an unexpected effect.

During our search through the trade journals, we found many references, often only one time, to patterns and pieces made by Hobbs. Unfortunately, we have not been able to find further information or illustrations of these items. For instance, Hobbs made much cut and engraved glass, but little is documented today. We also found mentions of baskets, knife handles, and numbered or named patterns which still remain mysteries. Hopefully, more information will come to light which will add to our knowledge about Hobbs, Brockunier & Co. and its products.

SAWTOOTH

Date: Unknown, ca. 1870 or earlier
Colors: Probably crystal; porcelain (opal)
Comments: One of the earliest patterns able to be positively attributed to Hobbs. Shards of this pattern have been found at the old Hobbs factory site. Other pieces in the pattern are likely. Many companies made almost identical patterns making exact identification almost impossible. Prices given are for items in porcelain (milk glass). Crystal pieces would be less valuable.

Sawtooth spoon, porcelain (opal).

Pieces	Prices
Celery	$45.00
Compotes, various sizes	75.00+
Table set:	
Butter & cover	50.00
Cream	45.00
Spoon	40.00
Sugar & cover	50.00

GRAPES WITH OVERLAPPING FOLIAGE

Date: 1870

Colors: Porcelain (opal), probably crystal

Comments: Some pieces found with legend "PAT FEB 1870." Patent No. 3,828 was granted February 1, 1870, and assigned to John H. Hobbs. The patent describes the design as "… a wreath or band of vine, with leaves, tendrils, and fruit closely clustered, and so arranged that the vines shall form the upper part of the figure, and the leaves, tendrils, and fruit shall all be below the vine."

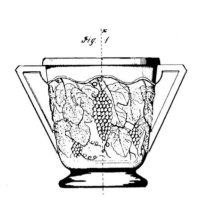

Grapes with Overlapping Foliage, illustration from patent.

Grapes with Overlapping Foliage spoon, porcelain (opal).

Grapes with Overlapping Foliage, illustration from patent.

Prices given are for pieces in porcelain (opal). Crystal items are valued lower. Other pieces in the pattern are likely.

Pieces	Prices
Celery	$45.00
Nappy, 4"	20.00
Nappy, 8"	40.00
Table Set:	
Butter & cover	65.00
Cream	50.00
Spoon	45.00
Sugar & cover	65.00

BEECH LEAF OVERLAPPING EGG CUP

This egg cup has the external appearance of Hobbs, Brockunier's opal, and turns the same color under black light. It has not been attributed to any other firm. There may be other pieces in the pattern, and it may exist in crystal glass.

Pieces	Prices
Egg cup, porcelain (opal)	$15.00

Beach Leaf Overlapping egg cup, porcelain.

BLACKBERRY

Date: 1870

Colors: Crystal, porcelain (opal)

Comments: Patented February 1, 1870, by William Leighton, Jr. Blackberry was assigned Design Patent No. 3,829. The patent described the design as "...A wreath or band of blackberries, leaves, and stems, intended to be placed upon the bowls of the various articles, or around the sides of dishes or upon the covers of dishes, in any manner that shall appear most ornamental." Some plain edged pieces have fine radial ribs on the rims. Lamps come on two type bases: opal, or clear glass with a pressed diamond pattern. Prices given are for porcelain (opal). Crystal items are valued less.

Reproductions: Several pieces were made by Westmoreland Glass Co. These have good quality but are more translucent in appearance, lacking the opacity of the original. Some Westmoreland pieces are marked WG.

Blackberry 8" covered comport, porcelain (opal). Courtesy of Huntington Museum of Art.

Covered sugar, spoon, cream, porcelain (opal).

Blackberry lamp, porcelain (opal) foot. Courtesy of Margaret Forkner.

Pieces	Prices
Celery, tall	$95.00
Celery	95.00
Champagne	75.00
Comport, high footed	150.00
Comport, high footed, covered	200.00
Comport, low footed	60.00
Comport, low footed, covered	150.00
Egg cup, single	50.00
Egg cup, double	55.00
Goblet	75.00
Nappy, 4"	22.00
Nappy, 4½"	22.00
Lamp, Blackberry font, 8½", crystal	120.00
Lamp, Blackberry font, 9½", crystal	150.00
Lamp, Blackberry font, 11½", crystal	185.00
Molasses can	260.00
Oval, 8"	38.00
Pitcher, ½ gallon, applied handle	450.00
Relish	38.00
Salt, open	40.00
Table set:	
Butter & cover, ice drainer	150.00
Cream	70.00
Spoon	55.00
Sugar & cover	90.00
Tumbler	100.00+
Wine	100.00+

PANELED WHEAT

Date: 1871
Colors: Crystal, porcelain (opal); light blue opaque reported.
Comments: Patented February 28, 1871. Design Patent No. 4,687, awarded to John H. Hobbs. The patent includes the description "... a series of sheaves of grain...inclosed by bands or shields...which are raised above the...surface...." Finials on covered pieces are shocks of wheat. A classic, plain pattern with excellent detail of wheat. The pickle dish has a naturalistic sheaf of wheat in the bottom of the dish.

Paneled Wheat, illustration
from patent

Paneled Wheat cream, crystal and porcelain.

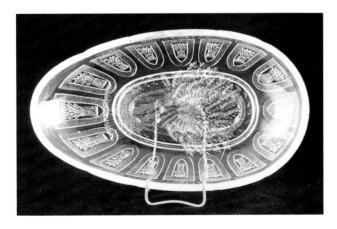

Paneled Wheat 8" pickle. Courtesy of Mart Groesser.

Prices given are for porcelain (opal). Crystal pieces are valued less.

Pieces	Prices
Comport, covered, 7"	$200.00
Comport, covered, 7½"	225.00
Comport, covered, 8"	250.00
Comport, low, 7"	75.00
Comport, low, 8"	85.00
Egg cup	55.00
Goblet	100.00+
Jug	200.00
Nappy, 4"	20.00
Pickle dish, 8"	45.00
Table set:	
Butter & cover, with ice drainer	150.00
Cream	60.00
Spoon	60.00
Sugar & cover	100.00
Sugar & cover, with spoon rack	175.00
Wine	100.00+

Paneled Wheat sugar with spoon rack
and cream. Courtesy of Mart Groesser.

NO. 53

Date: Unknown, but quite early, possibly the 1870s or earlier.
Colors: Crystal; cheese dish with ruby top.
Decorations: The cheese dish is known with Flamingo Habitat etching.
Comments: Note the star in the bottoms of ovals and salts. This plain pattern is one of the first we are able document that was made by J. H. Hobbs, Brockunier. The entire line may have been decorated with Hobbs' etchings and engravings. While No. 53 was probably a full line, including the table set, the items are so plain that they would be impossible to identify today unless a known J. H. Hobbs, Brockunier & Co. decoration is on them. The items listed survived into later catalogs, but certainly other items were also made.

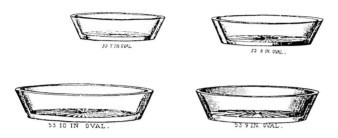

Catalog illustration of various size ovals.

Prices are for plain, undecorated pieces.

No. 53 cheese cover, ruby. Courtesy of Huntington Museum of Art.

Pieces	Prices
Celery	$18.00
Cheese & Cover	.65.00
Jar, apothecary, with ground stopper	.40.00
Oval, 7"	.10.00
Oval, 8"	.10.00
Oval, 9"	.12.00
Oval, 10"	.12.00
Salt, individual	.5.00
Salt, master	.7.00

PRESSED GRADUATES AND MEDICINE TUMBLERS

Crockery & Glass Journal, June 9, 1881:

"Hobbs, Brockunier & Co. have issued a circular to the trade in regard to the recent victory obtained by them in the United States District Court, in Pittsburgh, Pa., over M. M. Block, who was infringing a tumbler patent of Mr. J. H. Hobbs. In reciting the history of this suit and its termination in their favor, the firm says; 'Several parties have at various times infringed our patent, we entered suit in the Circuit Court of the United States, at Pittsburgh, against M. M. Block, who had most openly and extensively made tumblers infringing said patent: and we are gratified to say, after a fair and square fight, that the court sustained our patent in every particular, and allowed an injunction against Block and his manufacturers. We announce this result to the trade and to the manufacturers of glassware, and also our determination to at once prosecute any and every person violating this patent.'"

"Mr. J. H. Hobbs has obtained a patent for a set of medicinal glasses graduated on the inside of the glass, that for convenience and neatness surpass anything of the kind yet invented in this country. These glasses are graduated according to the United States Pharmacy standard. This firm surprised the state association of Druggists at its recent meeting in this city with a present of a set of these graduates to each member."

Comments: These wares, with measuring lines pressed on the inside of the piece, were patented in 1875. J. H. Hobbs, Brockunier & Co. had been making graduates with lines engraved on the outside before this time. The only other documentation relative to the engraved pieces is a comment in the company's book of engravings specifying what the lines looked like, and that "these lines go around the piece."

The law suit in the quote mentions tumblers, but M. M. Block was one of several competitors who had been making pharmacy tumblers with internal lines, and Hobbs, Brockunier & Co. chose them to take to court.

From this distance in time, there is no positive way to attribute any one particular graduate to Hobbs, Brockunier & Co. Graduates with pressed internal lines could have been made under the Hobbs' patent, but also could have been made by another firm after the patent expired. Engraved graduates were made before and after Hobbs, Brockunier & Co. patented the pressed wares; and again, there is no way to positively attribute them.

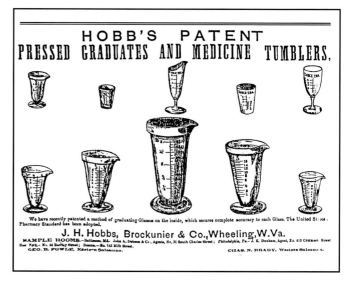

1875 ad showing some of Hobbs' "Pressed Graduates and Medicine Tumblers."

Group of pressed graduates made by the Hobbs' patent.

Prices of measuring glasses similar to those made by Hobbs usually are found in the $5.00 to $25.00 range.
Pieces
32 oz., marked in pounds and ounces
16 oz., marked in pounds and ounces
8 oz., marked in ounces only
4 oz., marked in ounces, with drams marked on first ounce
2 oz., marked in ounces and drams
1 oz., marked in ounces and drams
There are two stemmed and footed pieces marked in tablespoons and teaspoons, one with a pouring lip, the other with a plain rim.
Medicine glasses, marked in tablespoons and teaspoons:
    4 tablespoons
    2 tablespoons

FLOWER STAND AND BOUQUET HOLDER

On April 20, 1875, mechanical patent No. 162,234 was granted to John H. Hobbs and Charles W. Brockunier for the "manufacture of pressed glass flower and fruit stands." In essence, the patent says "Our improvement relates to the manufacture, by pressing, a series of glass articles to be united in a pyramidal structure for table or ornamental use, each such article having at its upper end a bowl or hollow or flat receptacle, and (except the upper most one) a socket or pin to receive and hold the next article above, and at its lower end (except the lowest one) a pin or socket by which to be united to and supported by the article next below." This patent was also used in the Tree of Life epergnes.

In November 1882, another mention of bouquet holders was made: "Among the many we noticed some very pretty designs of bouquet holders in ruby, sapphire, old gold and flame green."

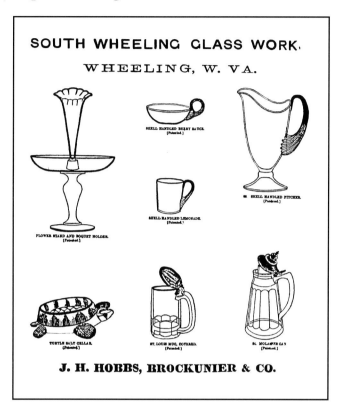

July 1875, ad illustrating various Hobbs' pieces including the patented shell handled pieces and the turtle individual salt. *Crockery & Glass Journal.*

SHELL HANDLED PIECES

On April 20, 1875, C. W. Brockunier was granted mechanical patent number 162,216 on the process of pressing one or more shell handles on a vessel. Prior to this, shell or ribbed handles were hand applied. These shell handled pieces had the appearance of hand finishing but the cost of pressed wares. On July 22, 1875, the above ad appeared in *Crockery and Glass Journal*, illustrating three pieces with shell handles, all mentioning that they were patented. The patent was apparently not broad enough since the next year King, Son & Co. of Pittsburgh patented shell feet and finials on an entire line of tableware which they called their "Centennial Ware."

While these pieces were introduced in 1875, before color production, the existence of a sapphire custard indicates that any of these pieces could have been made in any of the standard colors.

Shell handled custard, sapphire blue.

Pieces	Prices
Berry sauce	$10.00
Cup, custard	10.00
Lemonade, No. 75	15.00
Lemonade	15.00
Pitcher, No. 82	55.00

TURTLE SALT

The small turtle individual salt was covered by design patent No. 8,387, granted June 15, 1875, to Wm. Leighton, Jr. "My improved design for glassware consists of a glass dish made, in the base or supporting part thereof, of the form of a four-footed or flippered reptile, and made with a cavity, bowl, or other hollow shaped receptacle in or on the upper shell, back, or body of the same, such cavity having any desired capacity, according to the purpose for which it is intended." By stipulating the various bowl shapes this covers almost any glass article made in the form of a turtle.

The term of this patent was for fourteen years. After 1889, other companies were free to make their own turtle shaped objects. Adams & Co. made their Wildflower open salt, and Bellaire Goblet Co. their turtle salt dip. Campbell & Jones made a large turtle relish.

There is no evidence to indicate that J. H. Hobbs, Brockunier & Co. ever made anything but the turtle open salt, but they had protected other forms with their patent. The turtle salt is known in crystal and porcelain (opal).

Piece	Price
Turtle individual salt, in crystal	$75.00

Turtle open salt. Courtesy Jo and Bob Sandford.

No. 76 VIKING

Date: February, 1876
Colors: Crystal, opal (very scarce)
Decorations: Satin highlights on feet, faces, and finials; engraved. Seen with all-over satin, with three clear ovals with engraved flowers.
Trade Quotes:
Crockery and Glass Journal, February 22, 1877:
"*THE SOUTH WHEELING GLASS WORKS, J. H. HOBBS, BROCKUNIER & CO. In table ware they are making many very elegant styles. One of them, the '76' set has had a deservedly fine run in the market. The feet and handles of this set are in the shape of the head of a Roman warrior. The sides of the pieces are sharp, and the edges scolloped. These sets are either in engraved or plain crystal, and are highly ornate and rich.*"
Comments: The patent was filed on February 26, 1876, and Design Patent No. 9,647 was awarded to John H. Hobbs on November 21, 1876, term of patent, 14 years. It has been reported as Hobbs' Centennial pattern, but nothing we have seen indicates that this was an original name. Hobbs did have an exhibit at the Centennial Exposition in Philadelphia, and it is reasonable that they exhib-

ited their newest patterns, including Viking. All references in trade journals call the pattern simply No. 76, and describe it as having the head of a Roman warrior. In actuality, Roman might be a more accurate name for the pattern, but Viking has been used for many years. This pattern was originally inspired by various silver plate patterns, including those by Stimpson, Hall, Miller and Co., and E. G. Webster and Bro. Both water pitchers and table sets were made in silver plate.

Pitchers and creamers were made with and without faces under spouts and on handles. Bread plates come with and without the motto "Give Us This Day Our Daily Bread" in the bottom. An open jar is known which is made from the pickle jar. Also, a bottle, 7³/₄" tall, is known which is made from the apothecary jar. Interestingly, table set pieces are made in two varieties: one with three feet and the other with four. The four footed variety is more difficult to find.

No. 76 Viking 9" oval and cover.

Prices given are for plain pieces. Items with satin highlights will be valued at least 10% more. Interestingly, acid (satin) finish on glass became fashionable in this country after the Centennial Exhibition where several firms had extensive exhibits, including glass decorated with acid finish. Porcelain (opal) pieces have been seen priced in excess of $700. A shaving mug in opal glass is also known with a similar Viking head on the side of the mug.

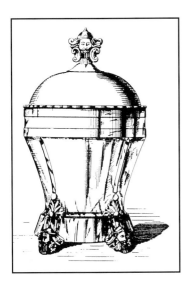

No. 76 Viking patent illustration.

No. 76 Viking covered sugar and cream.

Pieces	Prices
Bread plate, 9" x 12½", with motto	$135.00
Bread plate, 9" x 12½", without motto	125.00
Celery, tall, 7"	50.00
Comport & cover, high footed, 6"	225.00
Comport & cover, high footed, 7"	195.00
Comport & cover, high footed, 8"	195.00
Comport & cover, high footed, 9"	225.00
Comport & cover, low footed, 7"	85.00
Comport & cover, low footed, 8"	95.00
Comport & cover, low footed, 9"	115.00
Comport, 3½"	20.00
Comport, 4"	20.00
Comport, 4½"	22.00
Comport, 5"	25.00
Cream, individual, applied handle	100.00+
Cup, footed	100.00+
Egg cup	50.00
Jar, apothecary	125.00
Mug, applied handle	100.00+
Mustard, covered	150.00
Oval, covered, 7"	85.00
Oval, covered, 8"	95.00
Oval, covered, 9"	110.00
Pickle jar & cover	150.00

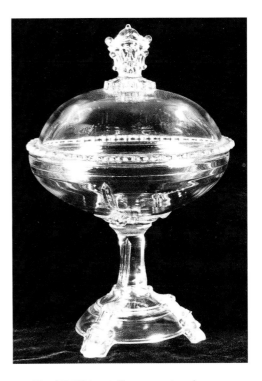

No. 76 Viking tall comport and cover.

Pitcher, ¹/₂ gallon, with face below spout & on handle 175.00
Pitcher, ¹/₂ gallon, plain under spout & on handle 195.00
Relish, 5¹/₂" x 8¹/₂" 45.00
Salver, 10³/₄" wide, 2" tall 110.00
Salver, 11¹/₄" wide, 2³/₄" tall 125.00
Salt, master 45.00
Sugar & cover, individual 95.00
Table set (3 foot):
    Butter & cover 85.00
    Cream, with and without faces on spout and handle 65.00
    Spoon 60.00
    Sugar & cover 75.00
Table set (4 foot):
    Butter & cover with ice drainer 200.00
    Cream 85.00
    Spoon 80.00
    Sugar & cover 100.00
Vase, 8" crimped top 175.00
Vase, 8" smooth top 150.00

No. 76 Viking water pitcher, satin decoration.
Courtesy of the Huntingtion Museum of Art.

No. 76 Viking bread plate with motto.

GOAT ALE

The *Wheeling Daily Intelligencer* of April 10, 1876, in describing wares sent to the Centennial Exhibition in Philadelphia includes this notation: "...two glasses, one...a rampant goat and prostrate beer drinker...." The article was devoted to cuttings, so we are speculating that the beer drinker was engraved on the piece, while the goat was pressed and frosted, as this one is.

Goat Ale. From the collection
of Joyce and Donn Appleman.

CENTENNIAL MUG

This beer mug was patented on April 11, 1876, Design Patent No. 9204, by George B. Fowle, and assigned to Hobbs, Brockunier & Co. Mr. Fowle was the Boston agent for the company. The design consists of a band of 13 stars "around the barrel of the glass mug" and vertical flutes above and below the central band. The word "Centennial" appears around the bottom plain band. There were at least two sizes. The patent notice is on the bottom of the mug.

Centennial Mug patent illustration.

No. 77

Date: Circa 1877

Colors: Crystal

Decorations: Engraving No. 89½; Engraving No. 237; Engraving No. 254; Engraving No. 257; Engraving No. 258; sandblast and cut; Flamingo Habitat etching

Comments: A plain line, including stemware, used for many J. H. Hobbs, Brockunier & Co. decorations. Without the distinctive stem on many pieces, this pattern would be difficult to properly identify. Pieces without stems are very similar to those made by other companies.

Catalog page illustrating No. 77 comports and ovals plus engravings Nos. 257 and 258.

Prices are given for plain pieces. For engravings, add 15 – 25%. For Flamingo Habitat etching, add 350 – 450%.

Pieces	Prices
Bowl, 3½"	$3.00
Celery	15.00
Champagne	10.00
Claret	10.00
Comport, 5"	8.00
Comport, 6"	8.00
Comport, 7"	9.00
Comport, 8"	12.00
Comport, 9"	12.00
Cordial	10.00
Dish, 8"	6.00
Dish, 9"	8.00
Dish, 10"	10.00
Egg cup	15.00
Goblet	10.00

Table set:
    Butter & cover 25.00
    Cream 15.00
    Spoon 12.00
    Sugar & cover 25.00
Wine .10.00

No. 77 comport, sandblasted and cut.

RUSSELL FLOWER POT

Date: Patent applied for March 7, 1877, and granted November 6, 1877

Colors: Color production at Hobbs, Brockunier & Co. unknown. It has been seen in an opaque blue, opaque purple, and chocolate glass. Shards have been found at Model Flint Glass Co. in Findlay of deep amethyst (almost black).

Trade Quote:

Crockery & Glass Journal, July 25, 1878:

"Another novelty is their glass flower-pot in one piece. This they have in various colors and decorations. We have seen nothing prettier of the kind."

Comments: This flower pot was patented by William F. Russell while he worked at J. H. Hobbs, Brockunier & Co. Mechanical patent No. 196,937 was assigned to the item. Russell did not assign this item to Hobbs but retained the rights for himself. The flower pot was also apparently made by at least two other companies. Shards have been found at the Model Flint Glass Co. factory site in Findlay, Ohio, in a deep, almost black, amethyst glass. An example is also known in chocolate glass, which indicates that after the National Glass Co. was formed, the flower pot was made again — possibly at McKee which is known to have made other chocolate glass as part of the National combine.

The references in the lone quote we have found are tantalizing — we can only wonder about the colors and decorations to which the writer was referring. Any example of the flower pot is very difficult to find today. Watch for the ogee scallop on the rim, which was typical of many J. H. Hobbs, Brockunier & Co. designs.

The patent illustration is not the same as actual known flower pots. The patent was for the making of the pot and saucer in one piece or formed in two pieces and joined together while hot, and design on the pot itself was not mentioned. Known flower pots have four flowers around the middle in two alternating designs.

Russell flower pot, chocolate glass.
Courtesy of Ross Trump.

Piece	Price
Flower pot, any color	$250.00+

No. 79 GOAT'S HEAD

Date: January, 1878
Colors: Crystal
Decorations: Satin finish on feet and finials
Trade Quotes:
Crockery and Glass Journal, July 25, 1878:
"Their new set, 'no. 79,' is very taking. The body is in crystal, etched bases, and relieved by goats' heads. In one variety of this pattern the pieces are supported by goats' heads. This is one of the handsomest designs offered in the market."
Comments: The patent was filed December 26, 1877. Design patent No. 10,392 was granted on January 8, 1878, assigned to J. H Hobbs — term of patent, seven years. This pattern is very similar to the popular Viking pattern in execution. It was also originally inspired by a silver plate piece. In addition to the items listed below, other pieces probably exist. It is much more difficult to find than Viking.

No. 79 Goat's Head patent illustration.

No. 79 Goat's Head covered sugar and cream, satin finish. Courtesy of the Huntington Museum of Art.

Prices given are for plain pieces. Add 15% for satin highlights.

Pieces	Prices
Comport & cover, low footed, 9"	$350.00
Oval, covered, 8"	350.00
Pitcher, ½ gallon	550.00+
Table set	
Butter & cover	250.00
Cream	150.00
Spoon	150.00
Sugar & cover	275.00

No. 79 Goat's Head 8" oval, covered.

Nos. 90, 98 TREE OF LIFE WITH HAND, TREE OF LIFE

Date: 1879

Colors: Crystal, old gold, canary, sapphire, marine green.

Decorations: Satin finish on finials, stems and feet of appropriate pieces

Non-footed items are allover Tree of Life except for the Little Samuel bowl/epergne.

Trade Quotes:

Crockery & Glass Journal, September 4, 1879:

"Their newest set, No. 898 [sic], is frosted ware in a very pretty design, the marked feature of which is a hand grasping a snowball. The set is made both plain and etched."

Comments: The trade quotation is in error with the number of the pattern, which should be No. 98, not 898. Tree of Life is not a true pattern but is an effect or finish on glass to imitate overshot glass. Overshot glass is made by rolling the hot article in powdered glass and expanding it into a mold. Tree of Life, a pressed pattern, was originally called "frosted," as was overshot ware, contributing to today's confusion about the two types of glass. Etched in the quote refers to the hand and ball being acid etched.

This pattern has been attributed to various companies over the years, including Portland Glass Co. and Geo. Duncan & Sons or another Pittsburgh area factory. In fact, the majority of the pattern, including all the pieces with the hand motif or the Little Samuel base, were exclusive J. H. Hobbs, Brockunier & Co. products. Hobbs, Brockunier, seems to have acquired four of the molds of the former Portland Glass Co. in Maine, but most of the items made were new designs in Tree of Life made only by Hobbs, Brockunier & Co. Known molds obtained from Portland were two sizes of comports (including one with a trumpet vase), and a finger bowl. These comports have "Davis" in the design. The Portland items have plain smooth rims, except for the vase for the comport. On the Little Samuel comport made by J. H. Hobbs, Brockunier & Co. only the bowl is of Portland origin (it has the name "Davis" intertwined in the pattern); but J. H. Hobbs, Brockunier & Co. added the Little Samuel base and a heavy ogee rim around the top of the bowl. (See Lighting for illustrations of Little Samuel pieces.) Epergnes and comports with P. G. Co. and the patent date are exclusive products of J. H. Hobbs, Brockunier & Co. even though they also have plain rims. This is confirmed since the patent date is after the close of the Portland Glass Co.

Three Tree of Life bowls used with silverplate holders from the 1886 – 87 Meridan Britannia Silver-plate catalog.

Tree of Life Little Samuel epergne with vase.

Other factories made Tree of Life patterns or patterns with portions in the Tree of Life motif. Portland Glass made stemware and tableware of very simple design with plain, smooth rims, sometimes marked either Davis or P. G. Co. Geo. Duncan and Sons made the popular Shell and Tassel pattern which has Tree of Life on the shells. An importer sold a boxed ice cream set, although the country of origin is not known at this time. The Boston & Sandwich Glass Co. is also reported to have made some pieces of Tree of Life. The Beatty-Brady Glass Co., of Dunkirk, Indiana, produced a rather extensive line in Tree of Life in a low quality glass around 1898.

J. H. Hobbs, Brockunier & Co. used an easily identifiable ogee scalloped rim on many pieces in Tree of Life and also in other patterns, i.e. No. 76 Viking and the Russell flower pot. Note that even the No. 90 leaf dish also has a broad ogee scallop.

The listed items are the only items we can document at this time as being made by J. H. Hobbs, Brockunier & Co. The items marked with an asterisk include the Hand as a portion of the design. The hand salvers do not have the Tree of Life motif on the tops. Other items are allover Tree of Life except for the Little Samuel comport and vase which is often missing from the comports. Original pattern numbers, when known, are listed after the entries.

Tree of Life was quite popular, and it is relatively easy to find today. Some pieces were widely used in elaborate silver plate holders made by Meriden Britannia Co. and probably many other silver mounting companies.

The No. 90 5" Tree of Life shade is one of the few pieces which continued in the line until U. S. Glass closed the plant in 1893.

Pieces have been found with stippling and stars on the balls, and with diagonal swirls, rather than Tree of Life, on the body. These are possibly of European origin. (See the chapter on Misleading Pieces for an illustration of this item.)

Prices given are for crystal pieces. Crystal pieces with frosted finials and stems are worth slightly more than all crystal items. For old gold (amber), add 20%; canary, 50%; marine green, sapphire, 100%. All pieces may not have been made in all colors.

Warren Glass Co., of Cumberland, Md. advertised a bouquet holder in August of 1882 utilizing a hand which resembles, and may be the same as, J. H. Hobbs, Brockunier & Co.'s hand used in comport and lamp stems. This item was patented although the patent covered the use of wires supporting small glass vessels for holding flowers. At this time there is no way of knowing what glass company made these hand bouquet vases or if there were any business arrangements between the two companies.

Illustration of Warren Glass Works bouquet vase using the hand stem found in Tree of Life with Hand, *Crockery & Glass Journal.*

Tree of Life with Hand 9" comport, marine green. Courtesy of the Huntington Museum of Art.

Reproductions and confusing pieces: The small leaf dish has been reproduced by L. E. Smith in crystal and possibly other colors. This piece has been seen in copper or selenium red, and this may be a Smith product. A similar leaf-shaped piece is sometimes found in true overshot glass, the top rim of which is cut and polished with gold applied. This item is probably of European origin and may have been the inspiration for the Hobbs piece.

5 m 90 Shade. Pressed

No. 90 Tree of Life 5" shade.

Tree of Life with Hand table set. Courtesy of Margaret Forkner.

Pieces	Prices
Bowl, 4"	$12.00
Bowl, 6"	15.00
Bowl, 8"	40.00
Bowl, 10"	50.00
Bowl with vase, 8"	250.00
Bowl with vase, 10"	350.00
Bowl with vase, Little Samuel base	575.00
Bowl, finger, No. 90	25.00
Bowl, finger, No. 98	25.00
Butter, individual	10.00
Comport, footed, 4" hand & snowball stem	40.00
Comport, footed, 6" *	65.00
Comport, footed, 8" *	75.00
Comport, footed, 10" *	95.00
Comport, footed, with vase, 8" *	325.00
Comport, footed, with vase, 10" *	375.00
Dish, leaf, 4$\frac{1}{2}$", No. 90	20.00
Dish, leaf, 5$\frac{1}{2}$", No. 90	25.00
Jug, $\frac{1}{2}$ gallon	225.00
Oval, 9"	30.00
Salver, cake, *	145.00
Shade, 5", No. 90	60.00
Table set: *	
Butter & cover	90.00
Cream	65.00
Spoon	50.00
Sugar & cover	80.00

* Hand included as portion of the design.

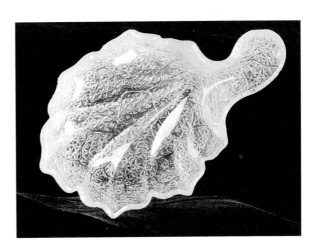

No. 90 Tree of Life leaf dish, canary.

Tree of Life 4$\frac{1}{2}$" bowl, old gold.

FLAMINGO HABITAT ETCHING

Date: 1880
Colors: Crystal
Trade Quotes:

Crockery and Glass Journal, March 25, 1880:

"This set exhibits an original design which has not been surpassed for elegance, beauty, or delicacy of workmanship by any pattern upon the most expensive glassware. It is in Japanese style — which has become so fashionable, and bids fair to retain a long hold on public favor, and is now on all kinds of furnishing goods. The stork, that picturesque bird, is represented on these wares in exquisite and elaborate patterns, which are durable as works of art, and strikingly graceful as forms of ornamentation. The work is varied upon each article of the set in such manner as not to weary the eye while the general unity of effect is preserved."

Comments: This plate etching was previously unattributed. Because of its occurrence on known J. H. Hobbs, Brockunier & Co. pieces and this trade quote, it can definitely now be attributed to J. H. Hobbs, Brockunier & Co. As noted in the quotation above, the etching design varies slightly between different pieces of glass, i.e., goblet and spoon, causing both to be collected as goblets today. Because it is a decoration rather than a pattern, per se, it occurs on several J. H. Hobbs, Brockunier & Co. patterns. The original pattern numbers are listed following each piece. Other pieces may exist.

Flamingo Habitat etched No. 77 three comports, various sizes.

Flamingo Habitat etched No. 53 cheese plate and cover.

Flamingo Habitat etched No. 77 table set covered sugar, spoon, cream.

Flamingo Habitat etched No. 77 wine and goblet.

Pieces	Prices
Champagne, No. 77	$35.00
Claret, No. 77	35.00
Cheese dish & cover, No. 53	150.00
Comport, 4", No. 77	20.00
Comport, 6", No. 77	35.00
Comport, 8", No. 77	50.00
Comport, 8", covered, No. 77	120.00
Goblet, No. 77	50.00
Pitcher, 1/2 gallon	225.00
Table set, No. 77:	
Butter & cover	95.00
Cream	60.00
Spoon	50.00
Sugar & cover	85.00
Tumbler	45.00
Wine, No. 77	35.00

Flamingo Habitat etching, detail of pattern.

DOLPHIN

Date: September, 1880

Colors: Crystal

Decorations: Sand blast finish on dolphins

Trade Quotes:

Crockery and Glass Journal, September 30, 1880:

"While in their sample rooms a few days ago, we were shown a new set, just finished for the trade, called the 'Dolphin,' which is one of the most elaborate and beautiful sets of glassware we have ever seen. The dolphin is the central figure in every piece, appearing now on the foot, again on the top, and once more upon the side; and each time the observer is struck by the ingenuity of the design, and the elegance of finish."

Comments: This pattern was previously unattributed as to its maker. The above quote and the similarity of the pattern to both Viking and Goat's Head confirm J. H. Hobbs, Brockunier & Co. as the maker. What at first glance appears to be a satin finish on the dolphins actually was done by sand blasting, not acid. J. H. Hobbs, Brockunier & Co. had just built a new sand blast building and this was one of the first patterns they decorated by sand blasting. Ruth Webb Lee listed a goblet (we have not seen one), but the spoon could easily be confused with a goblet. Other items may have been made in this pattern. A cologne bottle made from the pickle jar which has been necked in and fitted with a dolphin stopper is known. The pattern is quite difficult to find today.

Dolphin cream.

Prices given are for items with sand blast decoration.

Pieces	Prices
Celery, tall	$120.00
Comport, 8"	195.00
Comport, 9"	210.00
Comport and cover, 8"	220.00
Comport and cover, 9"	250.00
Jug	450.00+
Oval and cover, 7"	375.00
Oval and cover, 8"	375.00
Pickle jar and cover	325.00
Salt, master	50.00
Table set:	
Butter & cover	375.00
Cream	150.00
Spoon	125.00
Sugar & cover	375.00

Dolphin 8" comport.

Dolphin covered sugar. Courtesy of the Huntington Museum of Art.

Dolphin, detail of side motif, pickle jar.

Dolphin spoon. Courtesy of Nellie and Charles Huttunen.

CRAQUELLE

Date: September, 1881
Colors: Crystal, old gold, canary, marine green, sapphire, ruby
Decorations: Possibly enameled decorations
Trade Quotes:
Crockery & Glass Journal, September 8, 1881:
"Messrs. Hobbs, Brockunier & Co. This firm is now giving special attention to the manufacture of the old gold crackled ware that is at present creating such a furor among the trade. Orders began to come in immediately, and men sufficient to manufacture it as rapidly as ordered cannot be procured by the firm."
Crockery and Glass Journal, December 8, 1881:
"Hobbs, Brockunier & Co. have for some time been experimenting in the manufacture of ruby crackled pitchers. These pitchers are of a beautiful ruby color and have a crackled appearance. None of them have ever been manufactured in this country, and the few which have been imported have been sold at fancy prices. Yesterday the firm mentioned succeeded in turning out several dozen of these pieces, which have been pronounced equal to the finest imported work in tint, finish and workmanship. It is intended to continue the experiments, and to make a specialty of this work."
Crockery & Glass Journal, October 11, 1883:
"The beautiful craquelle ware made almost exclusively here is attaining a phenomenal popularity. Only a few specimens of this ware were made a year or two ago, more as an experiment than anything else, and now a number of shops are kept going exclusively on it."
Crockery & Glass Journal, March 27, 1884:
"Their lines of ware are quite handsome, their ruby, canary, and blue crackled wares especially so."
Comments: Craquelle is not truly a pattern but a decorative effect on glass which has been often confused with overshot glass. Techniques for making these two types of glass differ. Overshot is made by rolling the gather in frit (small glass particles) and then expanding the glass into a final mold form. The result is a rough, textured, sometimes sharp, surface on the glass. Craquelle (crackle) glass is made by quickly immersing the hot gather in a cold liquid causing the surface to crack because of the sudden change in temperature. The gather is then reheated and expanded in a finish mold resulting in glass with a relatively smooth exterior surface but having a web or network of tiny lines or fractures in the surface of the glass which were formed by the immersion. Because of these fractures, it is quite fragile and not much has survived, making it difficult to find today.

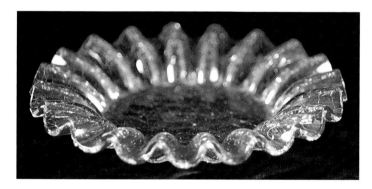

Craquelle underplate, ruby.

Craquelle finger bowls and underplates.

The original Hobbs, Brockunier & Co. shape numbers are listed after each item. Other pieces may exist.

Prices given are for crystal pieces. For old gold (amber) add 20%; canary 50%; marine green, sapphire, and ruby add 100%.

Reproductions: This type of ware has been made by many other companies, especially during the twentieth century. True craquelle has been made, as has a fake craquelle which is actually a pressed design. No Hobbs, Brockunier & Co. shapes are known to have been reproduced.

Pieces	Prices
Bitter, No. 309	$110.00
Bowl, finger, melon ribbed	.25.00
Bowl, shell footed, 8", No. 302	120.00
Celery, No. 314	.55.00
Cream, No. 305	.45.00
Dish, ice cream, No. 302	235.00
Mustard, No. 217	.65.00
Oil, No. 306	120.00
Pitcher, No. 319 (several sizes)	100.00+
Plate, melon ribbed, 6¾"	.20.00
Salt, No. 216	.25.00
Sugar, No. 305	.45.00

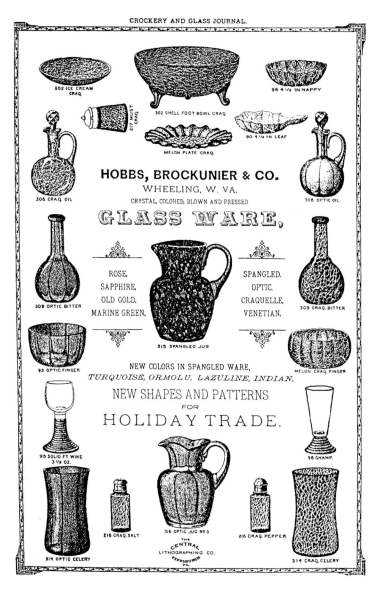

1883 Hobbs, Brockunier & Co. ad illustrating Craquelle, Spangled, and other wares. *Crockery & Glass Journal.*

VENETIAN

Date: Fall of 1882

Colors: White loopings on body with ruby or blue threading. Possibly other color combinations exist.

Comments: In late 1881 or early 1882, a large display of antique (fifteenth to seventeenth century) Venetian glassware was exhibited in New York. It is quite possible that this display inspired American glassmakers to experiment with Venetian style wares. The distinct loops or drapery of this ware was used by several American and European firms and called "Venetian" at that time.

Several companies contemporary with Hobbs, Brockunier & Co. illustrated Venetian patterns in their ads, all conforming to this type of glassware. Hobbs, Brockunier & Co. did not illustrate any items in Venetian, only mentioning the pattern in two ads, the first ad containing only text. The second ad had illustrations, but none showing Venetian. See page 62. These pieces in the photograph were possibly made by Hobbs, Brockunier & Co. but without original illustrations, positive attribution cannot be made. Venetian has been copied in ruby opalescent blown ware and possibly other colors.

The vase listed below belonged to the granddaughter of A. G. Frohme, the last manager of Factory H under U. S. Glass. Mr. Frohme had been with Hobbs, Brockunier & Co. for many years. The vase, now in the collection of the Oglebay Institute, is identical in manufacture to the tumbler and jug illustrated below. Other pieces may exist.

Pieces	Prices
Bowl, finger	.$700.00+
Jug	.1,800.00+
Tumbler	.850.00+
Vase, made from No. 314 celery	.1,200.00+

Venetian tumbler, ruby threaded; jug, blue threaded. Courtesy of the Huntington Museum of Art.

OPTIC

Date: Patent applied for November 33, 1882, granted February 20, 1883. Term of patent 14 years. Design Patent No. 13,645.

Comments: This decorative effect was patented by William Russell and assigned to the Hobbs, Brockunier & Co. The patent describes the design as: "The leading feature of my design consists of vertical or nearly vertical ribs and spiral or horizontal corrugations. The ribs may consist of comparatively thick portions which extend up and down the body of the glass article, inside or outside, or both, with intervening thinner portions, and the relative as well as absolute breadths and thicknesses of the thick and thin portions may be varied at pleasure."

This effect was used on a variety of blown wares, not as a pattern but as an optic effect. Russell patented not only the vertical ribs and broad areas, but also the fine spiral or diagonal optics shown in the patent illustration. The patent also covered horizontal ribbing. As broad as this patent is, any of these treatments may be found individually or in any combination.

Since the patent expired in 1897, and any company could have made these effects after then, we must rely on identifying Hobbs, Brockunier's optic wares from their shapes, not the optic. These wares may be found in any colors or stains made by Hobbs, Brockunier & Co. or Hobbs Glass Co. after the patent was applied for. See page 62 for ad showing optic pieces.

Patent illustration of Optic wares developed by William F. Russell.

EXTERNAL RIBS

Date: Patent applied for February 26, 1883, granted January 29, 1884. Mechanical Patent No. 292,765 for the manufacture of ornamental glassware.

Colors: Single layer and plated colors, sometimes with mica spangles. Any Hobbs, Brockunier color or color combination is possible.

Comments: This new method of forming glass was apparently important enough that the trade journals published an excerpt of the text of the patent.

Wm. F. Russell, Wheeling, W. Va., assignor to Hobbs, Brockunier & Co., same place.

1. Claim - The method herein described of ornamenting the exterior portion of glassware in the operation of forming the same, consisting of pressing the hot plastic glass of which the article is to be formed upon a ribbed or corrugated surface, twisting or bending the ribs or flutes thus formed in inclined or circumferential directions around the body of glass, and again pressing the glass upon a ribbed or corrugated surface, to impart a second set of ribs or flutes upon and across the first.

2. The method herein described of forming ornamented articles of glassware, consisting of first gathering the glass upon a blowers pipe, second, pressing such glass while attached to the pipe upon a corrugated wall or surface; third, bending or twisting the ribs thus made upon the body of glass; fourth, again pressing the glass upon a corrugated wall or surface forming a second set of ribs crossing the former ones, and then blowing and shaping the glass thus ribbed into the desired article.

3. The method herein described of ornamenting articles of glassware consisting in forming upon the exterior surface of the partially formed article inclined ribs, flutes, or corrugations, then pressing or imprinting upon such ribbed surface a second set of ribs, flutes, or corrugations, crossing those first formed, and finally shaping the glass thus impressed into the desired article.

4. A method herein described of ornamenting articles of glassware, consisting in forming upon the exterior surface of the glass one or more sets of ribs, flutes, or corrugations, the different sets being impressed or formed one upon another and inclined around the body of glass in different directions, then impressing another and larger set of corrugations upon and across those previously made, and finally shaping the glass thus impressed into the desired article.

5. The method herein described of ornamenting glassware, consisting in forming two or more sets of ribs or corrugations on the exterior surface of the glass article one set being impressed upon and across another."

While the patent specifies "two or more sets of ribs...one set being impressed upon and across another," we have not seen any articles with ribs crossing each other. We have, however, found several examples with one set of spiral ribs which were made in this manner.

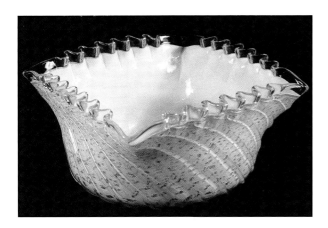

External Ribs bowl with square crimped top, canary spangle over opal inner plating.

External Ribs No. 205 7" bowl, ruby with opal edge.

SPANGLED

Date: Mid 1883

Colors: Blue, green, white, Indian (red-amber) and others. May be plated inside with opal (white).

Decorations: The glass has entrapped mica plated between the body with crystal or colored glass on the exterior. Satin finish according to Leighton color formula.

Trade Quotes:

Crockery & Glass Journal, August 30, 1883:

"The latest addition to the list of novelties is what they call spangled glass. A very unique effect is produced by flecking gold or silver foil on a ground of dark blue or green and then covering the spangles with a thin coating of crystal glass. Malachite effects are produced by taking a ground of malachite blue and flecking or spangling it with silver foil and coating in crystal. They are making a large line of tableware, globes, vases, etc., in this way and if the trade are in search of something quite out of the ordinary run they will do well to get a sample lot of these goods at once."

Crockery & Glass Journal, November 8, 1883:

"Their new ware, the 'spangled,' as they call it, is still more beautiful than the famous craquelle, and there is a very large demand for the various articles made from it. As a means of decoration the ware made from this goods is perhaps, at once the most unique and handsome of any that has been introduced in the last ten years."

Crockery & Glass Journal, November 15, 1883:

"In the line of spangle ware some very unique finger bowls, vases, bouquet holders, and other holiday goods are the most recent introduction."

Crockery and Glass Journal, January 1, 1884

"There is probably more craquelle and spangled ware here than at any other place in the country."

Patent illustration for spangled ware.

Spangled unknown pattern number jugs, one pint and three pint, deep blue base, amber plating on exterior. Courtesy of the Huntington Museum of Art.

Comments: The Design Patent was applied for on September 28, 1883, by William Leighton, Jr., granted February 12, 1884, and assigned No. 14,443. The Mechanical Patent was filed on September 26, 1883, and granted July 29, 1884, Mechanical Patent No. 292,663. These patents are broad enough to include any size of mica flakes and any arrangement, random or intentional.

This glass has entrapped mica plated between the first gather and crystal or colored glass on the exterior. Amber plating makes the mica appear to be gold; crystal glass makes it seem to be silver. Other colors could be obtained by using different colors to plate over the mica. Other color combinations include blue plated with red amber and blue plated with blue. Other companies also made spangled-type glassware. Sowerby's in Newcastle Upon Tyne in Great Britain made a line of ware in the early 1880s which they called Nugget — very similar to Hobbs' Spangled glass. Most of Sowerby's wares were pressed, while Hobbs, Brockunier's Spangled is blown. There are pieces of coral known with bits of mica between the amberina and the opal (white) ground.

See also page 62 for a jug in Spangled ware.

Pieces	Prices
Bowl, finger	$220.00
Cream, melon ribbed, applied handle, blue	250.00
Globes, shapes unknown	N.P.A.
Pitcher, No. 315, various sizes	350.00+
Pitcher, No. 316, various sizes	350.00+
Pitcher, No. 319, various sizes	350.00+
Pitcher, ringed neck, small	265.00
Pitcher, ringed neck, large	550.00
Salt, No. 216	200.00
Tumbler	140.00
Vase	260.00
Vase, melon ribbed	250.00
Vase, ring necked, large	400.00

Spangled No. 306 oil, deep blue base, amber plating on exterior. Courtesy of the Huntington Museum of Art.

Spangled, three tumblers: turquoise, opaque green, rose with amber overplate.

Spangled, vase, deep blue base with amber plating on exterior; cream, deep blue base with crystal plating on exterior.

SPATTER

Date: Mid 1883, based upon its combination with spangled glass.

Colors: Various combinations, base glass any transparent color with bits of color as spatters.

Comments: This glass was made by rolling the first gather in bits of broken glass, much like Spangled glass, then plating over this with another transparent color, then blowing it into the final form. Some Spatter glass also has mica inclusions.

Hobbs, Brockunier & Co. was not the only manufacturer of Spatter glass. Shapes and colors must be used to verify attribution. Otto Jaeger, after he left Hobbs, Brockunier & Co., and established Bonita Art Glass Co. in Indiana, may have made Spatter ware there.

Spatter may be found in any of Hobbs, Brockunier's standard blown shapes, tumblers, jugs, vases, etc.

Spatter No. 11 vase, ruffled top, ruby and opal; a very similar vase, turquoise spangled with crystal handles is in the Oglebay Museum; tumbler, ruby and opal.

Spatter tumbler and No. 319 jug, old gold and opal spatter with mica spangle, old gold over-plating.

POLKA DOT

Date: April, 1884

Colors: Crystal, old gold, sapphire, marine green, canary, ruby (cranberry), rubina, rubina verde, ruby amber, ruby sapphire, crystal opalescent, old gold opalescent, sapphire opalescent, marine green opalescent, canary opalescent, ruby opalescent, aurora (an unknown color or effect).

Decorations: Possibly enameling, engraving No. 5 on No. 290 tumblers

Trade Quotes:

Crockery & Glass Journal, April 17, 1884:

A new design called the 'Polka Dot' is having a very solid factory run. This design is of very recent invention and is as handsome as its name indicates.

Crockery & Glass Journal, June 5, 1884:

Among the many we notice a fancy vase in the Aurora colors, polka dot pattern, that is certainly magnificent.

Crockery & Glass Journal, October 9, 1884:

The 'Polka Dot' keeps pace with all the other products, and whether Aurora or ruby is beautiful.

Crockery & Glass Journal, November 20, 1884:

The 'Polka Dot' ware is now made in crystal, old gold, sapphire, marine green, canary, ruby, rubina-verde, and aurora.

Crockery & Glass Journal, March 19, 1885:

A neat little 'sugar' in colors in polka-dot with or without handles is attracting favorable attention.

Crockery & Glass Journal, March 25, 1886:

No. 290 tumblers, beautifully engraved, twelve different kinds in a box are also having a big sale.

Comments: This is not truly a pattern, but an optic effect for glass. Hobbs, Brockunier & Co. used many different numbered pieces with this effect. Original Hobbs, Brockunier & Co. numbers are listed after each piece below. The pitchers and some other pieces come in various sizes, designated by numbers 0 to 5, from smallest to largest. Many, many other companies have made this same type of ware, both in this country and abroad. The Polka Dot optic is still used by glassmakers today. Today's collectors often call this optic effect Inverted Thumbprint or IVT. Larger opalescent polka dots are sometimes called Coin Spot. We prefer to use the original terminology for this type of glass — Polka Dot. Please see the Lighting Section for globes and shades in Polka Dot.

The quotes in reference to Aurora colors are confusing. We have not been able to determine whether Aurora is indeed a color or colors or is a term for various shaded glasses such as ruby amber, ruby sapphire, etc.

The base of the cheese dish in this pattern is the No. 101 Daisy and Button 7" plate.

Remarkably, the boxed sets of tumblers are still known to exist — a set in the original box having been recently acquired by the Corning Museum of Glass.

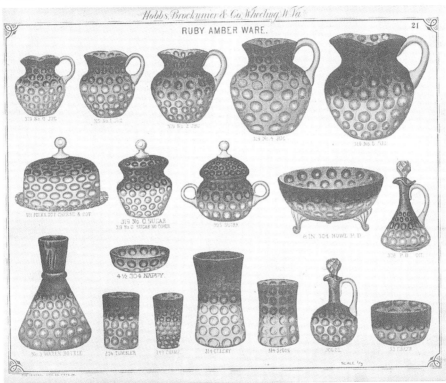

Catalog page — Polka Dot items in ruby amber. Top row, L to R: No. 319 Jugs, No. 0, No. 1, No. 2, No. 4, No. 5. Middle row, L to R: 101 Cheese & Cover, 319, No. 0 Sugar, 305 Sugar, 8 in. 304 Bowl PD, 308 PD Oil. Bottom row, L to R: No. 3 Water Bottle, 4½ 304 Nappy, 236 Tumbler, 247 Champ., 314 Spoon, 306 Oil, No. 93 Finger.

Polka Dot cheese and cover, rubina verde. Courtesy of Huntington Museum of Art.

Polka Dot No. 305 covered sugar and No. 319 cream, rubina verde. Courtesy of Huntington Museum of Art.

Prices given are for items in ruby, rubina, marine green, and sapphire. For pieces in crystal, old gold, and canary, deduct 25%. For pieces in rubina verde, ruby amber, and ruby sapphire, add 100% or more. For pieces with opalescence, add 20% to the above percentages.

Pieces	Prices
Bar bottle, No. 76	$225.00
Bar bottle, No. 89	225.00
Bitter, No. 309	195.00
Bowl, finger, No. 93	40.00
Bowl, shell feet, 8", No. 304	250.00
Celery, No. 314	70.00
Cheese & cover, No. 101	240.00
Cream, 1, No. 314, cylindrical neck and top	95.00
Custard, No. 507	30.00
Decanter, No. 42	95.00
Jug, 0, No. 319	85.00
Jug, 1, No. 319	95.00
Jug, 2, No. 319	110.00
Jug, 3, No. 319	160.00
Jug, 4, No. 319	200.00
Jug, 5, No. 319	250.00
Lemon (lemonade), No. 509	65.00
Molasses can, 12 oz., No. 97	175.00
Molasses can, 16 oz., No. 98	185.00

Polka Dot No. 236 tumbler and No. 319 jug, ruby amber. Courtesy of Huntington Museum of Art.

Catalog page — Polka Dot items in ruby, rubina verde, sapphire, and canary. Top row, L to R: No. 4 PD Decanter, Cut Stopper; 76 PD Bar Bot. Stop., Cut; 89 Optic Bar Eng. D. No. 236; 89 Bar Bottle, rubina verde; 319-0 Sugar & Cov., rubina verde; 309 Bitter, rubina verde; 509 Lemon PD, rubina verde; 507 Custard, rubina verde. Middle row, L to R: 98 PD Mol. Can, 16 oz.; 97 PD Mol. Can, 12 oz.; PD Bbl. Mustard; 4½ 304 Nappy, rubina verde; 5-304 Nappy, rubina verde. Bottom row, L to R: 216 PD Pepper; 216 PD Salt; 223 Salt, PD; 312 PD Oil; Sugar Sifter, ruby, PD; 101 PD Water Set, rubina verde.

Mustard, barrel with glass top 150.00
Nappy, 4½", No. 304 . . . . .25.00
Nappy, 5", No. 304 . . . . .25.00
Oil, No. 306 . . . . .130.00
Oil, No. 308 . . . . .130.00
Oil, No. 312 . . . . .130.00
Salt, No. 216 . . . . .70.00
Salt, No. 223 . . . . .70.00
Set: (cream & sugar)
    Cream, No. 314 . . . . .95.00
    Sugar & cover, No. 305 . . . . .140.00
Spoon, No. 314 . . . . .60.00
Sugar & cover, No. 319 . . . . .140.00
Sugar sifter 165.00
Tumbler, No. 236 . . . . .35.00
Tumbler, No. 290 . . . . .35.00
Tumbler, champagne, No. 247 . . . . .42.00
Vase (unknown shape, but probably No. 319) . . . . .N.P.A.
Water bottle, No. 3 . . . . .225.00

Polka Dot cheese and cover, ruby sapphire. Courtesy of Carol and Harvey Herbert.

Polka Dot No. 308 oils, ruby, rubina.

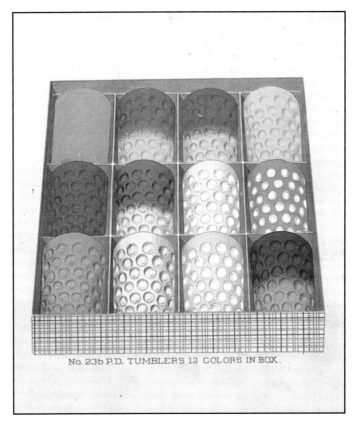

Catalog page — No. 236 Polka Dot tumblers in various colors and effects, shown in original box.

Polka Dot No. 314 spoons, rubina verde, ruby.

Polka Dot two tumblers, ruby sapphire, ruby amber, both engraved.

Polka Dot three No. 247 champagnes: ruby amber, rubina, rubina.

Polka Dot No. 507 custards, various opalescent colors.

NO. 290 TUMBLERS
Engd No. 5

THE CENTRAL LITH. CO. PITTS. PA.

Catalog page — No. 290 Polka Dot tumblers in various colors, engraved No. 5, shown in original box.

No. 101 DAISY & BUTTON

Date: October, 1884
Colors: Crystal, old gold, sapphire, marine green, canary, amberina, ruby
Decorations: Crystal is sometimes found with amber stain.
Trade Quotes:

Crockery & Glass Journal, October 9, 1884:

...The '101' set in all colors just now is the leading feature. The celery dishes, mostly in the shape of a shoe, fruit bowls so finely done in imitation of cut glass as to deceive the eye of all and make them in universal demand, the tumblers, nappies, and the score of other varieties of this serve to make it one great beauty.

Crockery & Glass Journal, October 30, 1884:

...Among their new goods this week is a new celery dish, very ingeniously fashioned into the form of a yacht. This dish in plain colors is one of the handsomest table ornaments yet brought out.... It is also in old gold, canary, and other colors.

Crockery & Glass Journal, March 19, 1885:

A set in colored imitation cut ware is the new '101.' It consists of a butter, sugar, cream, and spoon, each piece sets in a tray of very small proportions, but exquisitely pressed in imitation of cut ware.

Crockery & Glass Journal, July 9, 1885:

Hobbs, Brockunier & Co. have just introduced their new 101 Star Bowl, the richest berry bowl with saucers yet out.

Comments: This is a copy of the cut glass pattern known as Russian. Daisy and Button was, and still is, made by many, many companies. Hobbs, Brockunier & Co. originally called this pattern Hobnail Diamond.

Hobbs, Brockunier & Co. was licensed by the New England Glass Co. to make amberina in pressed ware only. The New England Glass Co. made blown amberina almost exclusively which it had developed and patented in July 1883. Note that Libbey (New England Glass Co.) did not give permission to make pressed amberina until long after Hobbs, Brockunier had begun making No. 101 Daisy and Button.

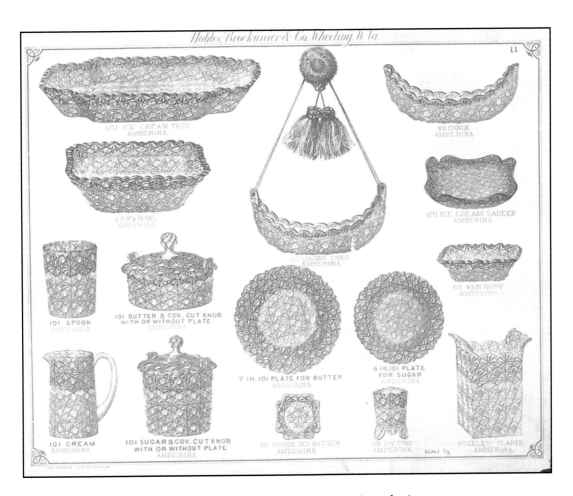

Catalog page — various No.101 items in amberina.

Gillinder & Sons made a flared, diamond shaped berry set in Daisy & Button in amberina, their No. 406 pattern. They als made other Daisy & Button items in amberina. The color of Gillinder & Sons' amberina is not as strong as that of Hobbs, Brocku nier — the red and amber are both lighter shades. Gillinder & Sons also made an oval table set in their No. 408 pattern which i very similar to the round one made by Hobbs, Brockunier & Co. This oval set is found with inserted metal finials.

The Star Bowl was not a Hobbs, Brockunier & Co. exclusive. Other companies made similar bowls. Hobbs, Brockunier's Sta Bowl, though round, is essentially a square with a pair of smooth grooves in each corner which meet at a point in the corner of th bottom. The manufacturer of the large shoe-shaped celeries has not been previously known. The 7" cheese plate was also use under the cheese (butter) in blown Polka Dot and Windows.

In addition to the pickle jars, the celeries (yachts and canoes) were fitted with elaborate silver-plated frames. Many other piece of Daisy & Button were also used in silver-plated frames.

A match holder in this pattern has been found in a purple slag glass. This piece is considered to have been made by the H Northwood Co. which occupied the factory 10 years after U. S. Glass closed the plant. There must have been at least two molds lef behind, since a piece of No. 331 has also been found in this same purple slag. These two pieces and others may be found in other Northwood colors.

See Lighting section for examples of No. 101 shades, page 145.

A bowl in ruby was illustrated in *Wheeling Glass* by Josephine Jefferson.

Reproductions: The toy tumbler or toothpick has been reproduced, both in Daisy & Button and the same shape with hobnails as the pattern. The reproduction toothpick or toy tumbler can be distinguished from the original by examining the feet. The original feet have two long points on each foot, the reproductions have four short points on each foot. The 9" oval crown bowl has beer made by Fenton Art Glass Co. in blue opalescent, among other colors. Many other items have also been reproduced. Original larger pieces usually have ground base rims. A 4" square nappy has been seen in a selenium or copper red. It is probably a product of either L. G. Wright or L. E. Smith.

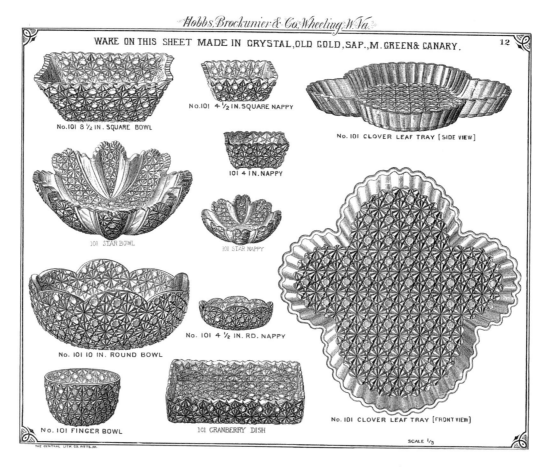

Catalog page — various No. 101 items.

Prices are for items in old gold, canary and crystal with amber stain. For crystal deduct 20%. For sapphire and marine green add 25%. For ruby and amberina add 500% or more.

Pieces	Prices
Bar bottle	$175.00
Bowl, finger	45.00
Bowl, round, 9½"	70.00
Bowl, round, 10"	70.00
Bowl, square, 6½"	40.00
Bowl, square, 8½"	65.00
Bowl, star	90.00
Bowl, star, footed	175.00
Bowl & cover, round, 8"	150.00
Butter, round individual	12.00
Butter, square individual	15.00
Butter and cover, small	125.00
Canoe	80.00
Canoe, hanging	90.00
Caster bottles:	
Mustard	30.00
Pepper	30.00
Vinegar	30.00
Catsup, cut stopper	120.00
Celery, flared	80.00
Celery, shoe, figured sole, 11¾"	125.00
Celery, shoe, plain sole, 11¾"	125.00
Celery, yacht, 13"	75.00
Cheese & cover (pressed)	150.00
Cologne, cut stopper	65.00
Dish, cranberry	35.00
Ice bowl & drainer	120.00

No. 101 Daisy and Button caster bottles, salt, mustard, amber stain on daisies.

No. 101 Daisy and Button cream and underplate, amberina. Courtesy of Huntington Museum of Art.

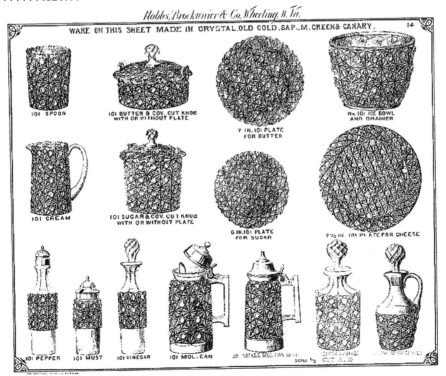

Catalog page — various No. 101 items.

Match safe 120.00
Molasses can 120.00
Molasses can, small, 10 oz 120.00
Nappy, round, 4¹/₂" 20.00
Nappy, square, 4" 20.00
Nappy, square, 4¹/₂" 20.00
Nappy, star 20.00
Oval, 10" 90.00
Oval, crown, 9" 90.00
Pickle, yacht, 8" 40.00
Pickle jar & cover 145.00
Plate, 6" for sugar 25.00
Plate, 7" for butter 25.00
Plate, 7¹/₂" for cheese 25.00
Salt, yacht, 3" .18.00
Saucer, ice cream 30.00
Shade, pan, 4" .90.00
Shade, pan, 4" crimped 90.00
Table set:
    Butter & cover 110.00
    Cream 60.00
    Spoon 60.00
    Sugar & cover 100.00
Tankard pitcher, quart 125.00
Tankard pitcher, 2 quart 150.00
Tankard pitcher, 3 pint 175.00
Tray, cloverleaf (water) 65.00
Tray, ice cream 80.00
Tumbler 35.00
Tumbler, 101-2 . . . . .35.00
Tumbler, toy (toothpick) 50.00
Whiskey 30.00

No. 101 Daisy and Button toy tumblers: crystal, amberina, marine green.

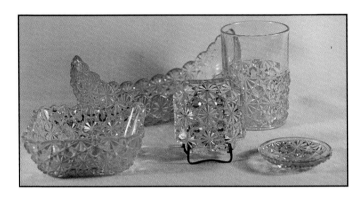

No. 101 Daisy and Button group in marine green; front: 4¹/₂" nappy, square individual butter, round individual butter; back: canoe, tumbler.

Catalog page — various No. 101 items in canary, old gold, and sapphire.

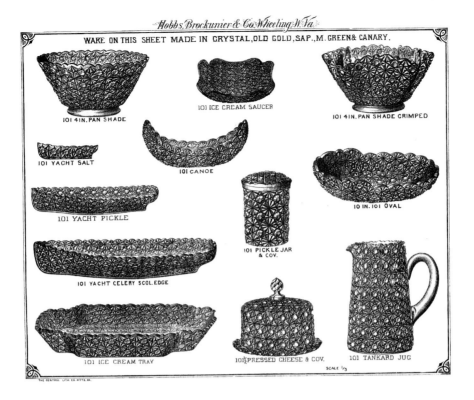

WARE ON THIS SHEET MADE IN CRYSTAL, OLD GOLD, SAP., M. GREEN & CANARY.

101 4 IN. PAN SHADE

101 ICE CREAM SAUCER

101 4 IN. PAN SHADE CRIMPED

101 YACHT SALT

101 CANOE

10 IN. 101 OVAL

101 YACHT PICKLE

101 PICKLE JAR & COV.

101 YACHT CELERY SCOL. EDGE

101 ICE CREAM TRAY

101 PRESSED CHEESE & COV.

101 TANKARD JUG

SCALE 1/3

THE CENTRAL LITH. CO. PITTS. PA.

Catalog page — various No. 101 items.

No. 101 Daisy and Button group in amberina, front: canoe, toy tumbler; middle: square nappy, cheese plate; back: ice cream tray.

No. 101 Daisy and Button group in sapphire; left to right: canoe, tankard jug, 101-2 tumbler.

77

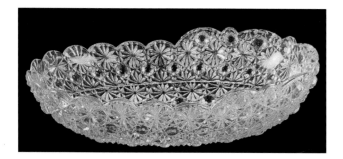

No. 101 Daisy and Button 10" oval, marine green.

No. 101 Daisy and Button canoe, amber stain on buttons.

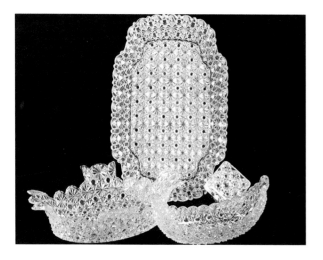

No. 101 Daisy and Button group in canary; front: 9" crown oval, canoe; back: ice cream tray, square individual butter.

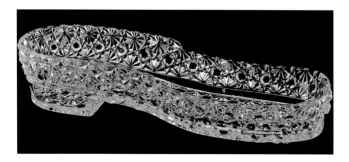

No. 101 Daisy and Button shoe celery, canary, allover pattern. Courtesy of Libby and Abe Yalom.

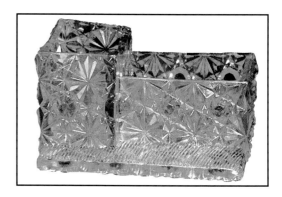

No. 101 Daisy and Button match safe, sapphire. Courtesy of Jo and Bob Sanford.

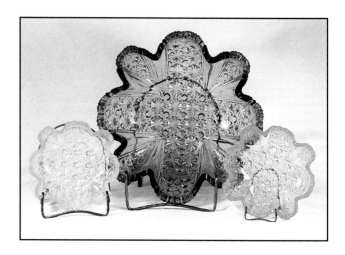

No. 101 Daisy and Button star bowls, canary, old gold, marine green.

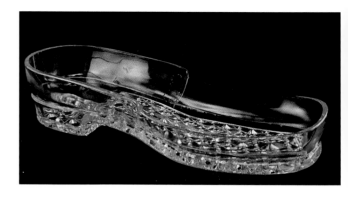

No. 101 Daisy and Button shoe celery, marine green, pattern on sole and heel, sides plain. Courtesy of Libby and Abe Yalom.

CORAL / PEACH BLOW

Date: 1886

Colors: Shaded amberina plated with opal

Decorations: Sometimes with allover satin finish. Some pieces have applied rigaree in amber. Handles and stoppers are also of amber glass.

Trade Quotes:

American Pottery and Glassware Reporter, November 26, 1885:

Among their latest novelties in the Coral ware, which for elegance of shape and beauty of coloring cannot be excelled anywhere. They have a line of pitchers in this ware of exquisite finish, the colors rivaling the bloom on the peach.... They are making many fancy articles in antique styles modeled from pieces taken from ancient ruins.

American Pottery and Glassware Reporter, December 3, 1885:

Still ahead. Hobbs, Brockunier & Co. The first to make the modern colors in Table and Fancy Glassware, we have continued adding to our variety. In addition to old gold, sapphire, canary, opalescent, ruby, amberina, we announce our newest and in many respects most beautiful coral ware, which will be ready for sale January 1, 1886. Pressed & Blown ware decorated in various designs.

Crockery and Glass Journal, March 25, 1886:

The 'Coral' goods are all new and are receiving the especial attention of the company.

Wheeling Daily Intelligencer, September, 1886:

When Thomas Webb, of England, made his first shipment of coral, or peachblow ware, to New York, Mr. Wm. Leighton, Jr., secured a piece of the ware and before the second shipment had been opened in New York, the always enterprising firm was turning out the same ware, which is being sold by some dealers as imported goods.

The best imitation of the famous $18,000 Morgan vase is manufactured by this firm, and although the first imitation was put on the market early this spring, the sales have been enormous and the demand for them is on the increase.

American Pottery and Glassware Reporter, November 25, 1886

The Coral and Peach Blow also continue in active request.

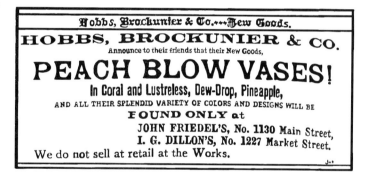

Ad for Peach Blow, *The Wheeling Daily Intellignecer*, August 4, 1886.

Coral/Peach Blow group.

Comments: In the minds of collectors today this is the ultimate art glass pattern made by Hobbs, Brockunier & Co. Both the gloss and satin finish items are today known as Wheeling Peach Blow. As noted above, the pattern was copied from Thomas Webb, c England.

The New England Glass Co. made and patented a ware now called "Plated Amberina" which, with the exception of its ribs, i virtually identical with Coral.

The sale of the Chinese porcelain Peach Blow vase for $18,000 in March of 1886 set the stage for Hobbs, Brockunier's introduction of Peach Blow glass. They produced a copy of the Morgan vase with a pressed amber stand. From the number of these vase: available in the antique market today, they must have been an instant success. The original porcelain vase had a wooden stand, but Hobbs, Brockunier made a stand in the form of five outward facing griffins in amber glass.

Most Coral is shaded from deep mahogany/fuchsia to a pale amber, the color of the gold ruby glass before reheating. Some pieces have been seen with the deep mahogany color all over. Many people consider this to be an overfiring, or an improper color but the application of dark amber handles and stoppers seems to indicate that the deep color was intentional. The company referred to the glossy finish as Coral and the satin finish as Peach Blow or lustreless.

There are several very unusual pieces in the Oglebay Museum collection, including a pair of vases with amber reeded handle: and mica inclusions, a banquet lamp, and a bowl with a lavender lining.

Catalog page — Peach Blow Morgan vase with griffin stand.

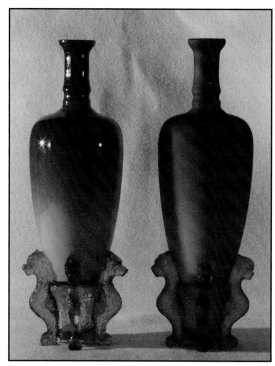

Two No. 22 Morgan vases with griffin bases, Coral on left, Peach Blow on right. Courtesy of Huntington Museum of Art.

Pieces	Prices
Bowl, finger, No. 1	$350.00
Bowl, finger, No. 2	350.00
Bowl, finger, No. 93	275.00
Caster set, No. 226 (salt & pepper, mustard)	1,400.00
Celery, No. 314	700.00
Custard, No. 507	275.00
Decanter, No. 4	1,400.00
Jug, No. 319, 0	650.00
Jug, No. 319, 1	650.00
Jug, No. 319, 2	750.00
Jug, No. 319, 4	1,300.00
Jug, No. 319, 5	1,600.00
Jug, claret, No. 322	1,900.00
Jug, Pelican, No. 324	2,500.00
Molasses can, No. 97	1,500.00
Mustard, No. 226	450.00
Oil, No. 306 (round)	1,600.00
Oil, No. 308 (funnel)	1,050.00
Oil, No. 312 (ovoid)	950.00
Salt, No. 226	400.00
Shade, 4", No. 1715	1,500.00+
Spoon, N0. 314	400.00
Sugar sifter	1,200.00

No. 228 salt and pepper, left Peach Blow, right Coral. Courtesy of Mary Ann and Dick Krauss.

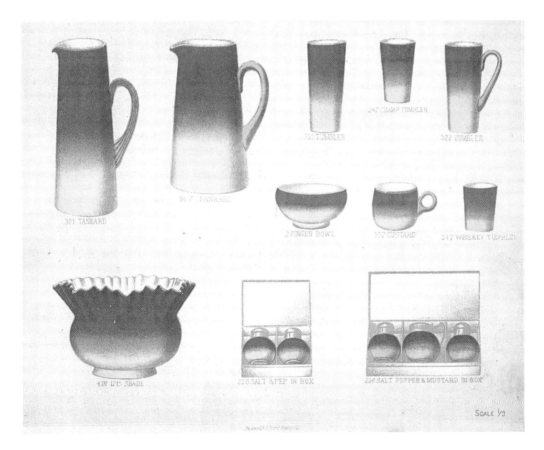

Catalog page — various items in Coral/Peach Blow.

Table set, No. 1
     Butter (open) 300.00
     Cream 550.00
     Spoon 500.00
     Sugar (open) 500.00
Tankard, No. 321 ....2,500.00
Tankard, No. 91-7 ....2,500.00
Tumbler, No. 236 ....325.00
Tumbler, No. 321 ....450.00
Tumbler, champagne, No. 247 ....350.00
Tumbler, handled, No. 322 ....650.00
Tumbler, whiskey, No. 247 ....350.00
Vase, No. 0 ....400.00
Vase, No. 1 ....50.00
Vase, No. 2 ....450.00
Vase, No. 4 ....700.00
Vase, No. 5 ....700.00
Vase, No. 6 ....1,200.00
Vase, No. 7 ....1,500.00+
Vase, No. 8 ....1,700.00+
Vase, No. 9 ....1,500.00
Vase, No. 11 ....750.00
Vase, No. 12 ....1,000.00+
Vase, No. 13 ....450.00
Vase, No. 13 (tall) 1,000.00
Vase, No. 14 ....1,400.00
Vase, No. 17 ....800.00
Vase, No. 18 ....950.00
Vase, No. 19 ....1,500.00+
Vase, No. 21 ....2,000.00+
Vase, No. 22-Morgan vase with griffin base 1,500.00
Vase, No. 22-Morgan vase without griffin base ..950.00
Vase, No. 23, may be No. 22 without neck 600.00
Water Bottle, No. 3 ....1,300.00

Dark Coral No. 312 oil, with dark amber handle.

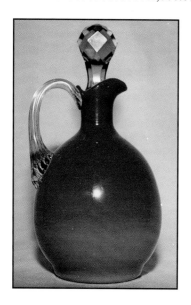

Coral No. 312 oil. Courtesy of
Huntington Museum of Art.

Coral No. 4 decanter. Courtesy of
Huntington Museum of Art.

Catalog page — various items in Coral/Peach Blow. Top row, L to R: Vases, No. 5, No. 4, No. 2, No. 1, No. 0. Middle row, L to R: No. 6 Vase, No. 7 Vase, No. 8 Vase, No. 322 Claret Jug, No. 11 Vase, No. 12 Vase. Bottom row, L to R: No. 1 Spoon, Cream, Sugar, Butter; No. 93 Finger Bowl, No. 1 Finger Bowl.

Coral No. 6 vase.

Coral No. 322 claret jug. Courtesy of Huntington Museum of Art.

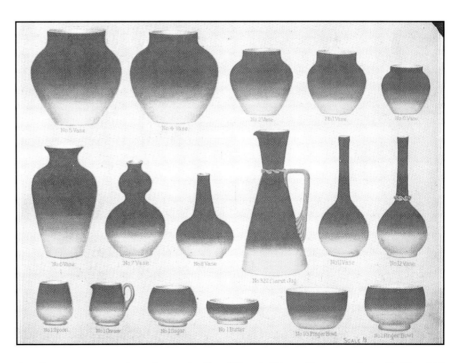

Catalog page — various items in Coral/Peach Blow. Top row, L to R: No. 319 Jugs, No. 5, No. 4, No. 2, No. 1, No. 0. Middle row, L to R: No. 4 Decanter, No. 3 Water Bottle, No. 314 Celery, No. 314 Spoon, No. 97 Mol. Can Plated. Bottom row, L to R: No. 13 Vase, No. 9 Vase, No. 236 Tumbler, No. 312 Oil, No. 308 Oil, Sugar Sifter.

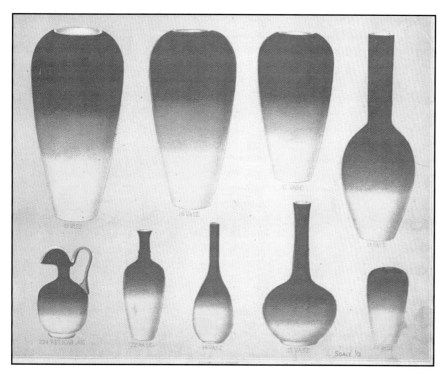

Coral parlor lamp. Courtesy of Oglebay Institute.

Catalog page — Various items in Coral/Peach Blow. Top row, L to R: Vases, 19, 18, 17, 21. Bottom row, L to R: 324 Pelican Jug, Vases, 22, 14, 12, 23.

No. 323 DEW DROP

Date: March, 1886

Colors: Crystal, old gold, sapphire, marine green, canary, ruby, rubina, ruby amber, ruby sapphire, rubina verde, canary opalescent, marine green opalescent, ruby opalescent, rubina opalescent, sapphire opalescent, ruby plated with alabaster, marine green plated with alabaster, sapphire plated with alabaster, sapphire plated with opal.

Decorations: Satin finish; Frances; No. 7, amber stain on rim

Trade Quotes:

Crockery & Glass Journal, March 25. 1886:

Hobbs, Brockunier & Co. are doing a very thriving business this spring, and well they may, for such a varied stock of glassware is seldom seen in the West. They have about twenty-five different colors and combinations of colors, and the varied hues and delicate tints in their sample rooms show that they believe variety is the life of trade as well as the spice of life. The display of pitchers, bowls, finger bowls and other goods in 'Dewdrop and Pineapple' excels anything of the kind ever produced in this section.... The 'Dewdrop,' 'Pineapple,' opalescents of all kind.... The delicate tints and rich, rare effect of the 'Dewdrop' form a superb combination that cannot fail to merit the admiration of all who appreciate the beautiful in art.

Crockery & Glass Journal, September 9, 1886:

The 323 'Richelieu' is a superb line, and the 323 'Rubina' is a very pretty combination.

Pottery & Glassware Reporter, November 25, 1886:

The demand is very large for their 323, or Pineapple in opalescents and parti-ruby colors.

Crockery and Glass Journal, February 24, 1887:

A. J. Beatty and Sons, of Steubenville, have been granted a license to handle ware under the patent of Hobbs, Brockunier & Co., on their nodule pattern in opalescent, and they have as fine a set of ware as is in the market this season in this vicinity.

American Pottery and Glassware Reporter, March 17, 1887:

…'323,' a full water set in crystal decorated, called 'Frances' in honor of Mrs. Cleveland, and '323' in Rubina, are beautiful goods and ought to sell well. They are still having a good run on opalescent.

Comments: Dew Drop was given mechanical patent No. 343,133, granted June 1, 1886, to William F. Russell and William Leighton, Jr. This pattern is now called Hobnail. The company first called the pattern Nodule. We feel that Dew Drop refers to non-opalescent glass, and Pineapple refers to opalescent wares, although references to these terms are confusing and incomplete. At this time, we re also uncertain exactly what is meant by Richelieu. It may be a color or a decorative effect, possibly ruby with white opalescence. Hobbs, Brockunier & Co.'s Dew Drop is a pressed, not blown, pattern. Much confusion has arisen over this, but the patent clearly states that the pattern is pressed and careful examination of pieces will reveal mold lines still present and smooth interior surfaces. Pieces such as the bitter bottles and pitchers have been hand tooled to form the necks and were not done in blown molds.

There were three molds used for the small berry dish. One mold had several rows of hobnails in the bottom, and the punty, where it was stuck up to crimp the top, was filled with a small hobnail prunt. Others were ground and polished where the punty had been attached. A third variety, found in Frances decoration, has uniformly large hobnails across the bottom. It is supposed the mold was made with a crimp, eliminating the hand operation of crimping.

Note that A. J. Beatty and Sons of Steubenville, Ohio, were licensed by Hobbs, Brockunier & Co. to produce Dew Drop opalescent glass. (See ad with No. 207 Murano, page 97.) At first they made only tumblers in Dew Drop opalescent, but soon they developed an entire line of Dew Drop opalescent, now called Over All Hobnail. They also expanded on the idea of opalescent glass patterns, patenting their Beatty Rib, Beatty Waffle, and a zig zag pattern.

Dew Drop bowls are sometimes found in elaborate silver-plate holders as bride's baskets.

See the Lighting section for Dew Drop shades and globes, see page 94 for No. 323 Dew Drop vase. The No. 324 Dew Drop Molasses can is shown on page 156 in the Miscellaneous chapter.

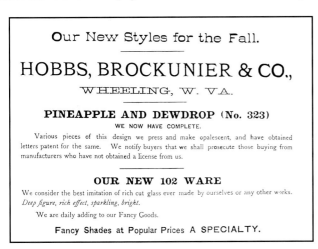

August 1886, ad for Pineapple and Dew Drop No. 323, *Crockery & Glass Journal.*

No. 323 Dew Drop jug group; left to right: No. 5 rubina verde opalescent, No. 2 sapphire plated opal, No. 4 rubina satin, No. 2 decorated No. 7, No. 3 crystal opalescent.

Prices given are for pieces with Frances decoration, canary, sapphire, and marine green-probably the most commonly encountere[d] versions of Dew Drop. For old gold and crystal, deduct 25%. For ruby and rubina, add 50%. For ruby amber, ruby sapphire, an[d] rubina verde, add 100% to 150%, depending on individual pieces. For opalescence or alabaster plating, add 20% to above values.

Reproductions: The tumbler and the bitter bottle have been reproduced by L. G. Wright in several colors, including some of th[e] original Hobbs' colors. Fenton Art Glass Co. of Williamstown, WV, has also reproduced many of the Dew Drop items, sometime[s] modifying them from the originals, i.e., making the covered butter into a footed, covered candy dish. All opaque pieces found ar[e] made by Fenton Art Glass Co. Fenton also made several pieces in original Hobbs' colors, including ruby opalescent, canary opales[-] cent, canary, blue, amber and probably others. Original Hobbs' pieces usually have a ground and polished pontil on the base[,] required to make the piece into its finished shape. Fenton pieces are not ground and polished, simply pressed, although usually th[e] pontil shapes are still evident on the bases. In the 1950s the Imperial Glass Corp. of Bellaire, Ohio, made a candy jar and cover i[n] milk glass and transparent colors that is very similar to Hobbs' Dew Drop covered sugar. Imperial also made this item with a foot.

Pieces	Prices
Bitter bottle	$145.00
Bowl, finger	.25.00
Bowl, round, 8"	.75.00
Bowl, round, 10" No. 305	.90.00
Bowl, round, shell footed, 8"	.250.00
Bowl, square, 8"	.75.00
Bowl, square, 9"	.85.00
Celery, tall	.70.00
Jug, No. 0	.235.00
Jug, No. 1	.190.00
Jug, No. 2	.190.00
Jug, No. 3	.160.00
Jug, No. 4	.175.00
Jug, No. 5	.175.00
Molasses can	.375.00
Nappy, round, 4½"	.25.00
Nappy, square, 4½"	.25.00
Oil	.425.00
Oval, 7"	.60.00
Oval, 8"	.70.00
Oval, 9"	.75.00
Pickle jar & cover	.175.00
Salt shaker	.150.00
Table set:	
Butter & cover	.80.00
Butter & cover, flanged	.250.00
Cream	.50.00
Spoon	.45.00
Sugar & cover	.65.00
Tray, water	.90.00
Tumbler	.45.00
Tumbler, toy	.65.00
Vase, No. 1	.85.00
Vase, ruffled top	.165.00
Water bottle	.135.00

No. 323 Dew Drop ruby amber tumbler, jug, satin.

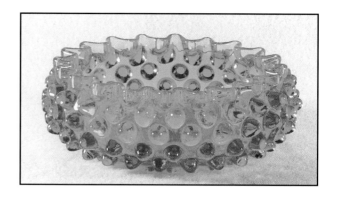

No. 323 Dew Drop small nappy, sapphire.

Catalog page — various items in No. 323 Dew Drop in old gold, sapphire, green, and Richelieu. Top row, L to R: 8 in. Square Bowl, 4½ in. sq. Nappy, Celery, 8 in. Round Bowl, 4½ in. Rd. Nappy. Middle row, L to R: 5 Jug, Mol. Can, Toy Tumbler, 4 Jug, Oil, Tumbler, 1 Jug. Bottom row, L to R: Sugar & Cov. Cream, Spoon, Butter & Cov.

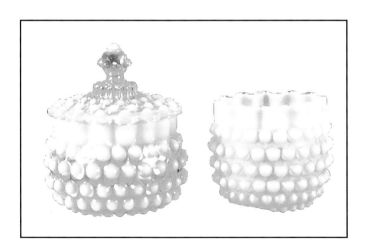

No. 323 Dew Drop covered sugar and spoon, sapphire opalescent.

No. 323 Dew Drop finger bowl, marine green, plated alabaster.

Catalog page — various items in No. 323 Dew Drop in canary opalescent, crystal opalescent, and ruby opalescent; old gold and ruby. Top, L to R: 8 in. Square Bowl, canary opal't; 4½ in. Sq. Nappy, crystal opal't; 4½ in. Rd. Nappy, ruby opal't.; 8 in. Round Bowl, ruby. Middle, L to R: Celery, ruby opal't.; Pickle Jar & Cov., canary opal't.; Mol. Can, ruby; Flanged Butter & Cov., old gold. Bottom, L to R: 9 in. Round Bowl, canary opal't.; Decanter, Cut Stop., rubina verde; Toothpick, old gold; Water Bottle, ruby.

No. 323 Dew Drop rubina verde group; left to right: celery, 4½" square nappy, opalescent satin No. 4 jug.

No. 323 Dew Drop 8" square bowl, ruby. Courtesy of Huntington Museum of Art.

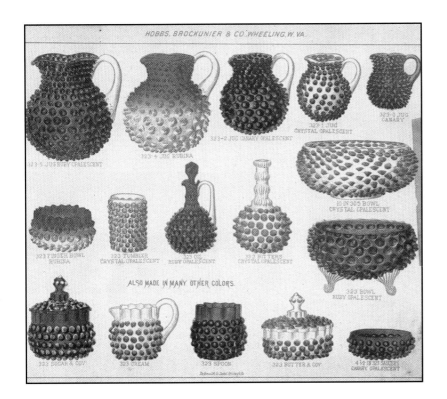

No. 323 Dew Drop tumbler, ruby sapphire.

Catalog page — various items in No. 323 Dew Drop in ruby opalescent, rubina, canary opalescent, crystal opalescent, and canary, also "many other colors."

No. 323 Dew Drop No. 5 jug, ruby sapphire, satin. Courtesy of Huntington Museum of Art.

No. 323 Dew Drop No. 5 jug, rubina verde opalescent.

No. 323 Dew Drop covered pickle, satin with old gold lid. Made to match pieces with Frances decoration.

Catalog page — items in No. 323 Dew Drop with Frances decoration. Top, L to R: 8 in. Square Bowl, 4½ in. Sq. Nappy, Mol. Can, Celery, Oil, 8 in. Round Bowl, 4½ in. Rd. Nappy. Middle, L to R: Ovals, 7 in., 8 in., 9. Bottom, L to R: Sugar & Cov., Cream, Spoon, Butter & Cov.

No. 323 Dew Drop cream, decorated Frances.

No. 323 Dew Drop covered butter, decorated Frances.

No. 323 Dew Drop No. 1 vase, canary plated with alabaster. Any jugs could be made into vases by leaving off handles. Courtesy Jo and Bob Sanford.

Catalog page — items in No. 323 Dew Drop with Decoration No. 7. Top, L to R: Jugs, 5, 4, 2, 1, 0. Middle, L to R: Tumbler, Toy Tumbler. Bottom, L to R: Finger Bowl, Tray, Flanged Butter & Cov.

No. 323 Dew Drop small nappies, canary with ground pontil, no prunt; ruby amber with Dew Drop prunt applied to pontil.

No. 323 Dew Drop toy water set, decorated No. 7. Courtesy of Jo and Bob Sanford.

No. 102 MALTESE AND RIBBON

Date: August, 1886

Colors: Crystal, old gold, canary, sapphire

Decorations: On crystal glass: amber stain on ribbons. No. 9 amber stain on fans.

Trade Quotes:

Crockery and Glass Journal, Augusts 12, 1886:

Among other things their new 102 ware, a beautiful set for design and pattern is a model, producing as it does the same effe[ct] as cut glass. The figures that give such a rich effect are a Maltese cross, cut very deep, with ribbons on either side, and it sparkle[s] like the genuine cut glass.

Pottery & Glassware Reporter, August 16, 1886:

HOBBS, BROCKUNIER & CO., of Wheeling, have out a new set, No. 102 which is an imitation of cut glass. They make it in a[ll] colors, also in crystal and decorated in amber. This is very beautiful ware and difficult to tell from cut.

Comments: This pattern was granted design patent Nos. 16,994 and 16,995 on November 23, 1886, granted to William Leighto[n] Jr. Term of patent 3½ years.

We have named this pattern Maltese and Ribbon based upon the description in the trade journals.

This pattern is very difficult to find, especially in colors. Several companies made patterns with a Maltese cross motif. Howeve[r] in the Hobbs, Brockunier & Co. pattern, the crosses are placed on a diagonal with ribbons dividing the rows. Pieces, except th[e] tumbler, also have a large fan-shaped motif on opposite sides. The tumbler is sometimes found with the legend "White River Flour" in the base. This flour was sold by a firm in Pittsburgh.

Prices are for items in crystal. For pieces in color add 150%.

Pieces	Prices
Bowl, finger	$30.00
Bowl, round, 8"	45.00
Bowl, round, 9"	45.00
Bowl, square, 7"	45.00
Bowl, square, 8"	45.00
Celery, tall	50.00
Nappy, 4"	20.00
Nappy, 4½"	20.00
Oval, 7"	35.00
Oval, 8"	35.00
Oval, 9"	45.00
Pickle dish	30.00
Pitcher, quart	100.00
Pitcher, ½ gallon	135.00
Salt, master, 3"x2"x1¼"	60.00
Shade, bowl	65.00
Shade, pan	65.00
Table set:	
Butter & cover	120.00
Cream	75.00
Spoon	65.00
Sugar & cover	100.00
Tumbler	40.00

No. 102 Maltese and Ribbon bowl shade with bottom intact, making it a bowl. Courtesy of Huntington Museum of Art.

No. 102 Maltese and Ribbon 7" square bowl, canary.

No. 102 Maltese and Ribbon tumbler. Tumblers do not have the large fans, only the Maltese crosses and ribbons.

Catalog page — No. 102 Maltese and Ribbon with Decoration No. 9.

No. 102 Maltese and Ribbon pickle dish with amber ribbons.

No. 102 Maltese and Ribbon 8" bowl, decorated No. 9. Courtesy of Mart Groesser.

Nos. 201, 203 DEW DROP

Date: 1886
Colors: Rubina verde opalescent. Probably many of the other colors and color combinations made during this period.
Decorations: Unknown, but possibly allover satin finish.
Trade Quotes:
Pottery & Glassware Reporter, August 26, 1886:
   They have also out a new line of fancy finger bowls and fruit bowls, as well as a new line of fancy globes and shades.
Crockery & Glass Journal, September 9, 1886:
   Hobbs, Brockunier & Co. have three furnaces in full blast, and in addition to the handsome lines already noted their fancy shaped bowls (203) their 201 and 202 finger bowls...
Comments: No. 202 and possibly No. 204 are likely variations of shape in both the finger bowl and underplate. These unusual finger bowls and plates are difficult to find today.

Prices given are for rubina verde opalescent.

Pieces	Prices
Bowl, finger (201)	$125.00
Bowl, finger (203)	125.00
Plate (201)	100.00
Plate (203)	100.00

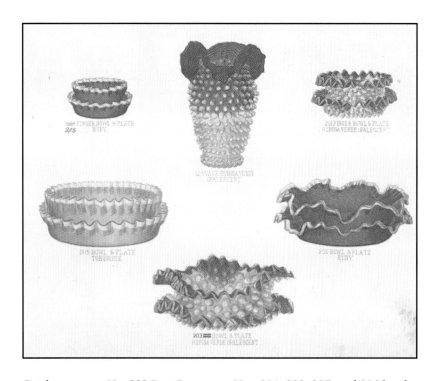

Catalog page — No. 323 Dew Drop vase, Nos. 201, 203, 205, and 206 bowls and plates.

No. 205

Date: 1886

Colors: Ruby with opal rim, turquoise Richelieu, pink Richelieu, ruby with yellow rim, canary with ruby rim, lemon yellow translucent with Ruby striped rim. It is likely that many other color combinations exist.

Decorations: Allover satin finish.

Trade Quotes:

Pottery & Glassware Reporter, August 26, 1886:

> *They have also out a new line of fancy finger bowls and fruit bowls, as well as a new line of fancy globes and shades.*

Crockery & Glass Journal, February 17, 1887:

> *...while the line of 505 and 506 bowls* [sic- but probably 205 and 206 were meant] *is simply superb.*

Comments: In this case the original Hobbs, Brockunier catalog page shows Richelieu as follows: turquoise Richelieu is turquoise with an opaque white rim, pink Richelieu is pink with a yellow rim.

These bowls are most often found hand crimped. In June of 1886, Wm. Leighton, Jr. patented a crimping machine, and some pieces of these patterns can be found with machine crimping. These pieces can also be found with diagonal external ribs.

The 7" bowls are often found in silver-plate holders.

Prices are for most colors, for ruby pieces, add 50%.

Pieces	Prices
Bowl, 7"	.$275.00
Bowl, finger	.125.00
Plate, finger bowl	.100.00
Plate, 7"	.225.00
Vase, trumpet shape, 10"	.275.00

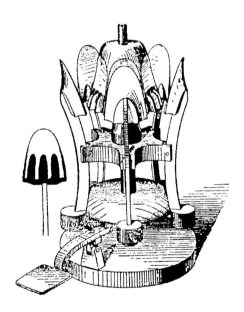

Detail of Leighton's crimping machine from the patent illustration.

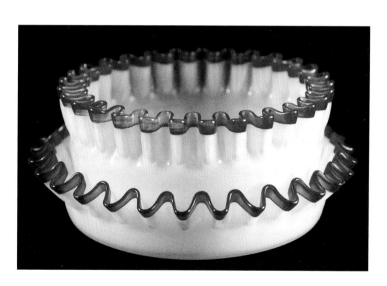

No. 205 bowl and plate, lemon yellow with ruby rim.

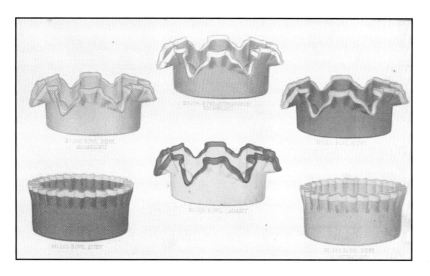

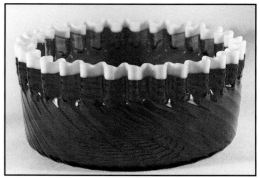

No. 205 bowl, ruby with opal edge and external ribs.

Catalog page — illustrations of Nos. 205 and 206 bowls in pink Richelieu, turquoise Richelieu, ruby, and canary. Top row, L to R: No. 206 Bowl, pink Rickelieu; No. 206 bowl, turquoise Richelieu; No. 206 Bowl, ruby. Bottom row, L to R: No. 205 Bowl, ruby; No. 206 Bowl, canary; No. 205 Bowl, pink Richelieu.

No. 206

Date: Ca. 1886

Colors: Ruby with white rim, turquoise Richelieu, pink Richelieu, ruby with yellow rim, canary with ruby rim, lemon yellow translucent with ruby striped rim, turquoise with yellow lining, yellow with turquoise lining. It is likely that many other color combinations exist.

Decorations: Satin finish

Comments: These bowls are most often found hand crimped. In June of 1886, Wm. Leighton, Jr. patented a crimping machine, and a few of these pieces can be found with machine crimping. The finger bowls illustrated in the photographs show a tighter crimp than the larger bowls on the catalog page.

Prices are for most colors, for ruby pieces, add 50%.

Pieces	Prices
Bowl, 7"	$325.00
Bowl, finger	175.00
Plate, 7"	250.00
Plate, finger bowl	125.00

No. 206 7" bowl, pink Richelieu. Courtesy of Huntington Museum of Art.

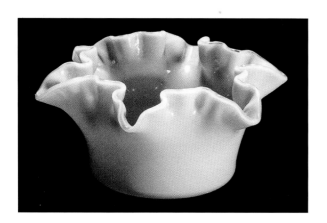

No. 206 finger bowl, yellow plated over pink.

No. 206 finger bowl and plate, turquoise plated with yellow interior.

No. 206 finger bowl and plate, yellow plated with turquoise interior.

No. 207 MURANO

Date: February, 1887

Colors: Crystal, old gold, sapphire, canary, ruby, ruby alabaster, canary alabaster, old gold alabaster, sapphire alabaster

Decorations: Satin finish all over, some pieces have satin finish on the inside as well.

Trade Quotes:

Crockery & Glass Journal, February 17, 1887:

　A handsome line of spiral glassware in delicate colors are among the new attractions that have taken a firm hold upon the trade.

Crockery & Glass Journal, February 24, 1887:

　Hobbs, Brockunier & Co. announce their new goods in this issue. The new blown pattern 'Murano' is indeed an attractive line of ware.

Crockery & Glass Journal, April 7, 1887:

　The blown pattern Murano is quite popular among those who appreciate the delicate tints, in fact lovers of real art in glass could not fail to appreciate this pattern.

Crockery & Glass Journal, April 21, 1887:

　At Hobbs, Brockunier & Co's trade is reported very good. The new 'Murano,' No. 207 blown pattern, is in splendid demand and has been sold in liberal quantities....

Pottery and Glass Reporter, July 7, 1887:

　They have also had a big demand in the 207 line.

1887 ad introducing No. 207 Murano, *Crockery & Glass Journal.*

No. 207 Muano group: ruby cream, crystal 2 quart jug, canary alabaster celery, all satin finish.

Comments: All Murano pieces have diagonal swirls, probably imparted by a dip mold. The oil and one salt illustrated on the catalog page carry a number (333) different from 207 and so are a different pattern. Murano is most often found with a satin finish and quite difficult to find.

Prices given are for crystal satin. For old gold, sapphire and canary, add 50%. For old gold alabaster, sapphire alabaster, and canary alabaster, add 65%. For ruby and ruby alabaster add 100%.

Pieces	Prices
Bowl, 8"	$40.00
Bowl, finger	25.00
Celery	35.00
Jug, ½ gallon No. 207½	85.00
Molasses can	115.00
Nappy, 4¾"	15.00
Salt	35.00
Table set:	
Butter & cover	75.00
Cream	40.00
Spoon	32.00
Sugar & cover	62.00
Tumbler	25.00

No. 207 Murano celery, ruby alabaster.

No. 207 Murano syrup, ruby satin. Courtesy of Huntington Museum of Art.

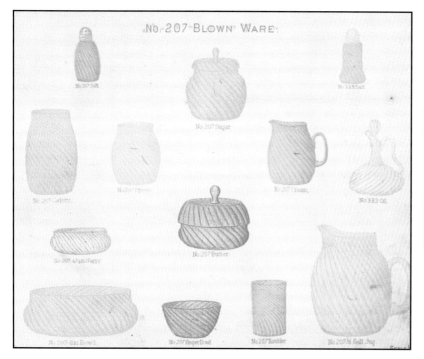

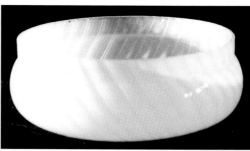

No. 207 Murano 8" bowl, canary. Courtesy of Huntington Museum of Art.

Catalog page — various items in No. 207 Murano and No. 333 Satina Swirl in old gold, ruby, canary, and sapphire. Top row, L to R: No. 207 Murano Salt, Sugar, No. 333 Satina Swirl Salt. Middle row, L to R: No. 207 Murano Celery, Spoon, Butter, Cream, No. 333 Satina Swirl Oil. Bottom row, L to R: No. 207 Murano 8 in. Bowl, Finger Bowl, Tumbler, ½ Gall. Jug.

No. 333 SATINA SWIRL

Date: February 1887
Colors: Crystal, ruby, sapphire, old gold, canary
Decorations: Satin finish
Comments: Probably other items exist, but existing catalogs show only the salt and oil.

Prices given are for crystal satin. For old gold, sapphire, and canary, add 50%. For Ruby, add 100%

Pieces	Prices
Oil	$250.00
Salt	50.00

No. 333 Satina Swirl oil, sapphire satin. Courtesy of Mary Ann and Dick Krauss.

No. 333 Satina Swirl salt shaker, canary. Courtesy of Marilyn and Charles Lockwood.

GREELEY

Date: Ca. 1887
Colors: Amber alabaster, canary alabaster, sapphire alabaster. Possibly other colors in combination with alabaster.
Comments: We have found these pieces in Hobbs, Brockunier & Co. shapes, and because of their distinctive ribs, have listed them as a separate line. The ribs on the exterior surface alternate between broad and very narrow. Pieces have been found with both left- and right-handed swirls. There are probably other pieces, possibly in Murano shapes, possibly in other blown shapes. All of the pieces seen have been plated with alabaster.

Pieces	Prices
Cup, custard	$75.00
Finger bowl	65.00

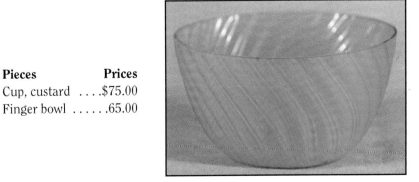

Greeley custard, old gold alabaster.

Greeley finger bowl, sapphire alabaster.

CHONCHA

Date: April, 1887
Colors: *"Rich Colors and delicate effects..."*
Decorations: Unknown
Trade Quotes:

Crockery & Glass Journal, April 28, 1887:

Hobbs, Brockunier & Co. are getting out a new line that has been christened the 'Choncha.' It is a delicately beautiful line ‹ goods, the rich tints producing an effect rarely seen in glassware.

Crockery & Glass Journal, May 12, 1887:

At Hobbs, Brockunier & Co.s everything is going along very satisfactorily. The new 'Choncha' line of rich colors and delicat‹ effects promises great results....

Crockery & Glass Journal, May 18, 1887:

At Hobbs, Brockunier & Co.'s business is moving along very actively. The new line of rich ware — Choncha — is now com‹ pleted, and a finer line of goods never decorated the sample room of this widely known firm. The skill of the artist and the judg‹ ment of the connoisseur is at once apparent, and the evident pride of that prince among glass men, Mr. Wm. Leighton, is indee‹ pardonable of the production of this rare line. It is one of the things that the conflict on prices will not reach, and yet it will be i‹ demand not more because of its variety than for the reason that it is truly beautiful.

Crockery & Glass Journal, June 2, 1887:

At Hobbs, Brockunier & Co.'s business is very fair, and they are still adding to their large and varied stock of fine goods. Th‹ sample room is now well filled, and the rich 'Choncha' ware, together with the elegant novelties displayed, make it indeed a ric‹ room to select fine and fancy ware from. Mr. C. W. Brockunier will be on duty this month, and will present the new lines in th‹ CROCKERY AND GLASS JOURNAL soon.

Comments: With the exception of the above quotations, there is nothing known about Choncha. It reigned for six weeks, and ther‹ was replaced by No. 230 Neapolitan which was introduced in mid-June. There were no further mentions of Choncha.

We have no information about its colors, shapes, or finishes.

SHELLS AND RIBS

Date: Ca. 1887
Colors: Rubina. Possibly others.
Comments: There is no documentation to support this pattern, but the floral prunt on the bottom of the bowls and rose bowl is‹ identical to prunts found on No. 230 Neapolitan, and the shell feet are identical in manufacture. This is a pressed bowl with hand‹ tooled features.

All pieces seen have been rubina. Other shapes may exist.

Pieces	Prices
Bowl, 8", 3 shell feet	$275.00
Bowl, 8" triangular, ruffled edge, 3 shell feet	300.00
Bowl, rose, 8" dia	200.00
Vase, trumpet, 9" applied foot	175.00
Vase, trumpet, 12" applied foot	225.00

Shells and Ribs, detail of center prunt and applied feet.

Shells and Ribs 8" bowl, rubina.

Shells and Ribs 8" triangular bowl, rubina.

SNOWSTORM

Date: Unknown, probably mid-1880s
Colors: Rubina overlaid with white Craquelle, possibly other colors.
Comments: Identification is based upon mechanically crimped top edge identical to other Hobbs' bowls and white border common to other Hobbs' bowls. Trumpet vases may exist.

Pieces	Prices
Bowl, 7" crimped, white edge	$400.00
Bowl, rose, 6½" dia., 5" opening, crimped edge	300.00
Bowl, rose, 6½" dia., 2¾" smooth opening	275.00

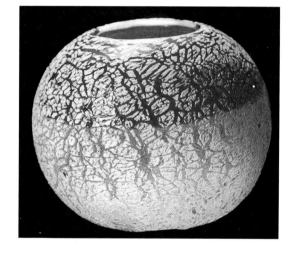

Snowstorm 6½" rose bowl, rubina with opal overlay.

Snowstorm 6½" rose bowl, crimped, rubina with opal overlay.

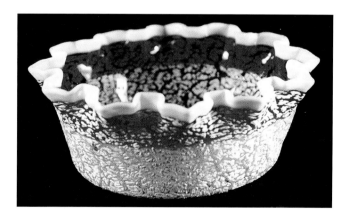

Snowstorm 7" bowl, crimped, rubina with opal overlay and applied edge.

No. 115 WHEELING

Date: June, 1887
Colors: Crystal
Decorations: No. 15 enamel, blue, pink, and white; No. 16 enamel, roses in pink, green, and brown or bronze on the leaves; No. 2(engraving; No. 201 engraving
Trade Quotes:
Crockery & Glass Journal, June 16, 1887:
> They have displayed in their sample room now a beautiful table line in crystal, plain and decorated, which is a rare im tation of cut ware, No. 115.

Pottery and Glassware Reporter, July 7, 1887:
> Their other new line of crystal, No. 115 (pressed) consisting of two designs of plain, two of engraved, and two of decora ed, are very pretty and are selling well.

Crockery and Glass Journal, July 28, 1887:
> The 115 pressed line with enamel decoration is very attractive and being liberally ordered.

Comments: Although this pattern was made in a full line of tableware, it is almost impossible to find today. We are giving what w feel are fair market values for the line, even though its rarity should suggest higher prices. For decorated pieces, add 20%.
See page 116 for additional shapes of this pattern.

Pieces	Prices
Bowl, 8"	$45.00
Bowl, 10"	55.00
Bowl, finger	25.00
Butter, individual	18.00
Celery, tall	40.00
Molasses can	120.00
Nappy, 4½"	15.00
Oval, 7"	30.00
Oval, 8"	30.00
Pickle dish	25.00
Pitcher, ½ gallon	90.00
Salt, table (master)	45.00
Table set:	
Butter & cover	85.00
Cream	50.00
Spoon	45.00
Sugar & cover	70.00
Tumbler	40.00
Tumbler, toy	70.00

Catalog illustration — No. 115 Wheeling with Engraving No. 200.

No. 115 Wheeling toy tumbler, Courtesy Mart Groesser.

Catalog illustration —Bowl in No. 115 Wheeling with Decoration No. 16.

Catalog illustration — No. 115 Wheeling with Decoration No. 15.

Catalog illustration — No. 115 Wheeling with Engraving No. 201.

No. 230 NEAPOLITAN

Date: June, 1887

Colors: Ruby with white rim, pink (ruby plated over white), possibly other colors and combinations

Decorations: *"etched and decorated"* — exact decorations unknown, etched probably refers to allover satin finish

Trade Quotes:

Crockery & Glass Journal, June 16, 1887:

...a new rich line of fine delicate colored ware, No. 230, called 'Neapolitan,' which is as fine a line as was ever shown to the trade anywhere.

Pottery and Glassware Reporter, June 23, 1887:

'Neapolitan' is the name of the blown set...in two colors, white and red...

Pottery and Glassware Reporter, July 7, 1887:

The Neapolitan, No. 230, plain, etched and decorated, richly colored, promises to sell better than anything they have ever introduced in the fancy line. These goods look better than the fine peach colored goods [Coral/Peach Blow] they have been making and for the reason that they are cheap for that class of goods they sell to the class of dealers who could not handle the peach goods. All the dealers who have seen the Neapolitan, have ordered it. In this line they have several pieces, richly decorated with small beads which are very striking.

Crockery and Glass Journal, August 18, 1887:

This city is not behind others in what seems to be a fashionable thing now of inviting the president to visit them, and the Glass Industry at once takes prominence in this invitation. The Chamber of commerce appointed a committee headed by Mr. C. W. Brockunier, of the well-known firm of Hobbs, Brockunier & Co., to prepare an appropriate invitation, and this committee decided upon a very unique souvenir to supplement the telegraphic invitation. The souvenir is a handsome glass vase, made by Hobbs, Brockunier & Co., which rests on a light ornamental base, and stands 13½ inches high. The vase is of ruby, plated on white. At the mouth the color is a deep ruby, and it is shaded down so that at the base it is a delicate rich pink. The style and shape of the vase is very graceful and pleasing. It is certainly a very admirable ornament. The mouth of the vase is fluted, and there are spiral ribs running from this fluting to the base, while the inscription is in black old English letters, enameled as follows:

To the President of the United States:

The Chamber of Commerce has instructed the undersigned to extend to yourself and Mrs. Cleveland a cordial invitation to visit this city as guests of this Chamber and to earnestly urge your acceptance.

C. W. Brockunier	*T. H. Logan*
C. B. Hart	*J. B. Taney*
T. N. Vance	*M. Reilly*
	C. W. Seabright
	Committee.

Wheeling, W. Va., August 5, 1887'

This was exhibited in one of the prominent jewelry stores of the city for a day or two before it was sent away, and large crowds flocked to see it and admire the exquisite taste displayed.

No. 230 Neapolitan nut bowl.
Courtesy of Oglebay Institute.

No. 230 Neapolitan 14"
vase, pink satin, Cleveland
Invitation. Courtesy of
Oglebay Institute.

Comments: This "Cleveland" vase, as it is now known, is Neapolitan. President and Mrs. Cleveland did not come to Wheeling despite the city's efforts to entice them. The "5" of the date is now missing from the vase.

A "table" in this pattern, about 14" in diameter and 30" tall, with a broken foot, is owned by the Oglebay Museum. It has a brown snake with red eyes wrapped around the support, and a set of white prunts above and below the snake. It is reported to have been found in a tavern near the Hobbs, Brockunier factory.

August 18, 1887, was the last quote relating directly to Neapolitan, but throughout the rest of the year fancy colored glassware was mentioned. On December 1 this quote "the finest combination of colors in glassware ever produced in this country" was published. Neapolitan was probably made until the end of the year 1887 when the company underwent a reorganization. Fancy art glass was not continued after this reorganization.

Neapolitan is a pattern of pink (ruby plated over white) glass, usually satin. It may or may not have swirls and hand tooled feet and rigaree of crystal glass. Prices are for all color combinations.

Pieces	Prices
Bowl, finger	$150.00
Bowl, fruit	325.00
Bowl, nut	325.00
Celery	225.00
Cream	225.00
Jug, No. 5	425.00
Sugar	350.00
Tumbler	225.00
Vase, Morgan, No. 22, with griffin stand	3,200.00
Vase, 14"	700.00
Water bottle, qt	350.00

No. 230 Neapolitan jug. Courtesy of Oglebay Institute.

No. 230 Neapolitan cream. Courtesy of Oglebay Institute.

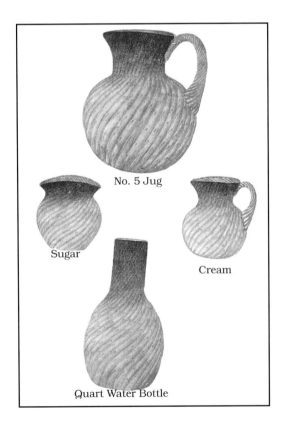

No. 5 Jug

Sugar

Cream

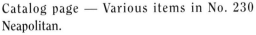

Quart Water Bottle

Catalog page — Various items in No. 230 Neapolitan.

No. 230 Neapolitan No. 22 Morgan vase with amber griffin base, pink. Courtesy of Huntington Museum of Art, Huntington, WV.

No. 230 Neapolitan fruit bowl. Courtesy of Huntington Museum of Art.

No. 230 Neapolitan 14" vase, ruby with opal rim. Courtesy of Huntington Museum of Art.

LEIGHTON

Neither the pattern number or name of this pattern has been found. We have chosen to honor the Leightons by naming this pattern after them because of its style and the ruby glass in which it comes.

This pattern is similar to Neapolitan, but the glass is transparent ruby and has no swirls. The shapes are different, but the feet and rigaree decoration are the same. This pattern may have been available in other colors, too. Other pieces may exist.

Pieces	Prices
Bowl, nut	$275.00
Bowl & cover, 8"	500.00
Celery	500.00
Jug	850.00
Table set:	
Butter & cover	450.00
Cream	300.00
Spoon	275.00
Sugar & cover	400.00

Leighton celery, ruby with crystal rigaree. Courtesy of Oglebay Institute.

Leighton jug, ruby with crystal rigaree. Courtesy of Oglebay Institute.

Leighton nut bowl, ruby with crystal rigaree. Courtesy of Oglebay Institute.

No. 293 STARS & STRIPES

Date: Fall, 1888

Colors: Crystal opalescent, sapphire opalescent, ruby opalescent

Comments: This pattern and No. 325 were the first two patterns produced by Hobbs Glass Co. after the reorganization. Stars an Stripes was also made by Beaumont Glass Co., ca 1899. There seems to be no way to distinguish between Hobbs and Beaumon production, nor really any reason to.

Prices are for ruby opalescent or sapphire opalescent. For crystal opalescent, deduct 40%.

Reproductions: All pieces except the globe have been made by Fenton Art Glass Co. in ruby opalescent.

Pieces	Prices
Bitter	.$450.00
Globe, squat	.500.00
Oil	.800.00
Tankard	.900.00
Tumbler	.190.00

Catalog illustrations of No. 293 Stars and Stripes, left to right top row: bitter, tumbler, tankard; bottom: globe.

No. 325 HOBBS' OPAL SWIRL

Date: September, 1888

Colors: Crystal opalescent, ruby opalescent, and sapphire opalescent, other colors may exist.

Decorations: Possibly satin finish

Comments: This is one of the first two patterns made by Hobbs Glass Co. after the reorganization. Hobbs, Brockunier & Co. molds were used in combination with the swirl opalescence probably developed by Nicholas Kopp. The pattern numbers of the pieces used were all changed to 325 for this pattern. The water set and the cheese dish use No. 101 Daisy & Button trays. Other companies have made similar opalescent swirl pieces, the Hobbs' shape must be the determining factor for identification.

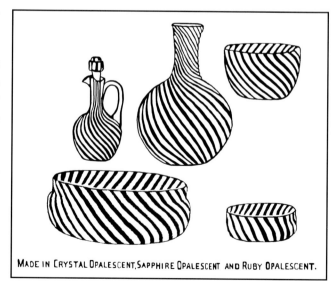

MADE IN CRYSTAL OPALESCENT, SAPPHIRE OPALESCENT AND RUBY OPALESCENT.

Catalog illustrations of items in No. 325 Hobbs' Opal Swirl.

Prices given are for ruby opalescent and sapphire opalescent, for crystal opalescent, deduct 50%.

Pieces	Prices
Bar bottle	.$650.00
Bitter	.450.00
Bowl, waste	.125.00
Bowl, round, 8"	.165.00
Caster set: 2 salts, 2 oils in metal holder	.1,250.00
Celery	.250.00
Cheese plate & cover (No. 101 plate)	.450.00
Custard	.125.00
Molasses	.450.00
Nappy, round, 4"	.85.00
Jug	.350.00
Oil	.600.00
Oil, small	.600.00
Salt	.150.00
Spoon	.185.00
Tumbler	.160.00
Water bottle	.385.00

No. 325 Hobbs' Opal Swirl tumblers, ruby opalescent satin and sapphire opalescent.

No. 325 Hobbs' Opal Swirl salt shaker, ruby opalescent. Courtesy of Hazel Tellier.

Catalog page of various items in No. 325 Hobbs' Opal Swirl, left to right, top row: oil, pepper, custard, salt, molasses; middle row: spoon, cheese & cover, bitter; bottom row: bar bottle, water set, celery.

No. 325 Hobbs' Opal Swirl custards, sapphire opalescent and ruby opalescent. Courtesy of Jo and Bob Sanford.

No. 325 Hobbs' Opal Swirl jug, sapphire opalescent. Courtesy of Huntington Museum of Art.

No. 326 SWIRL

Date: January, 1889
Colors: Crystal, crystal opalescent, sapphire opalescent, ruby opalescent
Decorations: Satin finish; No. 7, amber stain; Frances
Trade Quotes:

American Pottery & Glassware Reporter, January 17, 1889:

Wheeling-Goods that will be hard to excel are the three new lines of the Hobbs Glass Co. They are just out and they are 'rippers.' The numbers are 326, 327, and 328. The former is made in ten effects, namely, crystal, crystal opalescent, sapphire, ruby, these four colors in satin finish, decorated No. 7 and 'Frances.' In these they have a full line of tableware such as nappies, bowls, sugar sifters, molasses jugs, tumblers, pitchers, water bottles, finger bowls, celeries (boat and straight), salts, peppers, mustards, toothpicks, casters, also shades, oil bottles, etc. The shape is oval, entirely new, and all the articles named are made in this shape except tumblers.

Comments: This is the first new shape developed by Nicholas Kopp after the reorganization of the company. The opalescent colors are now called Windows. We have listed the Windows opalescent pieces not made in No. 326 Swirl below this entry for Swirl. The Windows opalescent effect is reported to have also been made by Beaumont Glass Co. Some pieces were also made with Coral or "Seaweed" opalescence. The No. 325 plates listed below appear to be identical to the plates in No. 326 pattern. The pieces marked (*) may be pressed.

Prices given are for Frances decoration and No. 7 decoration. Prices are also given for Windows in ruby and sapphire opalescent. For Windows in crystal opalescent, deduct 50%.

Reproductions: The covered sugar has been made by Fenton Art Glass Co. without a finial on the lid. They also made the cruet and salt and pepper. Fenton's colors include an opaque powder blue and ruby opalescent.

No. 326 Swirl small nappy with underplate, Frances decoration. Courtesy of Huntington Museum of Art.

Pieces	Prices Frances Dec. and No. 7	Prices Windows, Sapphire Opales. Ruby Opalescent
Bowl, 4"	$24.00	$55.00
Bowl, 8"	90.00	195.00
Bowl, finger	35.00	110.00
Bowl, waste	40.00	110.00
Caster set (2 oils, salt and pepper in metal frame)	750.00	1,800.00
Celery, flat	60.00	250.00
Celery, individual (relish or pickle)*	35.00	250.00
Celery, tall	90.00	325.00
Cheese & cover *	130.00	600.00
Molasses can	295.00	1,200.00
Mustard	95.00	500.00
Oil	250.00	1,000.00
Pitcher	225.00	1,200.00
Plate, 5" (sugar)-No. 325*	25.00	N/A
Plate, 6" (butter)-No. 325*	30.00	N/A
Sugar sifter	195.00	600.00
Salt	85.00	125.00
Shade, 4"	150.00	225.00
Shade, electric	175.00	250.00
Table set:		
Butter & cover	95.00	425.00
Cream	70.00	275.00
Spoon	55.00	300.00
Sugar & cover	85.00	325.00
Toothpick	160.00	325.00
Tray, candy, 9"*	60.00	N/A
Tumbler	45.00	185.00

Also found in Windows opalescence (not 326 Swirl):

Bitter Bottle	$550.00
Cheese & cover (No. 101 Plate, plain cover)	550.00
Molasses can	500.00
Pitcher, 1/2 Gal., No. 333	375.00
Tumbler, No. 333	135.00

No. 333 Windows Lemonade Set.

No. 326 Swirl salt shaker, Frances decoration. Courtesy of Mary Ann and Dick Krauss.

No. 326 Swirl tumbler and pitcher, Frances decoration.

No. 326 Swirl group: Windows celery, sapphire opalescent; Windows salt, ruby opalescent; Windows toothpick, crystal opalescent; Windows waste bowl, sapphire opalescent satin finish.

No. 326 Swirl mustard, Frances decoration.

Windows molasses can, ruby opalescent. Courtesy of Huntington Museum of Art.

No. 326 Windows Swirl tumbler, sapphire opalescent.

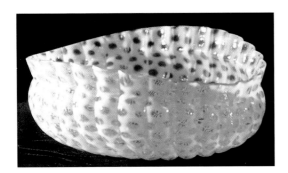

No. 326 Windows Swirl 8" bowl, sapphire opalescent. Courtesy of Huntington Museum of Art.

Windows cheese and cover, sapphire opalescent. The cheese plate in this pattern is borrowed from No. 101 Daisy and Button.

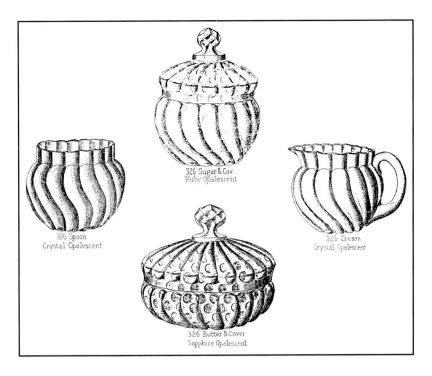

Catalog page No. 326 Swirl table set.

No. 327 QUARTERED BLOCK WITH STARS

Date: January, 1889

Colors: Crystal

Decorations: No. 7, amber stain; Frances

Trade Quotes:

American Pottery & Glassware Reporter, January 17, 1889:

...The '327' is made in crystal, imitation cut, pressed, and consisting of three different figures. It looks very much like cut goods and only experts can tell the difference. A full line of tableware is made in these goods.

Comments: This pattern is often confused with No. 330 pattern which does not have the stars. The pieces in this pattern are oval except for the tumbler. It is likely that the molds were reworked to make pattern No. 330. Perhaps these molds with the stars were difficult to maintain. Sometimes this pattern is called Hobbs' Block. See No. 330 for piece shapes common to both patterns.

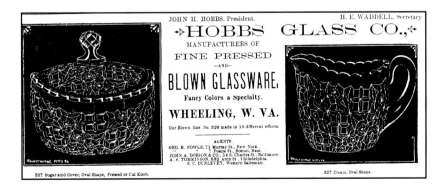

January 1889, ad introducing No. 327 Quartered Block with Star, *Pottery & Glassware Reporter.*

Prices are for pieces with Frances decoration. Pieces with No. 7, clear with amber rim, are 10% less.

Pieces	Prices
Bowl, 4"	$20.00
Bowl, 8"	65.00
Bowl, finger	40.00
Celery tray	60.00
Goblet	140.00
Molasses can	185.00
Nappy, 3"	20.00
Nappy, applied handle, 3"	50.00
Oil	175.00
Olive, 4½"	25.00
Oval, 7"	40.00
Oval, 8"	45.00
Oval, 9"	50.00
Oval, 10"	65.00
Pitcher	185.00
Salt shaker	60.00
Table set:	
Butter & cover	95.00
Cream	55.00
Spoon	45.00
Sugar & cover	75.00
Tumbler	45.00
Water bottle	100.00

No. 327 Quartered Block with Stars spoon, decorated No. 7.

No. 327 Quartered Block with Stars sugar and cover, cream, Frances decoration.

112

No. 328

Date: January, 1889

Colors: Crystal, crystal opalescent, sapphire opalescent, amber opalescent, pink opalescent (ruby)

Decorations: Satin finish

Trade Quotes:

American Pottery & Glassware Reporter, January 17, 1889:

...The 328 water sets consist of five colors, pearl satin finish, crystal opal, sapphire opal, amber opal and pink opal.

Comments: We have been unable to find illustrations of this line. Water set only.

No. 330 HOBBS' BLOCK

Date: July, 1889

Colors: Crystal

Decorations: No. 7, Amber stain, Frances

Trade Quotes:

Pottery and Glassware Reporter, July 18, 1889:

The three new fall lines of the Hobbs Glass Co. are taking well. They consist of No. 330, in imitation of heavy cut, No. 331 in ruby, pink, ornate, and crystal, blown, and No. 332 in crystal, plain and engraved, pressed.

Comments: The molds for this pattern were probably reworked from pattern No. 327, which is much like it. Also, a piece of cut glass is known which very closely resembles this pattern — maker unknown. This pattern is much more difficult to find than No. 327 Quartered Block with Stars.

Prices are for pieces in Frances decoration, pieces in No. 7 decoration, amber rim with unfrosted body, deduct 10%.

Reproductions: Pieces of this pattern have been made by the Fenton Art Glass Co. in light blue opaque, black, milk glass, and possibly others. Hobbs made this pattern only in crystal glass.

Pieces	Prices
Bowl, finger	$50.00
Bowl, round, 7"	65.00
Bowl, round, 8"	75.00
Bowl, round, 9"	85.00
Bowl, square, 8"	75.00
Celery boat	65.00
Goblet	155.00
Molasses can	200.00
Nappy, round, 4½"	25.00
Nappy, round, 5"	30.00
Nappy, square, 4½"	25.00
Oil	200.00
Olive, 4½"	30.00
Oval, 4½"	25.00
Oval, 7"	45.00
Oval, 8"	50.00
Oval, 9"	55.00
Oval, 10"	75.00
Rose bowl	85.00
Salt	65.00
Table set:	
Butter & cover	100.00
Cream	60.00
Spoon	55.00
Sugar & cover	85.00
Tankard, ½ gallon	200.00
Tumbler	50.00
Water bottle	120.00

Catalog page of various items in No. 330 Hobbs' Block.

No. 330 Hobbs' Block cream, Frances decoration. Courtesy of Huntington Museum of Art.

No. 331

Date: July, 1889

Colors: Crystal, ruby, pink, yellow opaque

Decorations: No. 363 Engraving, Satin, Frances, Ornate-unknown effect

Trade Quotes:

Pottery and Glassware Reporter, July 18, 1889:

The three new fall lines of the Hobbs Glass Co. are taking well. They consist of No. 330, in imitation of heavy cut, No. 331 in ruby, pink, ornate, and crystal, blown, and No. 332 in crystal, plain and engraved, pressed.

Comments: In Heacock's book III, a sugar sifter in purple slag is shown attributed to Northwood. A yellow opaque piece is also illustrated in Heacock. With these exceptions, we have only seen pieces in ruby. Pieces in this shape with other treatments can also be found under pattern No. 346.

Reproductions: The Fenton Art Glass Co. has used the cream shape to make items in Burmese and other colors. Fenton also made other pieces including a vase.

Prices are for pieces in ruby, for crystal items, deduct 50%.

Pieces	Prices
Bowl, 8"	$90.00
Bowl, finger	45.00
Jug, squat, 1/2 gallon	275.00
Jug, tall, 1/2 gallon	275.00
Lemonade or custard	35.00
Molasses can	190.00
Mustard	100.00
Nappy, 4 1/2"	35.00
Oil	225.00
Salt	75.00
Sugar sifter	220.00
Table set:	
Butter & cover	155.00
Cream	85.00
Spoon	65.00
Sugar & cover	120.00
Tumbler	35.00

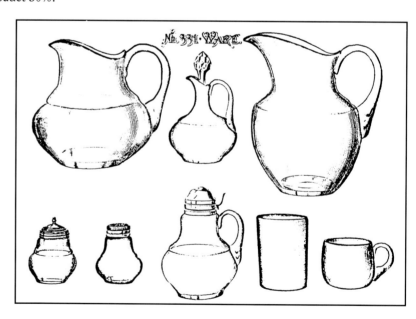

Catalog page of various items in No. 331, left to right, top row: 1/2 gallon squat jug, oil, 1/2 gallon tall jug; bottom row: mustard, salt, molasses can, tumbler, custard.

Catalog illustration of various items in No. 331 with Engraving No. 363.

No. 331 jug, ruby. Courtesy of Huntington Museum of Art.

No. 331 salt and pepper, ruby.

No. 332 OGLEBAY

Date: July, 1889
Colors: Crystal
Decorations: No. 361 Engraving
Trade Quotes:

Pottery and Glassware Reporter July 18, 1889:

The three new fall lines of the Hobbs Glass Co. are taking well. They consist of No. 330, in imitation of heavy cut, No. 331 i[n] ruby, pink, ornate, and crystal, blown, and No. 332 in crystal, plain and engraved, pressed.

Comments: This pattern is reworked from the No. 115 Wheeling molds. It is very difficult to find. We are giving what we feel ar[e] fair market values for the line, even though its rarity should suggest higher prices. For decorated pieces add 20%.

Pieces	Prices
Bowl, finger	$25.00
Bowl, round, 8"	45.00
Bowl, round, 10"	55.00
Celery, tall	40.00
Comport, tall, 8"	65.00
Comport & cover, tall, 8"	100.00
Jug, 1/2 gallon	90.00
Molasses can	120.00
Nappy, 4"	15.00
Nappy, 4 1/2"	15.00
Oval, 7"	30.00
Oval, 8"	30.00
Pickle dish	25.00
Salt, table (master)	45.00
Table set:	
Butter & cover	85.00
Cream	50.00
Spoon	45.00
Sugar & cover	70.00
Tumbler	40.00

Catalog page with various items in No. 332 Oglebay with Engraving No. 361; left to right, top row: spoon, covered sugar, cream, covered butter, middle: table salt, pickle, bottom: molasses can, celery, tumbler, 7" & 8" ovals.

No. 334 CRYSTALINA

Date: December, 1889
Colors: Crystal, pink, depression glass-type green, emerald green, and Dewey blue by U.S. Glass
Decorations: Amber on rims, gold on rims, satin finish, No. 20 (unknown)
Trade Quotes:

Pottery and Glassware Reporter, December 5, 1889:

Recently the Hobbs Glass Co. brought a brand new celery, the 'Autumn celery,' which has been selling like wild fire, in fact the works is kept hustling to make enough of them. It is one of the greatest selling articles in the market. It sells on sight. These celeries are made the shape of a leaf, in flint and old gold stain and autumn leaf, and white and satin finish and are as pretty as they can be. The number is 334 and this line will also be made in other table ware such as olives, pickles, bowls, etc.

Pottery and Glassware Reporter, March 20, 1890:

The Hobbs Glass Co. have ready two splendid new lines. These are No. 334 in crystal, gold finish and crystalina, and No. 335 in crystal, engraved and gold etching.

Pottery and Glassware Reporter, August 14, 1890:

Hobbs Glass Works has brought out a new effect in 334, the number of the latter is 20....

China, Glass and Lamps, December 31, 1890:

No. 334 of last year with new decorations will be a good seller.

omments: Crystalina is actually only the name of the amber decorated ware, not the pattern. A 7" plate in this pattern exists with struck ruby edge, appearing to be made from heat sensitive glass. This pattern is often confused with much later glass, especially ieisey's No. 1503 Crystolite, from the late 1930s. U. S. Glass continued to make some pieces of this pattern as late as the 1920s. ome pieces we have seen differ slightly from the catalog illustrations, for instance, the butter lid has a pattern similar to the sugar d, and the illustrations of the cheese dish finial vary between catalog and advertisement.

The design patent was applied for October 30, 1889, and granted No. 19,749 on April 1, 1890, to Hanson E. Waddell. It was not ssigned.

rices are for items with Crystalina decoration (amber stain on rims). Gold rim prices are the same, crystal pieces are 15% less. lobbs made this pattern only in crystal. All colors are by U.S. Glass.

ieces	Prices
Bread plate	$35.00
Butter, individual	8.00
Celery, flat	12.00
Cheese plate & cover	90.00
Cream, individual	20.00
Nappy, handled, 4½"	15.00
Olive	15.00
Pickle, 9"	15.00
Plate, 4" (underplate for sherbet)	8.00
Plate, 9"	18.00
Plate, 10"	25.00
Sherbet	15.00
Sugar, berry	15.00
Table Set:	
Butter & cover	85.00
Cream	50.00
Spoon	40.00
Sugar & cover	65.00

No. 334 Crystalina table set, amber stain on rims.

Catalog page showing various items in No. 334 Crystalina with gold finish.

May 1890, ad illustrating the No. 334 cheese plate and cover (note finial) and No. 335 sugar and cover.

No. 334 Crystalina group; front: olive, 6" round nappy, sherbet; rear: bread plate, all with amber stain on rims.

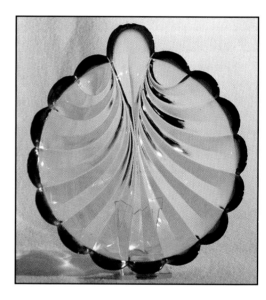

No. 334 Crystalina 6" plate, crystal with heat sensitive ruby rim. Courtesy of Huntington Museum of Art.

No. 334 Crystalina individual cream, emerald green by U. S. Glass Co.

118

No. 326

Date: November, 1890
Colors: Crystal. Other colors unknown.
Decorations: *"made in crystal and gold finished plate"*-probably meaning the plate had a gold rim.
Trade Quotes:
Pottery and Glassware Reporter, November 20, 1890:
    A new cheese cover, a three cornered affair, ribbed trust,[sic] and the shape of a slice of cheese, the number of which is 326, is the latest novelty of the Hobbs Glass Co. It is just out, and is not only useful but ornamental. It is made in crystal, and will doubtless become a fast seller.
Comments: From the catalog illustration this appears to be a pressed item. Most of No. 326 pattern is blown.

Pieces	Prices
Cheese and cover	$175.00

Illustration from catalog on No. 326 cheese and cover.

No. 335 HEXAGONAL BLOCK

Date: December, 1890
Colors: Crystal
Decorations: Amber stain; amber stain with etching; Engraving No. 364 (berry and leaf), ruby stain; ruby stain with engraving or etching
Trade Quotes:
Pottery and Glassware Reporter, December 5, 1889:
    This company has another new crystal line, No. 335, in which everything in tableware will be made. The line is half figured, the figure being entirely unique. This line will also be made in engraved and plain ware. A number of novelties will be made in No. 335 a little later on.
Crockery and Glass Journal, January 23, 1890:
    The Hobbs Glass Co., with their new 334 and 335 lines are meeting with phenomenal success. An entirely new feature has been added called the 335 gold etched novelties, and together they form a display at once popular and striking,
China, Glass & Lamps, July 22, 1891:
    No. 335 tableware pattern, in ruby etched and ruby cut is a magnificent line of goods, which cannot fail to meet the highest approval. They have it also in plain ruby.
Crockery & Glass Journal, November 26, 1891:
    The Hobbs Glass Co., which is now factory 'H' of the combine, continues to keep up the great reputation of these works, and has made a good hit with its crystal line nicely tipped with ruby.

Comments: This pattern was in production a year and a half before ruby staining was introduced, yet most pieces found are ruby stained. The engravings on this pattern lack the quality of the earlier Hobbs' engravings.

Prices are for ruby or amber stained pieces. For crystal, deduct 30%; for crystal etched or engraved, deduct 20%; for ruby or amber stain with etching or engraving, add 10%.

Pieces	Prices
Bowl, 7"	$35.00
Bowl, 8"	40.00
Bowl, 9"	40.00
Bowl, finger	30.00
Bowl, shallow, 7"	35.00
Bowl, shallow, 8"	40.00
Bowl, shallow, 9"	45.00
Celery, tall	60.00
Comport, 7"	45.00
Comport, 8"	55.00
Comport, 9"	65.00
Comport, covered, 7"	90.00
Comport, covered, 8"	100.00
Custard	25.00
Goblet	45.00
Jug, 1/2 gallon	155.00
Molasses can	250.00
Nappy, 4"	15.00
Nappy, 4 1/2"	15.00
Pickle jar, covered	65.00
Pitcher, tankard, 3 pt	130.00
Salt	45.00
Table set:	
Butter & cover	125.00
Cream	65.00
Spoon	45.00
Sugar & cover	100.00
Tumbler	35.00

No. 335 Hexagonal Block spoon, ruby stain.

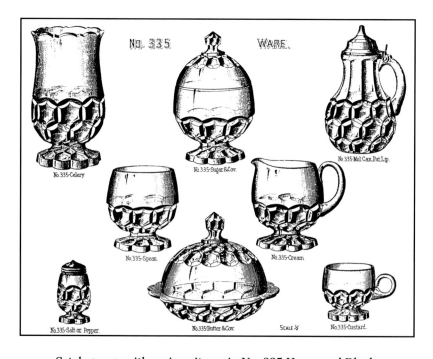

Catalog page with various items in No. 335 Hexagonal Block.

120

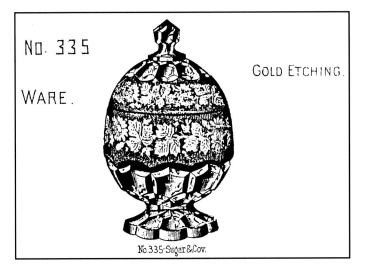

Catalog illustration of No. 335 Hexagonal Block covered sugar with gold etching.

No. 335 Hexagonal Block tumbler, ruby stain engraved.

Catalog illustration of No. 335 Hexagonal Block covered butter with ruby and etching.

Catalog illustration of No. 335 Hexagonal Block pickle jar and cover with Engraving No. 364.

No. 335 Hexagonal Block jug, gold etching. Courtesy of Huntington Museum of Art.

No. 336

Date: 1890
Colors: Crystal, ruby
Comments:
We have only these illustrations of this pattern. We do not know whether the circles drawn are meant to represent Polka Dots or an opalescent effect like Windows.

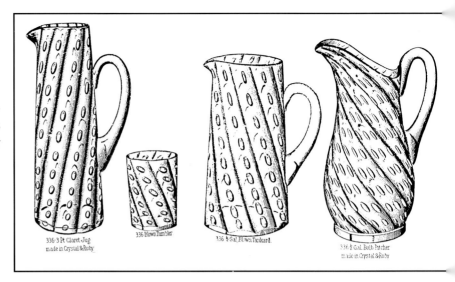

Catalog illustrations of No. 336, 3-pint claret jug, tumbler, 1/2 gallon blown tankard, and 1/2 gallon bulbous pitcher.

No. 337

Date: July, 1890
Colors: Crystal
Decoration: Amber stain on rim
Trade Quotes:
Pottery and Glassware Reporter, July 3, 1890:

Nos. 334 and 337, in table ware, are the latest new goods at the Hobbs Glass Works. They are made in crystal and decorated and are intended for the fall trade.

Comments: This short line resembles 334 Crystalina, and is quite difficult to find. There may be other pieces in the line.

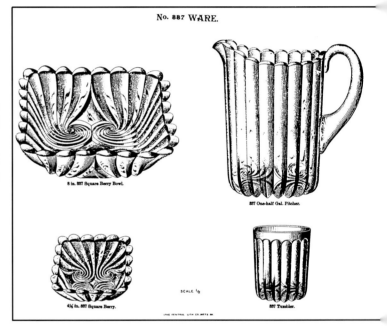

Catalog page of items in No. 337.

Prices are for pieces with amber rims.

Pieces	Prices
Bowl, 4¼" square	$20.00
Bowl, 8" square	65.00
Pitcher, ½ gallon	135.00
Tumbler	45.00

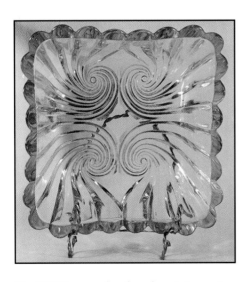

No. 337 8" square bowl, amber stain on rim.

122

No. 339 LEAF AND FLOWER

Date: November, 1890

Colors: Crystal

Decorations: No. 25 Etching on crystal, satin finish; No. 30 colored on plain crystal, amber stain on the flowers and leaves; No. 35 colored and etched, amber stain on the flowers and leaves combined with satin finish

Trade Quotes:

Pottery and Glassware Reporter, November 20, 1890:

Two new lines of table ware for the spring trade are in molds. They will be entirely different from anything ever made in this or any other country, and experts who have seen them pronounce then A No. 1.

Pottery and Glassware Reporter, January 1, 1891:

The Hobbs Glass Co. recently promised to bring out a line of ware that would be different from anything is this country or any other country, and they have kept their word. The number is 339, and it is made from different effects. The goods are made in crystal, with figured flowers and vines, and these are made in three different decorations, 25, 30 and 35, giving them four different effects for the new year. The shape and figures are entirely new. The crystal line, without any decoration, is very handsome, and was specially for the decorations selected. The 25 decoration is etched, the 30 decoration is colored on the plain crystal and the 35 decoration consists of etched and colored novelty. The line is entirely new, and there has never been anything like it anywhere. It is not a copy of anybody's goods in any shape, and is believed to be the richest line made for this year. Great preparations were taken in getting it up, and these people have succeeded admirably. Besides being complete in everything pertaining to tableware, the line is made in a patent molasses can and a four-bottled castor with an oak leaf base. The four bottles of the castor are intended for salt, pepper, mustard and vinegar. The little castor and the molasses can are among the handsomest things ever made in the way of novelties.

Comments: The small castor set is very difficult to find complete, as the bottles are completely plain and were often separated from the base. Catalog pages also indicate that the bottles were supplied in ruby.

Catalog page of various items in No. 339 Leaf and Flower.

No. 339 Leaf and Flower tankard pitcher, decorated No. 35.

Prices given are for amber stain or amber stain with satin. Satin items without stain should sell for 30% less.

Pieces	Prices
Bowl, berry, 7"	$50.00
Bowl, berry, 8"	60.00
Bowl, finger	35.00
Celery, handled (flat basket shape)	95.00
Celery, tall	60.00
Condiment set	
Plain salt, pepper, mustard, vinegar	
on leaf shaped tray	225.00
Molasses can	270.00
Nappy, 4½"	22.00
Nappy, 5"	22.00
Nappy, 7" (shallow)	35.00
Nappy, 8" (shallow)	40.00
Nappy, 9" (shallow)	45.00
Pitcher, tankard	150.00
Salt shaker	45.00
Table set	
Butter & cover	90.00
Cream	50.00
Spoon	45.00
Sugar & cover	70.00
Tumbler	40.00

No. 339 Leaf and Flower group: salt, decorated No. 30; leaf condiment tray, decorated No. 35; celery, decorated No. 30.

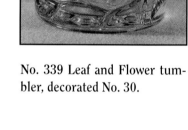

No. 339 Leaf and Flower tumbler, decorated No. 30.

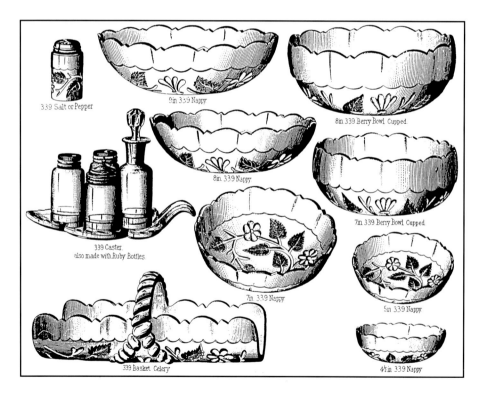

Catalog page of various items in No. 339 Leaf and Flower.

No. 342

Date: January, 1891
Colors: Crystal, ruby
Decorations: No. 96 cutting
Trade Quotes:

Pottery and Glassware Reporter, January 1, 1891:

 An individual water bottle and tumbler in blown, the number of which is 342, brought out for the holidays, is becoming very popular, and thousands will be sold. The bottle will hold enough water for one man, and is a mighty pretty thing.

Comments: Prices given are for plain pieces. Add 20% for cutting. Add 500+% for ruby.

Pieces	Prices
Carafe, individual	$15.00
Tumbler	5.00
Complete set	40.00

342 Blown Tumbler.
Made in
Crystal & Ruby.

342 Ind Carafe
Made in Crystal & Ruby.

Catalog illustrations of No. 342.

No. 343

Date: January, 1891
Colors: Crystal
Decorations: No. 96 cut star and miter.
Trade Quotes:

Pottery and Glassware Reporter, January 29, 1891:

 ...The number is 343, cut 96 and the goods are made in jugs, individual water bottles, salts, butter ..., etc.

Pottery & Glassware Reporter, February 26, 1891:

 The Hobbs Glass Co. are having a big run on 339 and 343 and other goods.

Comments: Little of this pattern is shown in original catalogs. The trade quote lists other items and implies even more to the line.

Prices given are for crystal items. For pieces with cutting, add 20%.

Pieces	Prices
Butter, unknown shape	N.P.A.
Carafe, with 342 tumbler	$40.00
Jug, No. 7 (tankard)	35.00
Salt, unknown shape	N.P.A.
Jug, sizes 1, 2, 3, 4, shape No. 314	70.00 to 125.00

342 Tumbler. Cut 96.

343 Carafe. Cut 96.

343-7 Jug. Cut 96.

314-2 Jug. Cut 96.

343 Water Bottle. Cut 96.

Catalog illustrations of Nos. 343 and 314 with No. 96 cutting.

No. 341 MARIO

Date: July, 1891

Decorations: Crystal etched No. 36; ruby stain; ruby stain engraved; ruby stain etched; amber stain; amber stain etched

Trade Quotes:

Pottery and Glassware Reporter, July 16, 1891:

   Several new and handsome lines have just been brought out by the Hobbs Glass Co. for the fall trade. No. 341, a full line, made in ruby stained, ruby etched and ruby cut, all of which are prettier than field daisies on which the girls all dote, and whic *will head the procession this season.*

China, Glass & Lamps, July 22, 1891:

   No. 341 pattern in crystal, etched No. 36, is a new one and a very new shape.

Comments: We have seen a small lamp which looks similar, but has a slightly different pattern on the font. This is probably not part of the Mario line, but may have been the inspiration for the design.

Prices given are for pieces with ruby or amber stain. Plain crystal would be 35% less. For etched or engraved pieces, add 20%.

Pieces	Prices
Bowl, 7"	$35.00
Bowl, 8"	.40.00
Bowl, finger	.35.00
Celery, tall	.60.00
Molasses can, ½ pint	.230.00
Molasses can, pint	.250.00
Nappy, 4½"	.22.00
Nappy, 5"	.22.00
Pitcher	.135.00
Salt	.45.00
Table set:	
Butter and cover	.100.00
Cream	.60.00
Spoon	.55.00
Sugar and cover	.80.00
Tumbler	.45.00

Catalog page showing various items in No. 341 Mario.

No. 341 Mario celery, etched No. 36; spoon, amber stain, etched.

No. 341 Mario tumbler, etched No. 36. Courtesy Huntington Museum of Art.

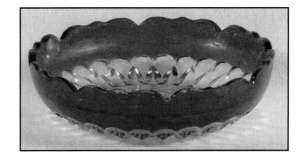

No. 341 Mario small nappy, ruby stain.

No. 341 Mario 8" crimped bowl, amber stain. Courtesy
Huntington Museum of Art.

NO. 346

Date: 1891

Colors: Crystal, ruby in optic ribbed pieces. Coral (seaweed) in crystal opalescent, sapphire opalescent, ruby opalescent.

Decorations: Amber stain on optic ribs; Engraved No. 384-only on optic ribbed pieces. Coral (Seaweed) pieces also are found with satin finish.

Comments: The optic effect, resurrected from the early '80s, consists of vertical ribs from the top to the bottom of the piece. Coral was the original name used by Hobbs Glass Co. for what collectors now call "Seaweed." The Coral or Seaweed items do not have the ribs as shown on one catalog page. See Lighting for lamps with Coral decoration.

This line was made of a combination of old and new molds. The table set and the half gallon jug are made from new molds while the remainder of the pattern used existing Hobbs' molds. Original pattern numbers are shown after each piece listing. This pattern was a transitional one made just prior to the merger with U. S. Glass and also made by U. S. Glass at Hobbs after the merger.

Prices are for ribbed optic pieces in ruby. For plain ribbed pieces, deduct 75+%. For ribbed items with amber stain, deduct 0%. Coral opalescent prices are for ruby and sapphire opalescent. For crystal opalescent, deduct 50%.

Reproductions: Heacock shows a cruet and a two quart pitcher that he attributes to someone other than Hobbs Glass Co. with Coral (Seaweed) opalescence. We feel that these pieces were produced shortly after the Hobbs Glass Co. closed in 1893, possibly by Beaumont Glass Co. Beaumont also made other Coral pieces. At this time, we know of no definite way to tell the difference between Hobbs' items and Beaumont ones except that Hobbs did not make crimped top pitchers.

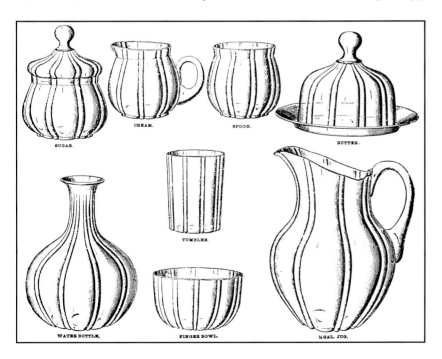

No. 346 half gallon jug, amber stain on
ribs.

Catalog page of No. 346 items with optic ribs.

Pieces	Prices Ruby ribbed	Prices Ruby opalescent; Sapphire opalescent
Bowl, 7"	$125.00	$225.00
Bowl, 8"	125.00	225.00
Bowl, finger	150.00	300.00
Celery, No. 314	225.00	325.00
Celery, hotel, No. 314	225.00	325.00
Jug, ½ gallon	450.00	800.00
Molasses can, No. 331	300.00	550.00
Nappy, 4½"	150.00	210.00
Oil, No. 331	375.00	585.00
Salt, No. 331	70.00	150.00
Sugar shaker, No. 331	400.00	500.00
Table set:		
Butter & cover	250.00	450.00
Cream	175.00	325.00
Spoon	195.00	425.00
Sugar & cover	225.00	400.00
Toothpick, No. 331		450.00
Tumbler	175.00	250.00
Water bottle	225.00	400.00

Pieces available with coral (seaweed) opalescence: (not part of No. 346)

Pieces		Price
Bitter bottle No. 308		$400.00
Bitter bottle, square		400.00
Oil No. 326		385.00
Pitcher, ½ gallon, No. 319		950.00

Catalog illustrations of No. 346 items with Coral (Seaweed) opalescent decoration.

No. 308 bitter bottle, sapphire
seaweed opalescent.

No. 346 Salt (331), tumbler, sapphire seaweed opalescent.

No. 346 Sugar and cover, seaweed opalescent.

Bitter bottle, ruby seaweed
opalescent. Courtesy Huntington Museum of Art.

Lighting

Lighting fixtures and lamps comprised a major portion of the products of Hobbs, Brockunier & Co. From the earliest docu mentation, lamps were important enough to warrant listing in Hobbs ads and in trade reports about the activities and products o the firm.

The first mention of lighting in journals described the patented method of joining a lamp font with a standard, especially o another color. This is in reference to the early Hobbs lamps made with usually crystal fonts on opal bases. These are connecte with a brass device which was patented by J. H. Hobbs in May of 1870.

One of the most important innovations in lighting made by Hobbs was the new method of making glass coverings for the tube carrying gas through a chandelier. This greatly improved the looks of the chandelier and also made it glisten even more — alway an asset in lighting fixtures. The company advertised that the lights in the chandeliers were available with from three to 24 light. Several remarkable examples of these chandeliers are still in existence in the Wheeling area, notably two in the Oglebay Mansio and two in the Mount de Chantal Visitation Academy. Those in the Academy are especially noteworthy: one using the Hand lamp base as the support for each light and the other using the Little Samuel lamp base.

In 1995 and 1996 both of the chandeliers in the Mount de Chantal Visitation Academy were restored by Duane Reeves and Harold Cusic with the assistance of the Pittsburgh chapter of the National Early American Glass Club. During the renovation, both chandeliers were completely disassembled, cleaned, and rewired. It was discovered that each piece was numbered, as mentioned in an 1878 brochure, an early example of do-it-your-self assembly following a numbered diagram. When the 24-light Hand chandelier had been electrified, sometime before 1906, the curved, glass covered arms and the hands had been installed upside-down. The light bulbs hung from the hands, surrounded by prisms (see page 131). This latest renovation restored the chandelier to its original form, with the hands supporting the light bulbs and shades.

These chandeliers were unusual enough to attract the attention of *Scientific American* in 1879: "Wheeling manufac-turers make the beautiful glass chandeliers which have become so fashionable of late, but they import the cut glass pendants from Switzerland, where the peasants make them by hand cheaper than they can be made by machinery in this country. Many of these chandeliers are sent to London, so the pendants make two voyages across the ocean."

While the chandeliers are the epitome of Hobbs lighting, many simpler designs were made primarily for use in public buildings. These ranged from large many-light fixtures with etched globes to one- or two-light fixtures for smaller areas and hallways. These simple fixtures did not have the glass coverings over the gas supply tubes and so are much less showy.

Twenty-four light Hand Chandelier after renovation. Courtesy Mount de Chantal Visitation Academy.

Hobbs had such success marketing their public lighting and chandeliers in this country and abroad that much of their output for many years was devoted to this area of the business. Even in later years, the company continued to make lamps, some matching tableware patterns and some only as lamp lines. The company also made many of the large and small dome shades for hanging lamps and cylinder shades for hall fixtures in many of their popular opalescent colors and in ruby glass.

Six-light Little Samuel chandelier after renovation. Courtesy Mount de Chantal Visitation Academy.

Detail of Hand and adjacent pieces prior to renovation, note that the hands are inverted. Courtesy Mount de Chantal Visitation Academy.

Framework of 24-light Hand chandelier during renovation. Duane Reeves and Howard Cusic. Courtesy Mount de Chantal Visitation Academy.

Twenty-four light Hand chandelier before renovation, examined by Duane Reeves. Courtesy Mount de Chantal Visitation Academy.

CHANDELIERS

Date: Ca. 1876
Colors: Crystal and opal for *"subdued lustre"*
Trade Quotes:

Crockery & Glass Journal, February 22, 1877:

Crystal chandeliers are a specialty with this house. These are got up in the most exquisite styles, and I should think the must win their way wherever good taste rules. The iron rods forming the body of the chandelier are concealed entirely by crystal tubes, finely cut; the iron being coated with tin cannot be seen, and the chandelier appears to be entirely composed of glass. In the first specimens made, the tube or iron was covered with nickel, and was only slightly visible, but tin being whiter has been found to assimilate entirely with the color of the glass. Not only chandeliers are got up in this way, but brackets, newel and hall lights, etc., in fine, every style of oil or gas chandelier or lamp formerly made in bronze. These are fitted out with crystal prismatic pendants or not, as may be desired. Some of the chandeliers are suitable for lighting stores and billiard rooms, and are made with the arms very wide spread. Crystal chandeliers can be obtained here with any number of lights desired, from two to twenty four. The Company have their patents on these goods. They have met with great success so far, and have the prospect of still greater triumphs before them. Not content with introducing them to the market here, they have initiated an outside trade and sent these chandeliers to fill orders from Australia, South America, and several other foreign countries.

Crockery & Glass Journal, January, 1878:

These manufacturers have just patented a press and molds for pressing glass in sections of a circle. This will be invaluable for parties making glass chandeliers, etc. Speaking of chandeliers, those crystal ones made at this factory sold enough to 'grace palatial halls' (that's a poetical compliment), look out for a run on them when trade begins.

Crockery & Glass Journal, February, 1878:

Inventions and Improvements Glass Chandelier Trimmings, John H. Hobbs, Wheeling, West Virginia. The mode of making open-topped glass trimmings for chandeliers, by blowing the same to shape in an open-topped mold, provided with one central and two or more radial cavities. Designs Glassware-John H. Hobbs, Wheeling, W. Va. Application filed December 26, 1877. Term of patent 7 years. [quoted from patent]

Crockery & Glass Journal, July, 1878:

One of their novelties is a new shaped globe. The effect of this is very fine, and the decorations are in admirable taste. These globes are etched and ornamented by the sand-blast process, and present a rich and beautiful appearance. These globes were used on the chandeliers and public lighting fixtures.

Crockery & Glass Journal, September 8, 1881:

The glass chandeliers manufactured by Hobbs, Brockunier & Co. are also having a tremendous run at present. A very large one was recently placed in one of the large public buildings of Nashville, Tenn., and the result was to create an immediate demand for them in that locality.

Crockery & Glass Journal, October 25, 1883:

The chandelier trade is also moderately brisk just now. The popularity of the articles as decorations for churches, theatres, and the gas fixtures for all public and private buildings, has become something phenomenal within a very few years. For globes of the finest description for interior gas jets there is a good demand.

Crockery & Glass Journal, January 17, 1884:

The chandeliers which are made in various designs cannot be supplied as rapidly as they are ordered. The ornaments for gas fixtures are just now in large demand on account of the variety of designs and their general beauty of manufacture. The shipments to the South American States in 1883 were large, as were some to the Australian cities.

Crockery & Glass Journal, April 10, 1884:

The globes for lamps and gas-lights in various colors are some of the recent products of this factory.

Comments: J. H. Hobbs patented many improvements and methods of making the various parts of the chandeliers over a period of about two years.

Patent Nos.

182,072	September 12, 1876	Pressed glass trimmings
182,073	September 12, 1876	Molds for pressing attachments
182,668	September 26, 1876	Pressed glass pendants

The chandeliers were also patented in Canada and England.

A company publication stated that *We make the Chandeliers, etc., in a large variety of patterns and in any number of lights from one to one hundred and more, and in spread and lengths as may be required.* They seem to have been willing to tackle any challenge.

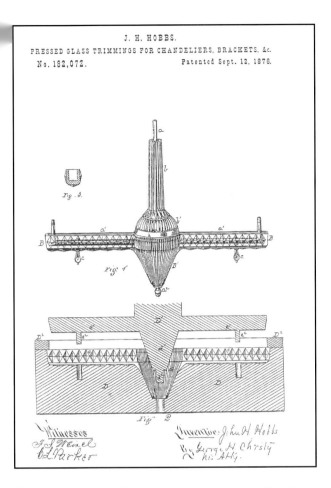

Illustration for brackets and glass trimmings for chandeliers from 1876 patent.

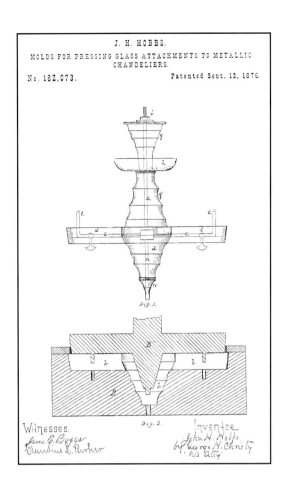

Illustration of molds for pressing glass attachments to chandeliers from 1876 patent.

March 1877 ad for J. H. Hobbs, Brockunier & Co. chandelier, *Crockery & Glass Journal.*

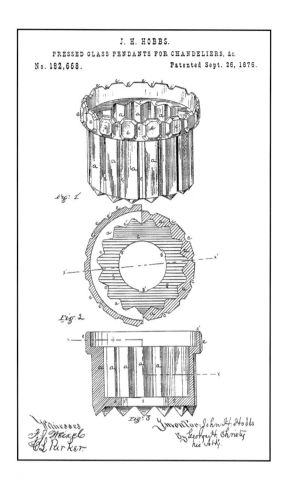

Illustration for joined prism cage for chandeliers from 1876 patent.

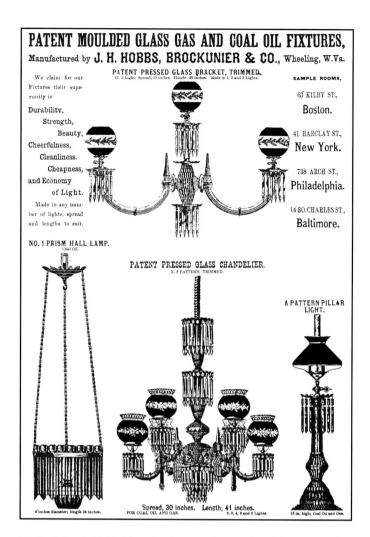

1879 ad for J. H. Hobbs, Brockunier & Co. chandeliers, *Crockery & Glass Journal.*

From a brochure of the J. H. Hobbs, Brockunier & Co.; note the Little Samuel figures in the chandelier.

CANDLESTICKS

ͻ. 3 CANDLESTICK
ate: Unknown, possibly 1870s
ͻlor: Crystal

ͺLVARY CANDLESTICKS
ate: 1883, possibly 1870s
ͺade Quotes:

ͼockery & Glass Journal, May, 1883:

Among the specialties at this factory are sacred candlesticks and her furniture used in Catholic churches all over the country....

ͻmments: Sacred or crucifix candlesticks were made by many glass fac-ries during the late 1800s. All are very similar and not easy to attribute specific companies. Hobbs No. 2 Calvary candlesticks have a cross on ch panel of the candle cup, which makes them easier to identify, but her companies may also have used this design. Usually the candlesticks ͼre made in crystal or opal.

Catalog illustration of No. 3 and Calvary candlesticks.

LAMPS

ͺPAL FOOTED LAMPS
ate: As early as 1870, possibly earlier
ͺade Quotes:

ͻe Crockery Journal, March 20, 1875:

We also observed a valuable improvement in the patent 'immovable socket for lamps.' The bowl and foot are connected with-ͺt the use of Plaster-Paris, by a series of notches and cross-notches fastening the parts together, and forming a better joint than ͼ the old method of cementing.

ͻe Crockery Journal, May 13, 1875:

Among many improvements peculiar to themselves we observed a very simple but effectual method of securing the connec-ͻn between lamp bowls and the foot stocks when the latter are of different material from the former, as in lamps with white ͼrcelain or metal stocks.

ͻockery & Glass Journal, July 5, 1883:

This firm has two new lines of lamps which have met with great success, and promise to ͼ a striking feature of the fall business.

ͻmments: The opal footed lamps made by J. H. Hobbs Brockunier & Co. are found with var-ͻus font designs and standards. On May 24, 1870, mechanical patent No. 103, 460 was grant-ͺ to John H. Hobbs. "My improvement consists in a metallic socket, fitting the pillar at one ͼd and the stem of the bowl at the other, and secured to each by pressing the metal into hor-ͻontal indentation in them, such socket being also provided with vertical ribs upon its interi-ͼ surface, fitting into corresponding grooves in the pillar and stem of the bowl, to prevent its ͼrning." This patented brass connector makes it possible to identify many of these early ͼmps.

Some lamps have blackberries or other fruit embossed on each corner of the base. The ͺ11 lamp is found with an opal or porcelain base and crystal or possibly a colored font. The ͺade quote, from July 1883, mentions two new lines of lamps, but we have been unable to ͼentify what lamps these were. In 1883, Hobbs Brockunier & Co. had not yet introduced ͻlka Dot, and it had been five years since the Tree of Life with Hand lamps had been intro-ͻced, so these are not the ones referred to. There are many varieties of both fonts and bases ͼund in these opal footed lamps.

Opal footed lamp, round font. Courtesy of the Huntington Museum of Art.

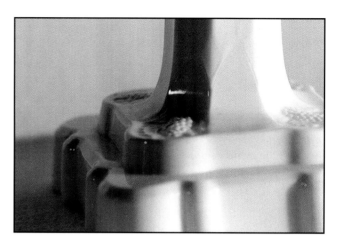

Opal footed lamp, ruby plain band font. Courtesy of the Huntington Museum of Art.

Detail of foot of lamp showing berry design. Courtesy of the Huntington Museum of Art.

Opal footed lamp with quatrefoil foot, plain font.

No. 7811 opal footed lamp, square foot, amber opalescent shade.

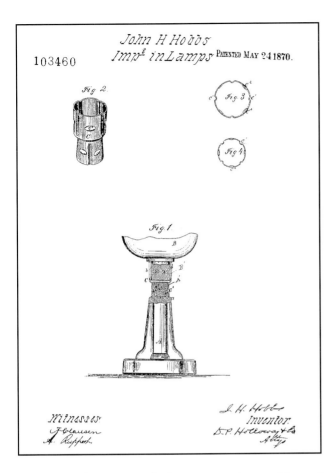

Illustration from patent for brass connector used in opal footed lamps.

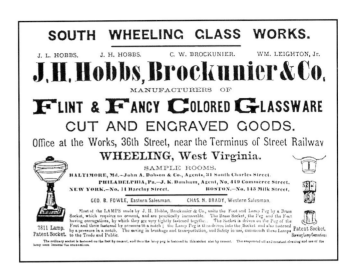

November 1875 ad illustrating No. 7811 lamp, *Crockery & Glass Journal.*

LITTLE SAMUEL

Date: 1877

Colors: Crystal and opal. Foot may be crystal, opal, or black.

Trade Quotes:

Crockery and Glass Journal, Feb., 22, 1877

The latest novelty they have in the lamp line has for the foot a figure of 'little Samuel' praying. This foot is either in plain or opal glass, the figure kneeling on a jet base.

Comments: This figure was introduced as a lamp base, but its use as a compote stem makes it far more available in that form. It has been found as a candlestick, with a bowl (the mold from Portland Glass) with "Davis" intertwined in the Tree of Life foliage, a paneled bowl, either cupped or flared, and with an epergne socket in the middle of its bowl. It has also been used as a figure on some of the chandeliers. See page 134 under Chandeliers.

Pieces	Prices
Candlestick	$300.00
Comport, flutes and punties	350.00
Epergne with vase	450.00
Lamp	350.00

Figure of Little Samuel, satin. Courtesy of Dean Six.

Little Samuel candlestick. Courtesy of
Huntington Museum of Art.

Lamp with Little Samuel base.
Courtesy of Dean Six.

Little Samuel comport, bowl with flutes and pun-
ties. Glass courtesy of Westward Ho Antiques. Photo
courtesy of Walt Adams.

Little Samuel epergne.

AND STEM LAMPS

Date: Ca. 1878

Colors: Crystal

Comments: Several fonts have been found on these lamps, some with engraving, some with pressed patterns. The lamp illustrated has the patent date of April 18, 1876, on the collar and "Pat'd. Sept. 29, 1863, Jan. 9, 1877" embossed on the font. See also Tree of Life With Hand in the Pattern section for compotes, cake stands, etc. (page 55).

Pieces	Prices
Lamp, kerosene, small	.$200.00
Lamp, kerosene, medium	.225.00
Lamp, kerosene, large	.300.00

Detail of etched font from Hand Stem lamp. Courtesy of Margaret Forkner.

Hand Stem lamp, etched font. Courtesy of Margaret Forkner.

Detail of hand stem.

FAIRY LAMPS, FIRE-FLY, AND ACORN LAMPS

Date: Fairy lamps — prior to 1887

    Acorn lamps — April, 1887

    Fire-fly lamps — July, 1887

Colors: Fairy Lamps — unknown colors

    Acorn Lamps — crystal, alabaster, old gold, canary, ruby, sapphire

    Fire-fly Lamps — crystal, old gold, canary, marine green, ruby, sapphire.

Trade Quotes:

Crockery & Glass Journal, April 28, 1887:

They have also ready for the trade a handsome new line of Acorn lamps in six colors, to take the place of the Fairy lamps.

Crockery and Glass Journal, July 14, 1887:

The fire-fly lamps in different colors are also popular with the trade....

Comments: These catalog illustrations are all we have been able to find of original material. We have not been able to find any illustrations of the Fairy Lamps. All of these lamps should be valued at $400.00 plus.

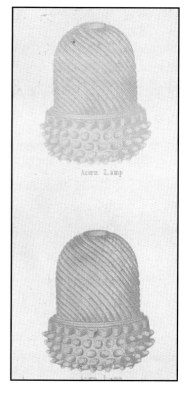

"Fire Fly" Lamp

Catalog illustration of the Acorn lamps in old gold, crystal, ruby, sapphire, canary, and alabaster.

No. 326

Date: May, 1889

Colors: Crystal, sapphire, old gold, possibly ruby; Windows: crystal opalescent, sapphire opalescent, ruby opalescent

Decorations: Frances on crystal, Windows opalescent

Trade Quotes:

Pottery & Glassware Reporter, May 23, 1889:

No. 326, the new line of fancy lamps of the Hobbs Glass Co., is a summer of the first water. These lamps are made in crystal opalescent, sapphire opalescent, ruby opalescent and plain crystal. There are five sizes, besides a night lamp.

Comments: Prices for plain crystal, deduct 50%. For sapphire and old gold add 20%. For crystal opalescent deduct, 40% from opalescent prices.

Pieces	Prices for Frances	Prices for Windows Opalescent
Lamp, hand, 0	$225.00	$375.00
Lamp, hand, A	250.00	400.00
Lamp, stand, A	250.00	400.00
Lamp, stand, A, No. 326½	250.00	400.00
Lamp, stand, B	275.00	450.00
Lamp, stand, C	300.00	500.00
Lamp, stand, D	325.00	550.00

Catalog illustrations of No. 326-0 Hand lamp and No. 326-A Hand lamp.

No. 326 Windows font lamp, sapphire opalescent. Courtesy of Huntington Museum of Art.

No. 338

Date: January, 1890

Colors: Crystal, may exist with ruby or sapphire fonts; Coral (seaweed) is found in crystal opalescent, sapphire opalescent, ruby opalescent,

Decorations: Crystal: Optic, No. 370 engraving, Gold etched. Coral (seaweed in opalescent colors).

Trade Quotes:

Pottery & Glassware Reporter, May 22, 1890:

Dealers should not fail to see the new fall lines of lamps of the Hobbs Glass Co., which are now ready. The lamps are just out, are very nobby and are bound to please the trade. The number of the new lamps is 338 and they are made in plain crystal optic, in gold etched and in coral made in three colors, red, white and blue. The shapes are unique and the effect is fine. Night and hand lamps are made to match and a decorated shade is made to match the etched goods. The 338 sewing lamp promised to be one of the most popular ones in the market. It is not only large but practical and is made so that the light is down close to the table — just where it is wanted. All of these lamps are a credit to the Hobbs Glass Co. and we predict a big sale.

Pottery & Glassware Reporter, June 19, 1890:

The crystal, optic, gold etched, white coral, blue coral and ruby coral lamps, in ten sizes, recently brought out by the Hobbs Glass Works, are selling very fast. Of their sewing lamps, made with Nos. 2 and 3 collars they are having a great run; also in the shades made to match the above goods.

Comments: The quote mentions 10 sizes of lamps, but does not specify what they were called. Also, it indicates that shades were available to match both the etched and opalescent wares. In 1892 the night lamp was advertised in amber and blue.

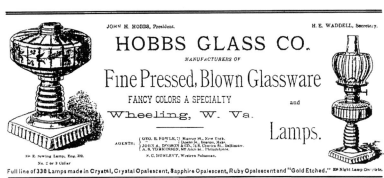

May 1890 ad illustrating No. 338 No. E Sewing lamp, engraved No. 310 and Night lamp with shade, *Crockery and Glass Journal.*

Prices for etched crystal, add 40%.

Pieces	Prices for Crystal	Prices for Coral Opalescent
Lamp, hand	$100.00	$225.00
Lamp, night	140.00	500.00
Lamp, sewing	100.00	400.00

No. 338 Night lamp without shade.

No. 341

Date: May, 1891

Colors: Crystal, crystal foot with sapphire or ruby fonts; daisy (Snowflake) opalescent: crystal opalescent, sapphire opalescent, ruby opalescent

Trade Quotes:

Pottery & Glassware Reporter, April , 1891:

A new line of lamps will be brought out by the Hobbs Glass Co. in a few days. They are square fluted, made in crystal opal, sapphire opal and ruby opal, with crystal feet, and a new combination, for which patent has been applied for.

Pottery & Glassware Reporter, May 7, 1891:

The new line of glass lamps of the Hobbs Glass Co. will be great sellers. The stand lamps are made in six sizes and the hand lamps in two sizes in crystal and opalescent colors, and in entirely new and novel designs. The bowls are square with round corners, fluted at the top and bottom, the figure being a daisy or clover leaf, giving the lamp a fine effect. The bowl and foot of these lamps are secured firmly together by a metal socket, which entirely obviates the excessive breakage attending all blown lamps. The socket is covered by a pressed glass sleeve, which completely conceals the metal, producing a brilliant effect and making practical an all glass lamp. The saving in breakage will make the dealer a handsome profit. For this device a patent has been applied for and no other factory can make it. The invention is an excellent one [which] makes the lamps much more desirable than other blown lamps for several reasons. The size stand lamps are as follows: 341½ A, 12 oz; 341B, 19 oz; 341C, (No. 2 collar) 30 oz.; 341D, Serving lamp [sewing] (No. 2 Collar) 30 oz.

No. 341 sewing lamp, ruby font, no glass collar.

mments: The *"daisy or clover leaf"* design mentioned in the trade quote refers to what are w called the Snowflake design in opalescent lamps. In addition to the standard square-aped fonts in Snowflake, a night lamp was made with a bell-shaped base and a matching . 338 Snowflake shade. Note that the trade quote mentions the volume of the lamps in nces, the only time we've found this done.

Night lamp with matching shade, ruby daisy (Snowflake) opalescent. Courtesy of Ray and Jennie Goldsberry.

r crystal lamps with ruby or other colored fonts, add 50%.

eces	Prices for Crystal	Prices for Snowflake Opalescent
amp, hand O (Flat)	$75.00	$450.00
amp, hand A (Footed)	75.00	450.00
amp, sewing D, No. 3 collar	125.00	950.00
amp, stand A	90.00	575.00
amp, stand A, No. 341½	90.00	575.00
amp, stand B	110.00	625.00
amp, stand C, No. 2 collar	110.00	650.00
amp, stand D, No. 2 collar	120.00	750.00
amp, night, with shade (unknown number)		1,000.00

GLOBES AND SHADES

rockery & Glass Journal, November 8, 1883:
While in the factory yesterday I was shown a variety of globes of most handsome design and still handsomer finish that this firm as just begun to manufacture. They are intended for use in parlors and small halls. Most of them are of the finest glass and are very xpensive.

rockery & Glass Journal, November, 1884:
The lamp and gas globes of various designs and beauty of finish are some of the prominent new features of the sample rooms.

This last quote, November 1884, probably deals with shades of No. 101 Daisy & Button. The previous quote (November 1883) may refer to olka Dot, but is unclear.

rockery & Glass Journal, January, 1885:
The opalescent ware will be one of the leading features of the new goods. Your correspondent noticed some designs in globes in colored glass hat are at once novel and beautiful. The shapes are as various as the colors, but all are attractive. These globes are in most instances rather xpensive compared, of course, with the common goods.

rockery & Glass Journal, March, 1885:
An umbrella-shaped dome gas shade of the same ware [Polka Dot, alabaster white glass] … is also one of the new varieties... A large hand-omely designed hall light in polka-dot in colors will be on the market in a few days. The rich colors of the shade shown up by a strong gas or oil ight give the shade an attractive appearance. A new cylindrical-shaped globe seven inches by nine in colors is in process of manufacture.

Crockery & Glass Journal, February, 1886:

Some exceedingly attractive shades tipped with brilliant ruby that gradually fades into a rich cream color or crystal. nev fail to attract attention....

These are probably the first Dew Drop (Hobnail) shades.

Pottery and Glassware Reporter, July 7, 1887:

This firm has just gotten out a new and unique line of shades in seven different colors, made in the shape of an acorn ar called Acorn gas shades. They are made to fit any gas holder and all who have seen them are highly pleased over them. The seve colors are alabaster, turquoise, canary, yellow, ruby, pink, green and amber. We have not seen these "Acorn" globes.

Comments: Globes and shades were an extremely important branch of Hobbs, Brockunier & Co.'s production. Major patterns suc as Daisy and Button, Windows, Polka Dot, and Dew Drop all had matching shades. Polka Dot, and Dew Drop were especially used i many varieties of globes and shades.

While Hobbs, Brockunier & Co. used shades and globes with their own lamps, the primary market for them was to the manu facturers of lamp fittings (the metal) who then marketed the entire lamp as their own product. This secondary market masquera ing as a primary manufacturer makes the identification of shades and globes difficult today. This is especially true since many glas companies produced shades and globes. Since the shades and globes were made for specific fittings, all companies made the sam basic sizes for their customers.

Polka Dot and Hobnail shades and globes are especially difficult to properly attribute as to manufacturer since so many compa nies made very similar shapes and colors. The following shades and globes have appeared in original Hobbs, Brockunier & Co. adve tisements and catalogs. Prices given are for shades only because fixtures and mountings vary greatly in quality and desirability.

LITHOPHANE LAMP SHADES

Date: 1871

Colors: Porcelain (opal)

Comments: Patent No. 114,140, Granted April 26, 1871, to J. H. Hobbs, C. W. Brockunier and W. Leighton, Jr.

This invention relates to shades for lamps, gas lights, and other lights; and... It consists in forming upon the surfaces of such shades, when made of hot-pressed porcelain or other semi-opaque and semi-liquid or vitreous substances, landscapes, vines, branch- es of trees, flowers, and other figures, by causing portions thereof to be of greater thickness than are other portions of the same fig- ures, in order that, when the light is caused to shine through the shades or the figures formed upon them, it shall be allowed to pass more freely at some points than at others, and thus gives the figure somewhat the appearance of a painting, the thicker por- tions appearing much darker than the thinner portions when viewed from the side which is opposite to the one upon which the light is shining.

This patent covered the concept of making an entire litho- phane shade in the final form, as opposed to making flat plates which could be mounted in a metal frame to become a shade.

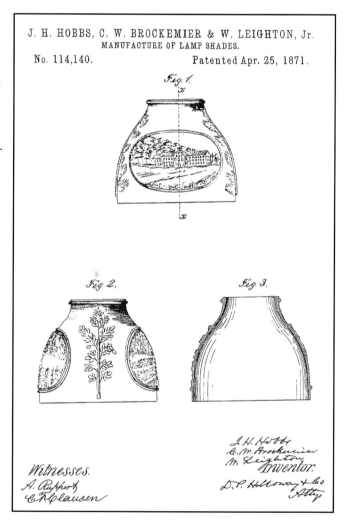

Illustration of lithophane lamp shade from patent.

No. 101 DAISY & BUTTON

Date: October, 1884

Colors: Old gold, sapphire, marine green, canary, ruby, amberina

Comments: Gillinder & Sons of Philadelphia also made various Daisy and Button shades in similar styles and colors. Other companies may also have made similar shades. Prices given are for all colors except amberina which should be priced 100% more.

Pieces	Prices
Shade, bowl, 4"	$175.00
Shade, bowl, 5"	175.00
Shade, crown, 5"	175.00
Shade, pan, 4"	175.00
Shade, pan, 5"	175.00
Shade, pan, crimped, 4"	175.00
Shade, pan, crimped, 5"	175.00

Catalog illustration of No. 101 Daisy & Button shades and No. 1700 Polka Dot shade in old gold, sapphire, marine green, canary, and ruby.

No. 323 DEW DROP

Date: About 1886

Colors: Ruby, ruby opalescent, crystal, old gold, sapphire, sapphire opalescent, canary opalescent, crystal opalescent.

Comments: See page 150 for 10" dome shade.

Pieces	Prices
Dome, 10"	$ 250.00
Dome, 14"	250.00
Shade, crimped, 4"	250.00
Shade, crimped, 5"	250.00
Shade, pan, 4"	250.00
Shade, pan, 5"	250.00

Catalog page of No. 323 4" and 5" pan and crimped shades, various colors.

No. 323 Dew Drop pan shade, Frances decoration. Courtesy of Huntington Museum of Art.

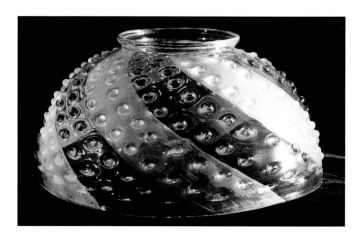

No. 323 Dew Drop dome shade, alternating amber stain and satin swirls. Courtesy of Huntington Museum of Art.

Hanging lamp with No. 323 Dew Drop dome shade, Frances decoration. Courtesy of Mary Ann and Dick Krauss.

No. 323 Dew Drop dome shade, rubina, clear portion satin. Courtesy of Mary Ann and Dick Krauss.

No. 325 HOBBS' OPAL SWIRL

Date: September, 1888

Colors: Ruby and sapphire opalescent, crystal opalescent possible.

Pieces	Prices
Dome, 10"	$375.00
Dome, 14"	375.00
Globe, crown, 4"	225.00
Globe, crown, 5"	225.00
Shade, tulip toilet, 4"	225.00
Shade, tulip toilet, 5"	225.00

Catalog illustrations of No. 325 Hobbs' Opal Swirl shades, 4" and 5" tulip toilet shades and 11" dome shades.

No. 326 WINDOWS

Date: January, 1889

Colors: Crystal opalescent, sapphire opalescent, ruby opalescent

Pieces	Prices Ruby opalescent Sapphire opalescent
Globe, electric	$250.00
Globe, squat, 5"	300.00
Globe, squat, 7½"	300.00
Shade, 4"	300.00
Shade, crimped, 5"	450.00
Shade, crown, 4"	375.00
Shade, dome, 10"	450.00
Shade, dome, 14"	500.00
Shade, toilet, 5"	425.00
Shade, tulip, 4"	425.00

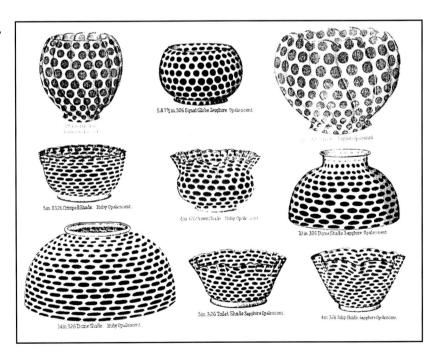

Catalog illustrations of No. 326 Windows shades and globes.

The following shades and globes are priced for ruby or ruby opalescent. Most shades and globes are very difficult to find and so are quite expensive. Other colors may or may not be less than prices listed.

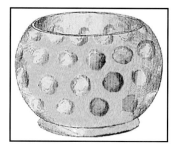

No. 1695 POLKA DOT

Date: Ca. late 1884
Colors: Old gold, sapphire, marine green, canary, ruby
See page 145 for illustration. Prices given are for ruby and ruby opalescent.

Pieces	Prices
Globe, 5" x 7½"	$225.00

No. 1695 Polka Dot globe.

No. 1700 POLKA DOT

Date: Ca. late 1884
Colors: Old gold, sapphire, marine green, canary, ruby
See page146 for illustration. Prices given are for ruby and ruby opalescent.

Pieces	Prices
Shade, 4"	$300.00

(Unnumbered) POLKA DOT

Date: March, 1885 for cylinder globe; March, 1885 for "umbrella domes"
Colors: Old gold, sapphire, marine green, canary, ruby
Prices given are for ruby and ruby opalescent.

Pieces	Prices
Globe, cylinder, 7" x 9"	$225.00
Shade, dome, 10"	275.00
Shade, dome, 14"	350.00

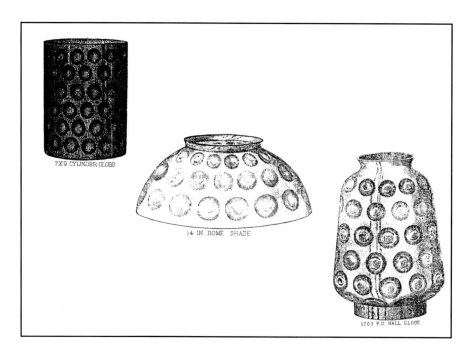

Catalog illustration of Polka Dot cylinder globe, dome shade, and No. 1703 hall globe.

w Drop (now called Hobnail) shades were first mentioned in Hobbs, Brockunier & Co. announcements in 1884. Hobbs made any varieties of these shades and globes, in different styles and different colors and color combinations. Most shapes of shades d globes are not unique to Hobbs. Many other companies also made Dew Drop shades in the same shapes and sizes as Hobbs, rockunier & Co. Prices given are for ruby and ruby opalescent.

o. 1703 DEW DROP
ate: Ca. 1886
olors: Old gold, sapphire, canary, marine green, ruby

Pieces	Prices
all globe	. . . . $350.00

o. 1706 DEW DROP
ate: Ca. 1886
olors: canary opalescent with red edge; crystal opalescent with red edge; ruby opalescent; Canary opalescent; Crystal opalescent. And a variety of other colors" according to catalog page.

Pieces	Prices
Globe, 4"	. . . . $400.00
Globe, 5"	. . . . .400.00

Catalog illustration of Nos. 1706, 1707, and 1708 Dew Drop globes in canary opalescent, red edge; crystal opalescent, red edge; canary opalescent; ruby opalescent; and crystal opalescent.

No. 1707 DEW DROP

Date: Ca. 1886
Colors: Canary opalescent with red edge; crystal opalescent with red edge; ruby opalescent; canary opalescent; crystal opalescent

Pieces	Prices
Globe, 4"	$ 200.00
Globe, 5"	.200.00

Pair of No. 1707 Dew Drop globes in crystal opalescent with red edge. Courtesy of Huntington Museum of Art.

No. 1708 DEW DROP

Date: Ca. 1886
Colors: Canary opalescent with red edge; crystal opalescent with red edge; ruby opalescent; canary opalescent; crystal opalescent

Pieces	Prices
Globe, 4"	$400.00 – 500.00
Globe, 5"	.400.00 – 500.00

No. 1709 DEW DROP

Date: Ca. 1886
Colors: Canary opalescent with red edge; crystal opalescent with red edge; ruby opalescent; canary opalescent; crystal opalescent; old gold opalescent, plated inside with canary. "These globes made for 4 in. or 5 in. holder. In a great variety of colors" according to catalog page.

Pieces	Prices
Globe, 4"	$300.00
Globe, 5"	.300.00

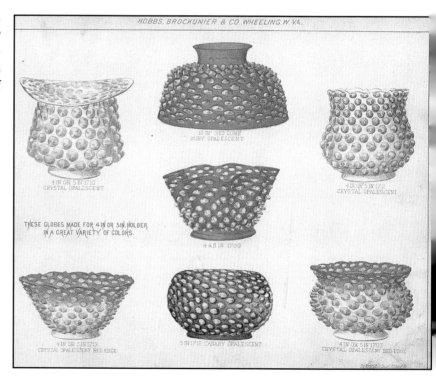

Catalog page of Nos. 323, 1707, 1709, 1710, 1711, 1712, and 1713 Dew Drop globes in ruby opalescent, crystal opalescent, crystal opalescent red edge, and canary opalescent.

No. 1709 Dew Drop 4" globe, old gold opalescent plated with canary.

o. 1710 DEW DROP

ate: Ca. 1886

olors: Canary opalescent with red edge; crystal opalescent with red edge; ruby opalescent; canary opalescent; crystal opalescent

Pieces	Prices
Globe, 4"	$400.00
Globe, 5"	.400.00

o. 1711 DEW DROP

Date: Ca. 1885 or 1886

Colors: Canary opalescent with red edge; crystal opalescent with red edge; ruby opalescent; canary opalescent; crystal opalescent

Pieces	Prices
Globe, 4"	$225.00
Globe, 5"	.225.00

No. 1712 DEW DROP

Date: Ca. 1885 or 1886

Colors: Canary opalescent with red edge; crystal opalescent with red edge; ruby opalescent; canary opalescent; crystal opalescent

Pieces	Prices
Globe, 5"	$225.00

No. 1713 DEW DROP

Date: Ca. 1885 or 1886

Colors: Canary opalescent with red edge; crystal opalescent with red edge; ruby opalescent; canary opalescent; crystal opalescent

Pieces	Prices
Globe, 4"	$225.00
Globe, 5"	.225.00

No. 2384 DEW DROP
Date: Ca. 1885 or 1886
Colors: Ruby

Pieces   Prices
Cylinder.........$350.00

Catalog illustrations on Nos. 2803, 2384, 2387, 2587, and 2590, cylinders and hall globe.

No. 2387 DEW DROP
Date: Ca. 1885 or 1886
Colors: Ruby

Pieces   **Prices**
Cylinder.........$350.00

No. 2584
Date: Unknown, but probably about 1885
Colors: Rubina verde opalescent, probably other colors

Pieces   **Prices**
Cylinder.........$250.00

ɔ. 2590

ate: Unknown, but probably about 1885
olors: Ruby opalescent, ruby
mments: 5⁷/₈" fitter fits Parker No. 1090, Ansonia No. 367, HBH No. 1522, and B&H No. 460.

eces	Prices
ade, 4¹/₂" fitter, 7¹/₂" diameter, 8 ¹/₄" high	$275.00
ade, 5⁷/₈" fitter, 9¹/₄" diameter, 9" high	.275.00

No. 2590 Hall Globe in ruby, top rim on this globe is metal.

No. 2803 DEW DROP

Date: Ca. 1885 or 1886
Colors: Ruby

Pieces	Prices
Cylinder.	$225.00

Dew Drop cylinder, old gold.

Unknown numbers:
Dew Drop cylinder, old gold, 7" diameter, 9" high
Ribbed Swirl cylinder, rubina verde opalescent, 5" diameter, 7" high

Ribbed Swirl cylinder, rubina verde opalescent in wrought iron frame.

⌇Miscellaneous Pieces and Groups⌇

The goods made here are as varied in pattern as they are in kinds...a full line of the goods of all grades, styles and designs; some in plain glass, and others cut and engraved in the most elegant and charming patterns. The stem ware, goblets, wines, etc., rival a soap bubble's transparency.... Finely engraved crystal ware of all kinds is made here, from table sets down to exquisite paper weights and ink stands.... The company...are bringing out novelties constantly.

Crockery & Glass Journal, February, 1887

They show lamps, decanters of all shapes, celery glasses, pickles, wines, champagnes, pitchers, footed goods, druggists ware, flower vases, ink stands, toilet sets, etc....

Crockery & Glass Journal, July, 1877

Hobbs, Brockunier & Co. made many items which do not fit into patterns. Many of these are groups of items, such a molasses cans or individual salts. Some are single items or very short lines which are not major patterns.

Many of these wares were made very early in the history of the company, and continued to be in the line until the end. Som were also continued by U. S. Glass. Many of these staple items are so plain as to be indistinguishable from the products of othe companies. We have included them to show the variety of products made by Hobbs, Brockunier & Co.

WHIMSEY BELLS

Glassworkers have always made whimsies on their own time. These bells resemble other items made by Hobbs, Brockunier & Co., and cannot otherwise be attributed. The bell on the left has the same swirls in the glass as do many other pieces of art glas made by the company, notably the No. 205 bowls and some of the lamp globes.

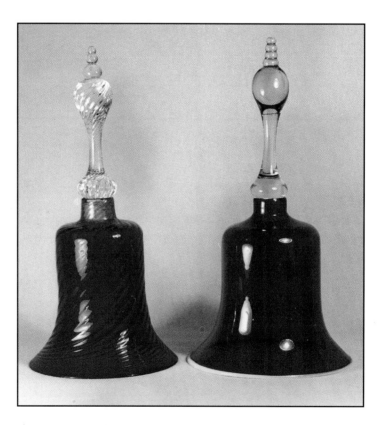

Two ruby bells of the type made by workers at Hobbs, Brockunier & Co.

BAR AND BITTER BOTTLES

These bottles were part of Hobbs, Brockunier & Co.'s stock in trade. With minor exceptions they are unexceptional and indis-tinguishable from the wares of other companies. Some or all of them could have been ordered with engravings or with the names various liquors engraved on them. No. 89 was available is several styles: Pearl, Butler, Choke Neck, and Optic. See Polka Dot, page 70 for an illustration of this in Blue Optic.

The No. 18 syrup bottle may have either a friction or two piece top of metal.

Only the No. 309 bitters is identifiable from other companies wares. It was continued through the life of the company and last appears in Coral (Seaweed) opalescence.

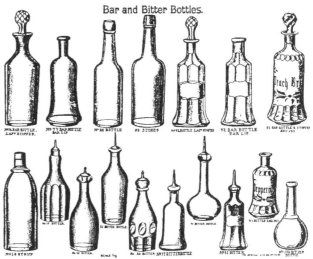

Catalog page of various bar bottles; L to R, top row: Nos, 76, 77, 88, 89 Stokes, 92, 92, 93, Engraved No. 263; L to R, bottom row: No. 18 syrup, bitters Nos. 14, 18, 75, 22, 77, 91, 93, Engraved No. 263, and 309.

MOLASSES CANS

These cans are now called syrups. Hobbs, Brockunier & Co. held two patents on the attachment of the lid to the glass body of the molasses can. Many of these cans may be found with the term "Pat'd" on the glass near the attachment of the lid. Some of these were continued by U. S. Glass until 1904 or later. The No. 96, now called Hercules Pillar, can be found in several of Hobbs, Brockunier & Co.'s colors, which leads us to conclude that many of these molasses cans may be found in color.

"We saw at Collins and Wright's the model of J. H. Hobbs, Brockunier & Co.'s new cream lid. It is much flatter than the old lid, and has an engraved belt around the top.... They will be manufactured in white metal and in colors. 600 dozen will be placed on the market as soon as they are ready...." — *American Pottery and Glassware Reporter*, June, 1881

The two covered creams shown were probably made for hotel or boarding house use. Since the numbers are not consecutive, there probably were other styles.

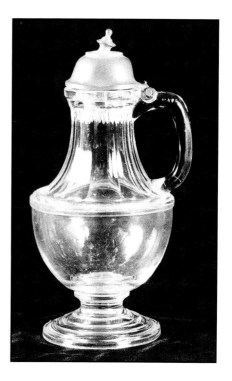

No. 94 Molasses can, ¹/₂ pint.

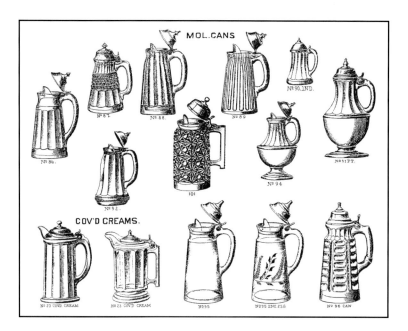

Catalog page of various molasses cans: L to R, top row: Nos. 86, 87, 88, 89, 90 individual, 91 pint; L to R, middle row: Nos. 92, 101, 94; L to R, bottom row: covered creams, Nos. 20, 23; molasses cans; Nos. 95, 95 Engraved No. 258 and 96.

Catalog illustration of No. 324 Dew Drop molasses can.

No. 96 Hercules Pillar molasses cans, old gold, sapphire.

No. 91 PITCHERS, BLOWN

These tankard pitchers were made in crystal and ruby and possibly other colors. It is interesting to note that these were listed st size 6½ oz. through eighth size, 61 oz. These all were available with shell handles and also listed as "ice jugs." One catalog ustration shows what is probably a ground pontil in the center of the bottom.

eces	Prices
g	.$250.00

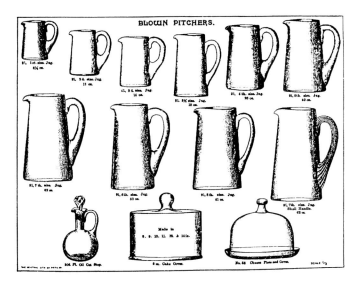

Catalog page of No. 91 blown pitchers. L to R, bottom row: No. 306 oil, cake cover, No. 53 cheese plate and cover.

No. 91 pitcher, ruby.

CAKE COVER

"The cake stands with covers (in crystal) are very handsome pieces. The covers of these are marked for their lightness, and he stands altogether are better finished, and cheaper than any heretofore made." — Crockery & Glass Journal, February, 1877.

This was made in six sizes from 8" to 14" diameter, for use on any salver or plate. Examples have been seen with a turned up ower rim which matches that on the No. 53 cheese covers.

For the No. 53 cheese plate and cover, see Flamingo Habitat. No 306 oil is shown with Coral/Peach Blow.

STEMWARE

Hobbs, Brockunier & Co. had several lines of stemware which they produced for many years. Some were full lines while oth-rs seem to have been only single items. It is unknown if any of these were made in colors other than crystal.

Full lines of stemware include No. 82, engraved No. 89½, No. 258 and No. 284; No. 103 (Hobbs' version of the Mitchell pat-ern) engraved with No. 89½ band and No. 237; No. 106; and No. 110.

Catalog page of various stemware. L to R, top row: No. 91 goblet; No. 103 goblet, champagne, claret, wine, cordial; L to R, middle row: No. 106 goblet, champagne, claret, wine; No. 110 goblet, champagne, claret, wine, cordial; L to R, bottom row: No. 98 cocktail, No. 114 cocktail, No. 105 Rhine wine, No. 75 lemonade PL. handle, No. 75 lemonade, shell handle.

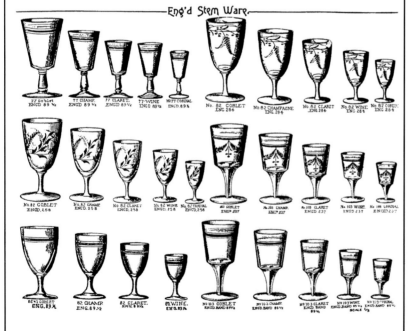

Catalog page of various stemware including engravings. L to R, top row: No. 77 goblet, champagne, claret, wine, cordial Engraved No. 89½; No 82 goblet, champagne, claret, wine, cordial Engraved No. 284; L to R, middle row: No. 82 goblet, champagne, claret, wine, cordial Engraved No. 258; No. 103 goblet, champagne, claret, wine, cordial Engraved No. 237; L to R, bottom row: No. 82 goblet, champagne, claret, wine; No. 103 goblet, champagne, claret, wine, cordial all Engraved Band No. 89½.

SALTS

Hobbs, Brockunier & Co. made several open salts, in table and individual sizes, as did most other glass manufacturers of the ~~ne~~. The salts illustrated in Hobbs, Brockunier & Co. catalogs were also made by many other companies and would be impossible ~~attribute~~. It is unknown if any were made in colors. In addition to open salts, it is now known that Hobbs, Brockunier & Co. ~~ade~~ the Alden Christmas salts after the close of the New England Glass Co.

Christmas salt, ruby. Courtesy of Marilyn and Charles Lockwood.

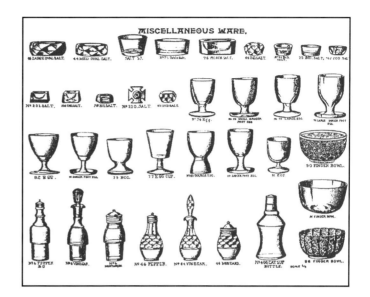

Catalog page of miscellaneous ware. L to R, top row: Open salts, Nos. 44 large oval, 44 medium oval, 53, 75 table, 76 block, 44 individual, 53 individual, 75 individual, 200; L to R, second row: individual salts Nos. 201, 204, 205, 210, and 211; egg cups Nos. 74, 74 small saucer foot, 74 large, 74 large saucer foot; L to R, third row: egg cups Nos. 82, 82 saucer foot, 75, 77, 89 double, 89 saucer foot, 91, No. 90 Tree of Life finger bowl; L to R, bottom row: caster bottles No. 6 pepper, vinegar, mustard; No. 44 pepper, vinegar, mustard; No. 400 catsup bottle; No. 96 finger bowl; No. 98 Tree of Life finger bowl.

EGG CUPS

With the exception of the No. 77, these egg cups would be impossible to attribute. It is unknown if any were made in colors. Nos. 74 large and small egg cups were continued by U. S. Glass and assigned numbers 14,007 and 14,008.

339 Egg

Catalog illustration of No. 339 egg cup.

CASTER BOTTLES

Hobbs, Brockunier & Co. made at least two styles of caster bottles, No. 6 and No. 44 in addition to ones in No. 101 Daisy Button. These were made to fit silver-plate holders. No. 6 probably came with various engravings, while the No. 44 may have co[...] cut over pressed in addition to pressed honeycomb. Both of these sets may have been made in color.

No. 400 CATSUP BOTTLE

This shape may be definitive enough to identify as a Hobbs, Brockunier & Co. product. It appears to have a two piece me[...] top, and it may have been made in color.

TUMBLERS

Most of the tumblers shown in old Hobbs, Brockunier & Co. catalogs are of standard shapes and designs which would be dif[...] cult to attribute to only one company. We are including them to show the types of standard wares made by the company. Most these tumblers would sell for about $10.00 to $25.00 in crystal. It is unknown if any were made in colors.

No. 288 is possibly identifiable, from its square shape and horizontal bands on the sides.

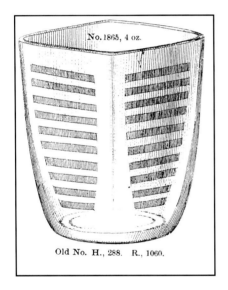

Catalog illustration of the No. 288 4 oz. bar glass.

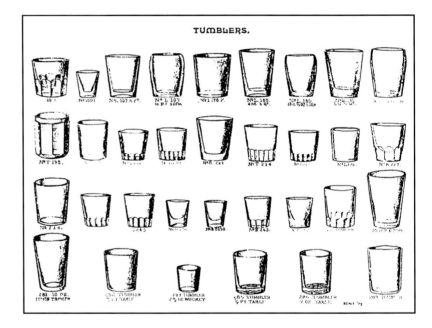

Catalog illustration of various tumblers. L to R, top row: Nos. 10F, 0101, L107, L107¹/₂ pint soda, L176, L180 small ¹/₃ qt., L180 small ¹/₃ qt. soda, L181 large ¹/₃ qt., and L181 large ¹/₃ qt. soda; L to R, second row: Nos. T195, L212, L210, B221, T224, L225, L226, and B227: L to R, third row: Nos. 234, 243, L243, B250, B0250, B263, B267, 275, and 276 lemon tumbler: L to R, bottom row: Nos. 281 10 oz. lemon tumbler, 232, 233, 285, 286, and 289.

CELERIES

At one time celeries were a standard feature on dining tables, as were table sets. Some of these celeries were all that were left
earlier patterns made by the company when this catalog was printed. For instance, Nos. 53 and 77 were certainly parts of exten-
e lines, No. 20, Huber, and No 74 may have been also.

20 CELERY.   No 53, CELERY.   No 74 Celery   77 CELERY

Catalog illustrations of Nos. 20, 53, 74, and 77 celeries.

CRUETS AND OILS

No. 315 was available with a cut neck and a cut star on top of the blown stopper. The Pullman oil was made with "cut neck,
utes (about the base) and (lapidary) stopper." These pieces appear only in a Hobbs Glass Co. catalog, ca. 1890, however, it is likely
ey were also made earlier.

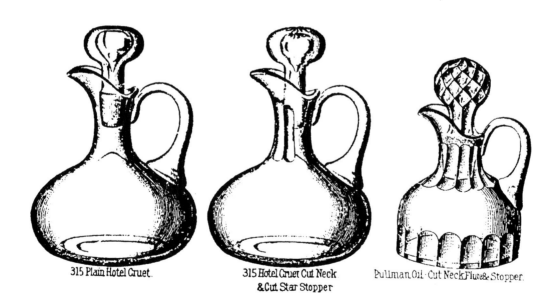

315 Plain Hotel Cruet.   315 Hotel Cruet Cut Neck   Pullman Oil Cut Neck Flute & Stopper.
&Cut Star Stopper

Catalog illustrations of No. 315 plain hotel cruet; hotel cruet cut neck, and cut star stopper;
Pullman oil, cut neck, flute, and stopper.

No. 95 FINGER BOWL

Date: From 1890 catalog, probably made earlier
Colors: Crystal, old gold, sapphire, ruby
Nos. 90 and 98 finger bowls are listed in the pattern section under Tree of Life.

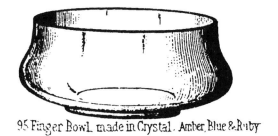

Catalog illustration of No. 95 finger bowl.

STRAW JAR AND COVER
It is not known if this was available in any color other than crystal.

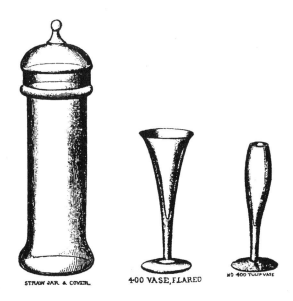

Catalog illustrations of straw jar and cover and No. 400
vase, flared and tulip.

VASES
No. 400 vases were available in two forms, flared and tulip. It is not known if these were available in any color other than crystal.

WATER BOTTLES

The No. 5 water bottle was available with cut star on the bottom and cut flutes on the neck. No. 340 was available with cut
tes on the neck. It is unknown if these were made in colors other than crystal.

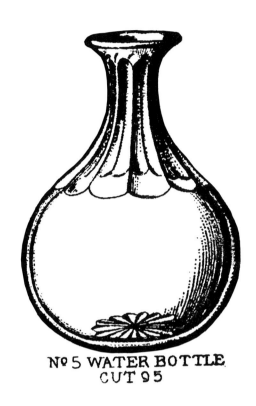

Catalog illustration of No. 5 water bottle, cut
No. 95.

Catalog illustrations of No. 340 water bottle,
cut neck.

⟨Confusing Patterns and Pieces⟩

During our research, we have encountered many patterns and types of glass attributed to Hobbs, Brockunier & Co. We haste to state that, especially in the case of unusual glass types, Hobbs, Brockunier & Co. certainly had the expertise to produce such wares, and may have done so. We would like to attribute some of these to the company; but with lack of evidence, we feel it more prudent to exclude them at this time. The following list contains some of these patterns which we have not been able to document as truly Hobbs and so have not included them in this book. It also includes some look-alikes and copies of Hobbs' patterns and other pieces which might be misleading. There are many others which could have been included, but we feel the following cause collectors the most problems in identification.

UNATTRIBUTABLE

"Mother-of-Pearl," or air-trap glass pieces have been attributed to Hobbs, Brockunier & Co. Joseph Webb, of Phoenix Glass developed the process for making air-trap glass in 1885. It is likely that Hobbs, Brockunier & Co. made some glass of this type, only as an experiment. Reportedly, shards of this type of glass were recovered from the factory site. Until documented Hobbs shapes in this type of glass are found, we feel it is likely that most air-trap glass was made by other companies.

William Heacock attributed several blown patterns to Hobbs, Brockunier & Co. based upon color, generally amberina and rubina. He failed to take into account Libbey's nearly exclusive right to amberina in blown ware, and the many imitations which have been imported since it became popular. To our knowledge, Hobbs, Brockunier made only pressed amberina, as per their agreement with Libbey.

We have found no overshot glass in Hobbs' shapes. Overshot has been widely confused with Hobbs' Craquelle due to illustrations in old ads which were unclear. We have seen pitchers similar to the No. 91 pitchers and matching tumblers in overshot, but these shapes are not distinctive enough to attribute only to Hobbs. The Boston & Sandwich Glass Co. did make much overshot glass, and also much has been imported, even recently.

We have also not found any documentation of the Diamond Quilted optic as being a Hobbs' product. The celery shown is similar in shape to those made by Hobbs, but the toothpick/vase shown is not a recognized Hobbs' form.

A vase and toothpick holder/small vase in Diamond Quilted with a copy of Pomona type decoration. Courtesy of the Huntington Museum of Art.

Pieces of mother-of-pearl glassware. Courtesy of the Huntington Museum of Art.

MISATTRIBUTIONS

Minnie Watson Kamm reported having found a pressed pattern she called "Diamond and Sunburst" in a Hobbs' catalog from e 1880s. That catalog was not available for our study. The ware she illustrates does not have the quality of Hobbs, Brockunier & .'s glass, and so we feel this pattern is not Hobbs.

Several authors have attributed a Klondike pattern to Hobbs, Brockunier & Co., even listing No. 321 as its original number. We el that this is in error, as we have found no original sources for No. 321 in Hobbs' material.

For many years an optic effect called Wheeling Drape has been attributed to Hobbs, Brockunier & Co., but its shapes and col- s do not correspond with other Hobbs' shapes and colors. We feel this is not a Hobbs, Brockunier & Co. product.

The popular Acorn salt shakers and toothpick holders have been attributed to Hobbs. The only references we have seen to corn in Hobbs' glass are the Acorn night lights and globes. Again, the Acorn salts/toothpicks come in a variety of colors not usual- associated with Hobbs, Brockunier & Co., and so we feel they are another company's product. Also, this is true of the shaded nk to white opaque glass in which they are often found.

The pattern called Gonterman Swirl usually has a patent date embossed in the glass. Research shows that on this date a patent as issued to Hobbs, Brockunier & Co. dealing with joining the bowl and stem of a goblet. According to other researchers, Gonter- an Swirl was made by Ætna Glass Co. in Bellaire, Ohio, in the mid 1880's. It may have been made under license from Hobbs, rockunier & Co., but it was not made by them.

Diamond and Sunburst cream.

Acorn salt shaker, black opaque. Courtesy of Mary Ann and Dick Krauss.

Tumbler, pink to white opaque glass.

SIMILAR PATTERNS

Not all Polka Dot was made by Hobbs, Brockunier & Co. Geo. Duncan & Sons of Pittsburgh, among others, made a full line of Polka Dot, both blown and pressed. They also made a line of jugs, or pitchers, which resemble Hobbs' No. 319 jugs with square tooled tops. Fortunately, the applied handles differ slightly between the two companies. The handles on Duncan's pitchers are more nearly circular while Hobbs' are more oval in shape.

Polka Dot covered cheese made by Geo. Duncan & Sons, Pittsburgh in 1884.

Rubina verde Polka Dot jug, Geo. Duncan & Sons. Courtesy Jo and Bob Sanford.

The cheese cover illustrated below is considerably heavier than the Hobbs' product. Also, the bottom edge is ground but not polished. The knob, or finial, is ground and polished, as are some Hobbs' finials, but this one is considerably larger and is crystal while the finials on Hobbs' cheese covers are the same color as the bodies.

The pattern Hand and Ball closely resembles Hobbs, Brockunier & Co.'s No. 98, Tree of Life with Hand. The ball, instead of being smooth, is stippled and has tiny six-pointed stars on it. The body of the pattern is covered with pressed swirls rather than the frosted effect of Tree of Life. This pattern is probably an European import and has been found in crystal and amber.

Polka Dot cheese cover in blue with crystal faceted finial.

Hand and Ball covered butter, amber. Courtesy of Linda Sandell.

In 1898 Harry Northwood, in his own plant in Indiana, PA, developed a pattern he called "Klondyke" in honor of the site of the —ld discovery in the Yukon. This is a pressed pattern consisting of shell feet with simulated rigaree above them, a simulated daisy —unt in the center of the bottom, fans about the top edge, and threading around the body. Handled pieces have pressed handles —mulating shell or reeded applied handles. With the exceptions of the top edge fans and the threading, this could easily be a copy Hobbs' No. 230 Neapolitan pattern, and while it should never confuse anyone, we feel it should be noted as a similar pattern.

Simulated flower prunt on bottom of Klondyke.

Klondyke cream from Northwood ad, 1898.

While Hobbs, Brockunier & Co. did make the majority of spangled wares in this country, there were others making them, too. —hese two pieces of pink spangled resemble Hobbs' pieces, but because the patterns and colors are not contemporary we feel they —ere made by some other factory. The shape is only similar to No. 326 Swirl, not identical. Also, when Spangled was being made, —o. 326 hadn't been developed. By the time No. 326 was being made, the company had been reorganized and Spangled was no —onger being made.

Pink spangled tumbler and oil.

Daisy and Button, a pressed copy of the cut glass Russian pattern, arguably has been made by most companies who ma[de] pressed glass. The Star Bowl, a name Hobbs, Brockunier & Co. applied to their large bowl and comport, was also probably a copy [of] a particular cut glass piece. Several companies copied this style of bowl, with plain radial grooves, and with or without a foot.

BERRY DISHES.

Catalog page showing Cloverleaf bowl by Richards & Hartley, ca. 1885.

Gillinder and Sons, of Philadelphia, was one of the companies which made a Daisy and Button pattern. The table set in th[is] pattern was remarkably like that of Hobbs, Brockunier & Co. The only differences were that the Gillinder set was oval while Hobb[s] was round, and the Gillinder set had metal, rather than glass, finials. Two berry sets in amberina, one diamond shaped and th[e] other square, were thought to be Hobbs because of the Libbey license allowing Hobbs to make amberina. These two berry sets we[re] Gillinder's, as they appear in a catalog of that company.

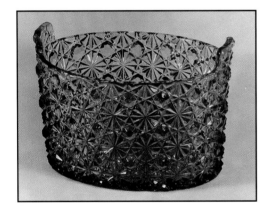

Catalog illustration of No. 406 Daisy and Button flared bowl, Gillinder & Sons, ca. 1886. Courtesy of Dorothy Lee Jones.

Daisy and Button oval sugar without lid, amber, Gillinder & Sons, ca. 1886

Hobnail. This Hobnail pattern is similar to Hobbs' Dew Drop. This pattern has small, tiny hobs on the top portion of the ruffle which Hobbs' does not. The ruffle on the tops of these pieces is entirely pressed while on Hobbs' pieces it was usually hand tooled. It may not be confusing to collectors, but some pieces are remarkably similar to the Hobbs' pattern.

Hobnail cream, crystal opalescent.

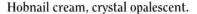

☙ Bibliography ☙

American Pottery & Glass Reporter, various issues, Journal of Industry Co, Pittsburgh, PA: 1883 – 1888.

Baker, Gary Everett. *The Flint Glass Industry in Wheeling, West Virginia, 1829 – 1865.* master's thesis, 1986.

Baker, Gary E., et. al. *Wheeling Glass 1839 – 1939.* Wheeling WV: Oglebay Institute,1994.

Bredehoft, Neila M., George A. Fogg, and Francis C. Maloney. *Early Duncan Glassware.* Boston, MA: 1987.

China, Glass and Lamps, various issues. Pittsburgh, PA: Barker, Wiberg & Co., 1892 – 1904.

Crockery & Glass Journal, various issues, New York, NY: Geo. Whittemore & Co., 1874 – 1902.

DiBartolomeo, Robert D. *The Public and Private Lives of Wheeling Glass Makers.* Address before the Blue Pencil Club, Wheeling, W.Va.

Garrison, Myrna and Bob. *Imperial's Vintage Milk Glass.* Arlington, TX: Author, 1992.

Heacock, William. *Opalescent Glass from A to Z.* Marietta, OH: Richardson Printing Corp., 1977.

———. *Syrups, Sugar Shakers & Cruets from A to Z.* Marietta, OH: Antique Publications, 1976.

———. *Ruby-Stained Glass from A to Z.* Marietta, OH: Antique Publications, Inc., 1986.

———. *Oil Cruets from A to Z.* Marietta, OH: Antique Publications, 1981.

———. *Fenton Glass The First Twenty-five Years.* Marietta, OH: O-Val Advertising Corp., 1978.

———. *Fenton Glass The Second Twenty-five Years.* Marietta, OH: O-Val Advertising Corp., 1980.

———. *Fenton Glass The Third Twenty-five Years.* Marietta, OH: O-Val Advertising Corp., 1989.

Heacock, William and Fred Bickenheuser. *U. S. Glass from A to Z.* Marietta, OH: Antique Publications, 1978.

Heacock, William and William Gamble. *Cranberry Opalescent from A to Z.* Marietta, OH: Antique Publications, 1987.

Heacock, William, James Measell and Berry Wiggens. *Harry Northwood, The Wheeling Years, 1901 – 1925.* Marietta, OH: Antique Publications, 1991.

History of West Virginia, Old and New, and West Virginia Biography New York and Chicago: The American Historical Society, 1923.

Jefferson, Josephine. *Wheeling Glass.* Mount Vernon OH: The Guide Publishing Co., 1947.

Jenks, Bill, and Jerry Luna. *Early American Pattern Glass, 1850 – 1910.* Radnor, PA: Wallace Homestead Book Co., 1990.

Kamm, Minie Watson. *Eight Pitcher Books.* Gross Point, MI: Author, Fifth Printing, 1970.

Lee, Ruth Webb. *Victorian Glass.* Northboro, MA: Author, Seventh Edition, 1944.

_____. *Early American Pressed Glass*. Northboro, MA: Author, Thirteenth Edition, 1946.

Lewis, Clifford M. S. J. *Salvage Archeology on the Site of a Wheeling Glass Plant*. Wheeling College, address before the Society Historical Archeology, Tallahassee, Florida, January 1972. Printed in the *West Virginia Archeologist*, No. 24.

Peterson, Arthur G. *Glass Patents and Patterns*. De Barry, FL: Author, 1973.

Revi, Albert Christian. *Americana Pressed Glass and Figural Bottles*. New York: Thomas Nelson & Sons, 1964.

Salverson, John F. *Those Fascinating Little Lamps*. Marietta, OH: Antique Publications, 1988.

Thuro, Catherine M. V. *Oil Lamps — The Kerosene Era in North America*. Des Moines, IA: Wallace Homestead Book Co., 1976.

_____. *Oil Lamps II: Glass Kerosene Lamps*. Paducah, KY: Collector Books, 1983.

Tilveston, Geo. A. *Directory of the City of Wheeling and Vicinity*. 1859.

Welker, John W. and Elizabeth F. *Pressed Glass in America, Encyclopedia of The First Hundred Years. 1825 – 1925*. Ivyland, P. Antique Acres Press, 1985.

Wheeling Daily Intelligencer, various issues.

Williams & Co. Williams' Wheeling Directory for 1867-'8. J. C. Orr & Co. 1867.

_____. *Williams' Wheeling Directory for 1868-'9* A. W. Paull & Co. 1868.

~Index~

COLLECTOR BOOKS

Informing Today's Collector

For over two decades we have been keeping collectors informed on trends and values in all fields of antiques and collectibles.

DOLLS, FIGURES & TEDDY BEARS

4707	A Decade of Barbie Dolls & Collectibles, 1981–1991, Summers	$19.95
4631	Barbie Doll Boom, 1986–1995, Augustyniak	$18.95
2079	Barbie Doll Fashions, Volume I, Eames	$24.95
3957	Barbie Exclusives, Rana	$18.95
4632	Barbie Exclusives, Book II, Rana	$18.95
4557	Barbie, The First 30 Years, Deutsch	$24.95
4657	Barbie Years, 1959–1995, Olds	$16.95
3310	Black Dolls, 1820–1991, Perkins	$17.95
3873	Black Dolls, Book II, Perkins	$17.95
1529	Collector's Encyclopedia of Barbie Dolls, DeWein	$19.95
4506	Collector's Guide to Dolls in Uniform, Bourgeois	$18.95
3727	Collector's Guide to Ideal Dolls, Izen	$18.95
3728	Collector's Guide to Miniature Teddy Bears, Powell	$17.95
3967	Collector's Guide to Trolls, Peterson	$19.95
4571	Liddle Kiddles, Identification & Value Guide, Langford	$18.95
4645	Madame Alexander Dolls Price Guide #21, Smith	$9.95
3733	Modern Collector's Dolls, Sixth Series, Smith	$24.95
3991	Modern Collector's Dolls, Seventh Series, Smith	$24.95
4647	Modern Collector's Dolls, Eighth Series, Smith	$24.95
4640	Patricia Smith's Doll Values, Antique to Modern, 12th Edition	$12.95
3826	Story of Barbie, Westenhouser	$19.95
1513	Teddy Bears & Steiff Animals, Mandel	$9.95
1817	Teddy Bears & Steiff Animals, 2nd Series, Mandel	$19.95
2084	Teddy Bears, Annalee's & Steiff Animals, 3rd Series, Mandel	$19.95
1808	Wonder of Barbie, Manos	$9.95
1430	World of Barbie Dolls, Manos	$9.95

FURNITURE

1457	American Oak Furniture, McNerney	$9.95
3716	American Oak Furniture, Book II, McNerney	$12.95
1118	Antique Oak Furniture, Hill	$7.95
2132	Collector's Encyclopedia of American Furniture, Vol. I, Swedberg	$24.95
2271	Collector's Encyclopedia of American Furniture, Vol. II, Swedberg	$24.95
3720	Collector's Encyclopedia of American Furniture, Vol. III, Swedberg	$24.95
3878	Collector's Guide to Oak Furniture, George	$12.95
1755	Furniture of the Depression Era, Swedberg	$19.95
3906	Heywood-Wakefield Modern Furniture, Rouland	$18.95
1885	Victorian Furniture, Our American Heritage, McNerney	$9.95
3829	Victorian Furniture, Our American Heritage, Book II, McNerney	$9.95
3869	Victorian Furniture books, 2 volume set, McNerney	$19.90

JEWELRY, HATPINS, WATCHES & PURSES

1712	Antique & Collector's Thimbles & Accessories, Mathis	$19.95
1748	Antique Purses, Revised Second Ed., Holiner	$19.95
1278	Art Nouveau & Art Deco Jewelry, Baker	$9.95
4558	Christmas Pins, Past and Present, Gallina	$18.95
3875	Collecting Antique Stickpins, Kerins	$16.95
3722	Collector's Ency. of Compacts, Carryalls & Face Powder Boxes, Mueller	$24.95
4655	Complete Price Guide to Watches, #16, Shugart	$26.95
1716	Fifty Years of Collectible Fashion Jewelry, 1925-1975, Baker	$19.95
1424	Hatpins & Hatpin Holders, Baker	$9.95
4570	Ladies' Compacts, Gerson	$24.95
1181	100 Years of Collectible Jewelry, 1850-1950, Baker	$9.95
2348	20th Century Fashionable Plastic Jewelry, Baker	$19.95
3830	Vintage Vanity Bags & Purses, Gerson	$24.95

TOYS, MARBLES & CHRISTMAS COLLECTIBLES

3427	Advertising Character Collectibles, Dotz	$17.95
2333	Antique & Collector's Marbles, 3rd Ed., Grist	$9.95
3827	Antique & Collector's Toys, 1870–1950, Longest	$24.95
3956	Baby Boomer Games, Identification & Value Guide, Polizzi	$24.95
3717	Christmas Collectibles, 2nd Edition, Whitmyer	$24.95
1752	Christmas Ornaments, Lights & Decorations, Johnson	$19.95
4649	Classic Plastic Model Kits, Polizzi	$24.95

4559	Collectible Action Figures, 2nd Ed., Manos	$
3874	Collectible Coca-Cola Toy Trucks, deCourtivron	$
2338	Collector's Encyclopedia of Disneyana, Longest, Stern	$
4639	Collector's Guide to Diecast Toys & Scale Models, Johnson	$
4651	Collector's Guide to Tinker Toys, Strange	$
4566	Collector's Guide to Tootsietoys, 2nd Ed., Richter	$
3436	Grist's Big Book of Marbles	$
3970	Grist's Machine-Made & Contemporary Marbles, 2nd Ed.	$
4569	Howdy Doody, Collector's Reference and Trivia Guide, Koch	$
4723	Matchbox® Toys, 1948 to 1993, Johnson, 2nd Ed	$
3823	Mego Toys, An Illustrated Value Guide, Chrouch	$
1540	Modern Toys 1930–1980, Baker	$
3888	Motorcycle Toys, Antique & Contemporary, Gentry/Downs	$
4728	Schroeder's Collectible Toys, Antique to Modern Price Guide, 3rd Ed.	$1
1886	Stern's Guide to Disney Collectibles	$1
2139	Stern's Guide to Disney Collectibles, 2nd Series	$1
3975	Stern's Guide to Disney Collectibles, 3rd Series	$1
2028	Toys, Antique & Collectible, Longest	$1
3979	Zany Characters of the Ad World, Lamphier	$1

INDIANS, GUNS, KNIVES, TOOLS, PRIMITIVES

1868	Antique Tools, Our American Heritage, McNerney	$
2015	Archaic Indian Points & Knives, Edler	$1
1426	Arrowheads & Projectile Points, Hothem	$
4633	Big Little Books, Jacobs	$
2279	Indian Artifacts of the Midwest, Hothem	$1
3885	Indian Artifacts of the Midwest, Book II, Hothem	$1
1964	Indian Axes & Related Stone Artifacts, Hothem	$1
2023	Keen Kutter Collectibles, Heuring	$1
4724	Modern Guns, Identification & Values, 11th Ed., Quertermous	$1
4505	Standard Guide to Razors, Ritchie & Stewart	$
4730	Standard Knife Collector's Guide, 3rd Ed., Ritchie & Stewart	$1

PAPER COLLECTIBLES & BOOKS

4633	Big Little Books, Jacobs	$1
1441	Collector's Guide to Post Cards, Wood	$
2081	Guide to Collecting Cookbooks, Allen	$1
4648	Huxford's Old Book Value Guide, 8th Ed.	$1
2080	Price Guide to Cookbooks & Recipe Leaflets, Dickinson	$
2346	Sheet Music Reference & Price Guide, 2nd Ed., Pafik & Guiheen	$1
4654	Victorian Trading Cards, Historical Reference & Value Guide, Cheadle	$1

GLASSWARE

1006	Cambridge Glass Reprint 1930–1934	$1
1007	Cambridge Glass Reprint 1949–1953	$1
4561	Collectible Drinking Glasses, Chase & Kelly	$1
4642	Collectible Glass Shoes, Wheatley	$1
4553	Coll. Glassware from the 40's, 50's & 60's, 3rd Ed., Florence	$1
2352	Collector's Encyclopedia of Akro Agate Glassware, Florence	$1
1810	Collector's Encyclopedia of American Art Glass, Shuman	$2
3312	Collector's Encyclopedia of Children's Dishes, Whitmyer	$1
4552	Collector's Encyclopedia of Depression Glass, 12th Ed., Florence	$1
1664	Collector's Encyclopedia of Heisey Glass, 1925–1938, Bredehoft	$2
3905	Collector's Encyclopedia of Milk Glass, Newbound	$2
1523	Colors In Cambridge Glass, National Cambridge Society	$1
4564	Crackle Glass, Weitman	$1
2275	Czechoslovakian Glass and Collectibles, Barta/Rose	$1
4714	Czechoslovakian Glass and Collectibles, Book II, Barta/Rose	$1
4716	Elegant Glassware of the Depression Era, 7th Ed., Florence	$1
1380	Encyclopedia of Pattern Glass, McClain	$1
3981	Ever's Standard Cut Glass Value Guide	$1
4659	Fenton Art Glass, 1907–1939, Whitmyer	$2
3725	Fostoria, Pressed, Blown & Hand Molded Shapes, Kerr	$2
3883	Fostoria Stemware, The Crystal for America, Long & Seate	$2
3318	Glass Animals of the Depression Era, Garmon & Spencer	$19
4644	Imperial Carnival Glass, Burns	$18

COLLECTOR BOOKS
Informing Today's Collector

46	Kitchen Glassware of the Depression Years, 5th Ed., Florence	$19.95
14	Oil Lamps II, Glass Kerosene Lamps, Thuro	$24.95
15	Pocket Guide to Depression Glass, 10th Ed., Florence	$9.95
14	Standard Encyclopedia of Carnival Glass, 5th Ed., Edwards	$24.95
15	Standard Carnival Glass Price Guide, 10th Ed.	$9.95
74	Standard Encylopedia of Opalescent Glass, Edwards	$19.95
81	Stemware Identification, Featuring Cordials with Values, Florence	$24.95
26	Very Rare Glassware of the Depression Years, 3rd Series, Florence	$24.95
49	Very Rare Glassware of the Depression Years, 4th Series, Florence	$24.95
32	Very Rare Glassware of the Depression Years, 5th Series, Florence	$24.95
56	Westmoreland Glass, Wilson	$24.95
24	World of Salt Shakers, 2nd Ed., Lechner	$24.95

POTTERY

30	American Limoges, Limoges	$24.95
12	Blue & White Stoneware, McNerney	$9.95
58	So. Potteries Blue Ridge Dinnerware, 3rd Ed., Newbound	$14.95
59	Blue Willow, 2nd Ed., Gaston	$14.95
16	Collectible Vernon Kilns, Nelson	$24.95
11	Collecting Yellow Ware – Id. & Value Guide, McAllister	$16.95
73	Collector's Encyclopedia of American Dinnerware, Cunningham	$24.95
15	Collector's Encyclopedia of Blue Ridge Dinnerware, Newbound	$19.95
58	Collector's Encyclopedia of Brush-McCoy Pottery, Huxford	$24.95
72	Collector's Encyclopedia of California Pottery, Chipman	$24.95
11	Collector's Encyclopedia of Colorado Pottery, Carlton	$24.95
33	Collector's Encyclopedia of Cookie Jars, Roerig	$24.95
23	Collector's Encyclopedia of Cookie Jars, Volume II, Roerig	$24.95
29	Collector's Encyclopedia of Cowan Pottery, Saloff	$24.95
38	Collector's Encyclopedia of Dakota Potteries, Dommel	$24.95
09	Collector's Encyclopedia of Fiesta, 7th Ed., Huxford	$19.95
18	Collector's Encyclopedia of Figural Planters & Vases, Newbound	$19.95
61	Collector's Encyclopedia of Early Noritake, Alden	$24.95
39	Collector's Encyclopedia of Flow Blue China, Gaston	$19.95
12	Collector's Encyclopedia of Flow Blue China, 2nd Ed., Gaston	$24.95
13	Collector's Encyclopedia of Hall China, 2nd Ed., Whitmyer	$24.95
31	Collector's Encyclopedia of Homer Laughlin China, Jasper	$24.95
76	Collector's Encyclopedia of Hull Pottery, Roberts	$19.95
73	Collector's Encyclopedia of Knowles, Taylor & Knowles, Gaston	$24.95
62	Collector's Encyclopedia of Lefton China, DeLozier	$19.95
10	Collector's Encyclopedia of Limoges Porcelain, 2nd Ed., Gaston	$24.95
34	Collector's Encyclopedia of Majolica Pottery, Katz-Marks	$19.95
58	Collector's Encyclopedia of McCoy Pottery, Huxford	$19.95
63	Collector's Encyclopedia of Metlox Potteries, Gibbs Jr.	$24.95
13	Collector's Encyclopedia of Niloak, Gifford	$19.95
37	Collector's Encyclopedia of Nippon Porcelain I, Van Patten	$24.95
89	Collector's Ency. of Nippon Porcelain, 2nd Series, Van Patten	$24.95
65	Collector's Ency. of Nippon Porcelain, 3rd Series, Van Patten	$24.95
36	Nippon Porcelain Price Guide, Van Patten	$9.95
47	Collector's Encyclopedia of Noritake, Van Patten	$19.95
32	Collector's Encyclopedia of Noritake, 2nd Series, Van Patten	$24.95
37	Collector's Encyclopedia of Occupied Japan, Vol. I, Florence	$14.95
38	Collector's Encyclopedia of Occupied Japan, Vol. II, Florence	$14.95
88	Collector's Encyclopedia of Occupied Japan, Vol. III, Florence	$14.95
19	Collector's Encyclopedia of Occupied Japan, Vol. IV, Florence	$14.95
35	Collector's Encyclopedia of Occupied Japan, Vol. V, Florence	$14.95
64	Collector's Encyclopedia of Pickard China, Reed	$24.95
11	Collector's Encyclopedia of R.S. Prussia, 1st Series, Gaston	$24.95
15	Collector's Encyclopedia of R.S. Prussia, 2nd Series, Gaston	$24.95
26	Collector's Encyclopedia of R.S. Prussia, 3rd Series, Gaston	$24.95
77	Collector's Encyclopedia of R.S. Prussia, 4th Series, Gaston	$24.95
34	Collector's Encyclopedia of Roseville Pottery, Huxford	$19.95
35	Collector's Encyclopedia of Roseville Pottery, 2nd Ed., Huxford	$19.95
57	Roseville Price Guide No. 10	$9.95
65	Collector's Encyclopedia of Sascha Brastoff, Conti, Bethany & Seay	$24.95
14	Collector's Encyclopedia of Van Briggle Art Pottery, Sasicki	$24.95
63	Collector's Encyclopedia of Wall Pockets, Newbound	$19.95
11	Collector's Encyclopedia of Weller Pottery, Huxford	$29.95
52	Coll. Guide to Country Stoneware & Pottery, Raycraft	$11.95
77	Coll. Guide to Country Stoneware & Pottery, 2nd Series, Raycraft	$14.95
34	Coll. Guide to Hull Pottery, The Dinnerware Line, Gick-Burke	$16.95

3876	Collector's Guide to Lu-Ray Pastels, Meehan	$18.95
3814	Collector's Guide to Made in Japan Ceramics, White	$18.95
4646	Collector's Guide to Made in Japan Ceramics, Book II, White	$18.95
4565	Collector's Guide to Rockingham, The Enduring Ware, Brewer	$14.95
2339	Collector's Guide to Shawnee Pottery, Vanderbilt	$19.95
1425	Cookie Jars, Westfall	$9.95
3440	Cookie Jars, Book II, Westfall	$19.95
3435	Debolt's Dictionary of American Pottery Marks	$17.95
2379	Lehner's Ency. of U.S. Marks on Pottery, Porcelain & China	$24.95
4722	McCoy Pottery, Collector's Reference & Value Guide, Hanson/Nissen	$19.95
3825	Puritan Pottery, Morris	$24.95
4726	Red Wing Art Pottery, 1920s–1960s, Dollen	$19.95
1670	Red Wing Collectibles, DePasquale	$9.95
1440	Red Wing Stoneware, DePasquale	$9.95
3738	Shawnee Pottery, Mangus	$24.95
4629	Turn of the Century American Dinnerware, 1880s–1920s, Jasper	$24.95
4572	Wall Pockets of the Past, Perkins	$17.95
3327	Watt Pottery – Identification & Value Guide, Morris	$19.95

OTHER COLLECTIBLES

4704	Antique & Collectible Buttons, Wisniewski	$19.95
2269	Antique Brass & Copper Collectibles, Gaston	$16.95
1880	Antique Iron, McNerney	$9.95
3872	Antique Tins, Dodge	$24.95
1714	Black Collectibles, Gibbs	$19.95
1128	Bottle Pricing Guide, 3rd Ed., Cleveland	$7.95
4636	Celluloid Collectibles, Dunn	$14.95
3959	Cereal Box Bonanza, The 1950's, Bruce	$19.95
3718	Collectible Aluminum, Grist	$16.95
3445	Collectible Cats, An Identification & Value Guide, Fyke	$18.95
4560	Collectible Cats, An Identification & Value Guide, Book II, Fyke	$19.95
1634	Collector's Ency. of Figural & Novelty Salt & Pepper Shakers, Davern	$19.95
2020	Collector's Ency. of Figural & Novelty Salt & Pepper Shakers, Vol. II, Davern	$19.95
2018	Collector's Encyclopedia of Granite Ware, Greguire	$24.95
3430	Collector's Encyclopedia of Granite Ware, Book II, Greguire	$24.95
4705	Collector's Guide to Antique Radios, 4th Ed., Bunis	$18.95
1916	Collector's Guide to Art Deco, Gaston	$14.95
3880	Collector's Guide to Cigarette Lighters, Flanagan	$17.95
4637	Collector's Guide to Cigarette Lighters, Book II, Flanagan	$17.95
1537	Collector's Guide to Country Baskets, Raycraft	$9.95
3966	Collector's Guide to Inkwells, Identification & Values, Badders	$18.95
3881	Collector's Guide to Novelty Radios, Bunis/Breed	$18.95
4652	Collector's Guide to Transistor Radios, 2nd Ed., Bunis	$16.95
4653	Collector's Guide to TV Memorabilia, 1960s–1970s, Davis/Morgan	$24.95
2276	Decoys, Kangas	$24.95
1629	Doorstops, Identification & Values, Bertoia	$9.95
4567	Figural Napkin Rings, Gottschalk & Whitson	$18.95
3968	Fishing Lure Collectibles, Murphy/Edmisten	$24.95
3817	Flea Market Trader, 10th Ed., Huxford	$12.95
3976	Foremost Guide to Uncle Sam Collectibles, Czulewicz	$24.95
4641	Garage Sale & Flea Market Annual, 4th Ed.	$19.95
3819	General Store Collectibles, Wilson	$24.95
4643	Great American West Collectibles, Wilson	$24.95
2215	Goldstein's Coca-Cola Collectibles	$16.95
3884	Huxford's Collectible Advertising, 2nd Ed.	$24.95
2216	Kitchen Antiques, 1790–1940, McNerney	$14.95
3321	Ornamental & Figural Nutcrackers, Rittenhouse	$16.95
2026	Railroad Collectibles, 4th Ed., Baker	$14.95
1632	Salt & Pepper Shakers, Guarnaccia	$9.95
1888	Salt & Pepper Shakers II, Identification & Value Guide, Book II, Guarnaccia	$14.95
2220	Salt & Pepper Shakers III, Guarnaccia	$14.95
3443	Salt & Pepper Shakers IV, Guarnaccia	$18.95
4555	Schroeder's Antiques Price Guide, 14th Ed., Huxford	$12.95
2096	Silverplated Flatware, Revised 4th Edition, Hagan	$14.95
1922	Standard Old Bottle Price Guide, Sellari	$14.95
4708	Summers' Guide to Coca-Cola	$19.95
3892	Toy & Miniature Sewing Machines, Thomas	$18.95
3828	Value Guide to Advertising Memorabilia, Summers	$18.95
3977	Value Guide to Gas Station Memorabilia, Summers & Priddy	$24.95
3444	Wanted to Buy, 5th Edition	$9.95

Schroeder's
ANTIQUES
Price Guide

. . . is the #1 best-selling antiques & collectibles value guide on the market today, and here's why . . .

Schroeder's ANTIQUES Price Guide

OUR #1 BEST SELLER!

Identification & Values Of Over 50,000 Antiques & Collectibles

8½ x 11, 608 Pages, $12.95

• *More than 300 advisors, well-known dealers, and top-notch collectors work together with our editors to bring you accurate information regarding pricing and identification.*

• *More than 45,000 items in almost 500 categories are listed along with hundreds of sharp original photos that illustrate not only the rare and unusual, but the common, popular collectibles as well.*

• *Each large close-up shot shows important details clearly. Every subject is represented with histories and background information, a feature not found in any of our competitors' publications.*

• *Our editors keep abreast of newly developing trends, often adding several new categories a year as the need arises.*

If it merits the interest of today's collector, you'll find it in *Schroeder's*. And you can feel confident that the information we publish is up to date and accurate. Our advisors thoroughly check each category to spot inconsistencies, listings that may not be entirely reflective of market dealings, and lines too vague to be of merit. Only the best of the lot remains for publication.

Without doubt, you'll find
SCHROEDER'S ANTIQUES PRICE GUIDE
the only one to buy for
reliable information and values.

COLLECTOR BOOKS
A Division of Schroeder Publishing Co., Inc.